Theatres of the Troubles

Theatres of the Troubles is the first book to document the grass roots popular theatres which developed from within the working-class Republican and Loyalist communities of Belfast and Derry during the latest phase of the four hundred year conflict between Ireland and Britain.

Bill McDonnell explores the history of one of the most important periods of political theatre activity in post-war Europe. In this significant study, he seeks to show how these theatres within the Republican and Loyalist communities related, first to each other, and then to European traditions of radical theatre and to the liberation models developing in neo and post colonial contexts in the South.

'[*Theatres of the Troubles*] should prove accessible to general readers interested in Northern Ireland, and will be especially valuable to students and scholars of Irish theatre, political theatre and community and applied theatre. The detailed case studies are framed by wider philosophical and theoretical discussion which should be of broad appeal. I believe that as well as expanding enormously our understanding of the cultural dimension of the Northern Ireland Troubles, it also serves as a model for how experience as a practitioner and direct witness can enrich and validate academic discourse.'

David Grant, Head of Drama Studies,
Queen's University Belfast

Bill McDonnell is Senior Lecturer in Theatre at the University of Sheffield. He has worked both as an actor and writer and was founder and co-director of Theatreworks, Sheffield. He is co-author of *Social Impact in UK Theatre* (with Dominic Shellard, Arts Council England, 2006).

Exeter Performance Studies

Series editors: Peter Thomson, Professor of Drama at the University of Exeter; Graham Ley, Professor of Drama and Theory at the University of Exeter; Steve Nicholson, Reader in Twentieth-Century Drama at the University of Sheffield.

From Mimesis to Interculturalism: Readings of Theatrical Theory Before and After 'Modernism'
Graham Ley (1999)

British Theatre and the Red Peril: The Portrayal of Communism, 1917–1945
Steve Nicholson (1999)

On Actors and Acting
Peter Thomson (2000)

Grand-Guignol: The French Theatre of Horror
Richard J. Hand and Michael Wilson (2002)

The Censorship of British Drama, 1900–1968: Volume One, 1900–1932
Steve Nicholson (2003)

The Censorship of British Drama, 1900–1968: Volume Two, 1933–1952
Steve Nicholson (2005)

Freedom's Pioneer: John McGrath's Work in Theatre, Film and Television
edited by David Bradby and Susanna Capon (2005)

John McGrath: Plays for England
selected and introduced by Nadine Holdsworth (2005)

Theatre Workshop: Joan Littlewood and the Making of Modern British Theatre
Robert Leach (2006)

Making Theatre in Northern Ireland: Through and Beyond the Troubles
Tom Maguire (2006)

"In Comes I": Performance, Memory and Landscape
Mike Pearson (2006)

London's Grand Guignol and the Theatre of Horror
Richard J. Hand and Michael Wilson (2007)

Theatres of the Troubles

Theatre, Resistance and Liberation in Ireland

Bill McDonnell

UNIVERSITY
of
EXETER
PRESS

First published in 2008 by
University of Exeter Press
Reed Hall, Streatham Drive
Exeter EX4 4QR
UK
www.exeterpress.co.uk

British Library Cataloguing in Publication Data
A catalogue record for this book is available
from the British Library.

Paperback ISBN 978 0 85989 794 5
Hardback ISBN 978 0 85989 793 8

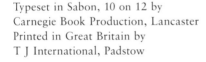
Typeset in Sabon, 10 on 12 by
Carnegie Book Production, Lancaster
Printed in Great Britain by
T J International, Padstow

FSC
Mixed Sources
Product group from well-managed
forests and other controlled sources

Cert no. BGB-COC-2482
www.fsc.org
© 1996 Forest Stewardship Council

Dedicated to my parents, Agnes and Bill McDonnell, whose lives are part of the long history of the Irish diaspora

Contents

PART FOUR: 'NOT A PROFESSION BUT A MOVEMENT'

Illustrations

Cover illustration taken from the H Block production of *The Crime of Castlereagh*, directed by Tom Magill

Acknowledgements

I owe a great debt to many courageous and visionary individuals. Chief amongst them are Joe and Margaret Reid and family, and Fr Des Wilson and Sister Noelle Ryan – a debt stretching back over two decades. They have offered intellectual inspiration, generous company, irreplaceable primary sources, and, when necessary, free accommodation and very strong tea. They have also shaped, in lasting ways, my understanding of theatre and politics, and the complex relationship between them. I am also indebted to the inspiration and warm friendship of the performers, activists and teachers of Springhill Community House, especially Marie McKnight, Pat and Jim McGlade, Tony Flynn and Gerard McLaughlin.

Laurence McKeown, Pam Brighton, Anne Marie Evans, Michael Hall and Tom Magill all gave of their time to be interviewed, and were generous in providing information, and precious copies of unpublished scripts, pamphlets, production notes and other ephemera. I could not have written the book without their help, and I owe them a huge debt of gratitude. My absolute reliance on these sources makes this study feel less the product of individual authorship than an act, or series of acts, of transcription and mediation. A feeling expressed by Raphael Samuel, who writes in *Theatre and Memory*:

> History is not the prerogative of the historian, nor even, as postmodernism contends, a historian's 'invention'. It is, rather, a social form of knowledge; the work in any given instance of a thousand different hands.[1]

Generous assistance was also received from Hugh Odling Snee and the staff at Belfast's Linenhall Library, and staff at the Working Class Movement Library, Salford. I am grateful also for the support of the series editors. To David Grant and Tom Maguire, who read the MS, and offered detailed advice and feedback I also wish to express a very sincere gratitude. Notwithstanding, any faults and omissions are mine alone. Finally, this book would never have been written if it had not been for a fifteen-year partnership with John Goodchild, whose vision, ethics and innovatory workshop methods made our joint work possible, and led to the encounters which provided the inspiration for its writing.

My infinite gratitude goes to my sons, Robin and Joe, and my partner, Julie, for their patience, support and understanding.

Chronology of key events

1919	After winning the majority of seats in all Ireland elections, Sinn Féin forms the first, illegal Dail Eireann.
1919–20	Irish War of Independence against Britain.
1920	The Government of Ireland Act leads to the partitioning of Ireland.
1921	Anglo-Irish Treaty signed and the first NI parliament formed.
1949	Ireland leaves the Commonwealth and the Republic of Ireland is founded.
1951–56	IRA border campaign, which ends in failure.
1967	Northern Ireland Civil Rights Association is formed.
1968	First civil rights march takes place. NI Prime Minister Terence O'Neill ushers in a reform package in bid to address Nationalist grievances.
1969	RUC is armed and O'Neill mobilizes the 'B' Specials. O'Neill resigns and is succeeded by James Chichester Clark. Rioting in Belfast and Derry. Battle of the Bogside. Peace lines erected in Belfast. IRA establishes no-go areas. IRA splits to form Provisional and Official wings.
1970	Nationalist Falls Road area of Belfast is placed under curfew while army carries out searches for arms.
1971	Internment without trial introduced.
1972	'Bloody Sunday' in Derry when British Paratroopers kill fourteen unarmed civilians during a civil rights march. Widgery Report largely exonerates the army. 'Bloody Friday' in Belfast, in which IRA bombs kill nine and injure hundreds. This prompts Operation Motorman, the largest mobilization of British forces since Suez as the Army attempts to regain control of Republican areas.
1974	Special Category status granted to Loyalist and Republican prisoners of war. Ulster Worker's Council strike brings down the power-sharing executive formed under the Sunningdale Agreement of 1973.

1976   'Ulsterisation': the war against Republican insurgency is reframed as a civil law and order issue. Political status is withdrawn from Republican and Loyalist POWs. Republican prisoners begin the 'Blanket' protest in the Long Kesh prison in response.

1978   Beginning of the 'No Wash' protest by Republican POWs in Long Kesh prison.

1979   Margaret Thatcher leads Conservatives to victory in British general election.

1980   The first hunger strike by Republican prisoners in Long Kesh. Called off under misapprehension that their demands had been met.

1981   The second hunger strike by Republican prisoners in Long Kesh begins in May and leads to the death of ten hunger strikers before relatives end it in October. The first to die, Bobby Sands, is elected to the British Parliament as MP for Fermanagh–South Tyrone during his fast.

1985   Anglo-Irish Agreement signed.

1988   SDLP leader John Hume and Sinn Féin's Gerry Adams begin talks. British Home secretary announces a broadcasting ban on members of Sinn Féin.

1989   Guildford Four released by the Court of Appeal.

1990   Margaret Thatcher replaced by John Major as leader of the Conservative Party.

1993   Hume–Adams joint statement on what would become the Peace Process.

1994   First IRA ceasefire: this is followed by Loyalist cease-fires.

1996   IRA ceasefire ends with bomb attack on Canary Wharf, London.

1997   Tony Blair elected as British Prime Minister as Labour secure landslide victory. Second IRA ceasefire announced.

1998   Tony Blair announces setting up of the Saville inquiry into 'Bloody Sunday'.
         Good Friday Agreement signed and an elected Northern Ireland assembly takes over devolved government of the north. Real IRA bomb in Omagh kills 29 people.

1999   Patten Report on policing proposes far-reaching changes. An executive for the NI Assembly is formed.

2005   Irish Government formally amends Articles 2 and 3 of Eire's constitution which lay territorial claim to NI. The IRA declares an end to all military activities and undertakes a final act of decommissioning.

2007   Sinn Féin and DUP reach an historic accommodation which restores the NI Assembly.

Glossary of terms and acronyms

B-Specials. The B-Specials was a part time unit attached to the Ulster Special Constabulary (USC). Formed after partition, the predominantly Protestant USC and the B-Specials were disbanded in 1970 following the Hunt Report, and replaced with the Ulster Defence Regiment (UDR).

Castlereagh. The RUC Special Branch holding centre outside Belfast. It was here that illegal interrogation methods, including torture, were refined and used up to the mid-1980s.

Derry. The name originally came from the Irish *Daire*. The city was renamed Londonderry during the Plantation of Ulster of the early seventeenth century. In recent times Derry has been the Nationalist/Republican designation, though often now used also by Protestants. For convenience the name Derry is generally used in this book.

Democratic Unionist Party (DUP). Formed in 1971 by Ian Paisley, the DUP is a political party committed to the maintenance of the Union. Once the standard bearer of the anti-Good Friday Agreement forces within the Northern Ireland assembly, 2007 has seen an historical realignment with Sinn Féin.

H-Blocks at H.M. Maze Prison (formerly Long Kesh). Named after their cellular layout, the H-Blocks were the main holding prison in the north of Ireland for both Republican and Loyalist prisoners. Republicans continue to use the term Long Kesh, and I follow that convention here.

Irish Republican Army/Oglaigh n hEireannn (IRA). Formed in 1919, the IRA fought ever after for a 32 county, united Ireland. It was the armed wing of Sinn Féin (Ourselves Alone). In 1969 the organization split into Official and Provisional sections. The latter, as the Provisional IRA (PIRA), prosecuted a military struggle against the British state between 1970 and 1994, and again from 1996 to 1997. I follow common usage in using the acronym IRA for the Provisional IRA or 'Provos'.

North of Ireland. Republicans use this term, rather than Northern Ireland, as it indicates not a state, but a geographical area, and so underlines their sense of the statelet as an illegal construct.

Northern Ireland Civil Rights Association (NICRA). A predominantly middle-class and Catholic civil rights pressure group in the 1960s, NICRA was superseded by the more radical People's Democracy during the crucial period 1968–70.

Northern Ireland Office (NIO). After the imposition of direct rule in 1972, the NIO was the British state's administrative structure within the north of Ireland.

People's Democracy (PD). launched by left-wing students from Queen's University, Belfast in 1968, the PD was aligned with the IRA in the early days of the Troubles, and maintained a broadly Trotskyite analysis of the struggle.

Prevention of Terrorism Act (PTA). The term PTA refers to the 1974 act, which was promulgated in the wake of the Birmingham bombings of the same year, and which was renewed annually until 1998. A highly contentious piece of legislation, the act provided for the detention of suspects for seven days without judicial review. It also allowed the state to deport from Britain or deny entry to Britain anyone the security forces alleged was a threat to state security.

Royal Ulster Constabulary (RUC). Until 2001, the RUC was the overwhelmingly Protestant police force for the six counties. It was renamed the Police Service of Northern Ireland (PSNI) following the 1999 Patten Report.

Sinn Féin (Ourselves Alone) (SF). Founded 1905. Despite having little role in its organization or prosecution, Sinn Féin was identified in popular mythology as a lead player in the Easter Rising. From 1918 it has been the political wing of the IRA.

Social Democratic and Labour Party (SDLP). Founded in 1970 as the political voice of moderate, middle-class, Catholic opinion in the north of Ireland, the SDLP was in favour of a British withdrawal, but supported the Loyalist community's veto over re-unification. The Good Friday Agreement can be seen, essentially, as the triumph of its values.

Special Air Services (SAS). The elite undercover unit of the British Army, the SAS was blooded in a series of colonial wars, and was noted for its extrajudicial assassinations of IRA volunteers.

Stormont. Seat of the Northern Ireland government 1922–72, Stormont is now home to the new cross-party Northern Ireland Assembly.

Ulster Defence Association (UDA). Loyalist paramilitary group, which was responsible for the majority of assassinations against Catholics and Republicans during the conflict. It operated under the guise of the Ulster Freedom Fighters.

Ulster Defence Regiment (UDR). A unit of the British army that was the local regiment for Ulster. The UDR replaced the B-Specials in 1970, and was a predominantly Protestant regiment.

Ulster Unionist Party (UUP). Until 2003 the largest Unionist party, which ruled the north of Ireland uninterrupted, 1921–72. The UUP was formed in the 1890s to resist Home Rule.

Ulster Volunteer Force (UVF). The militia raised by Sir Edward Carson in 1912 to prevent the creation of a united Ireland. Revived by Loyalist paramilitaries in the 1970s, the UVF was a particularly vicious sectarian death squad.

United Irishmen. The Republican revolutionary movement led by Wolfe Tone in the 1790s. It was a uniquely non-denominational group, and was crushed after an abortive rising in 1798.

Young Ireland. Active in the 1840s, Young Ireland was formed by radical intellectuals and was influenced by the pan-European Nationalist movement of the period. The group launched an unsuccessful rising in 1848

PART ONE

CONTEXTS

The Research Context

War, revolution, poverty, hunger; men reduced to objects and killed from lists; persecution and torture; the many kinds of contemporary martyrdom: however close and insistent the facts, we are not to be moved in a context of tragedy. Tragedy we know is about something else.[1]

Before it was enacted the 1916 Easter Rising in Ireland was first imagined, in poetry, prose and, above all, in drama. Declan Kiberd writes that 'no previous Irish insurrection had been imagined in such avowedly theatrical terms'.[2] It was therefore perhaps inevitable that the first to fall in the Rising should have been an actor, Sean Connolly, who had appeared at Dublin's Abbey Theatre. Inevitable also, perhaps, that W.B. Yeats should have wondered at the historical agency of his own works: 'Did that play of mine send out/Certain men the English shot?' he asks rhetorically, going on to conflate the Abbey Theatre and the Rising, theatre and history, stage actors and political actors:

> Come gather round me, players all
> Come praise Nineteen Sixteen,
> Those from the pit and gallery
> Or from the painted scene
> That fought in the Post office
> Or round the City Hall,
> Praise every man that came again
> Praise every man that fell.[3]

Some 80 years later, during the Troubles in the north of Ireland, between 1969 and 1999, Irish Republican Army volunteers would also act in plays as part of what they intended to be the final act of the Rising, the completion of the historical drama of Irish unity. In 1996, as in 1916, the link between theatre and politics, between stage and insurrection, would be made. The Irish, who would later be instructed in liberatory methods by messengers from the former colonial centre, were also the first subalterns to recognize the symbiosis between political struggle and cultural renewal, just as they were the first to invent urban guerrilla warfare, and the first to achieve (partial) freedom from the imperium. This partial success, concretized in partition, would lead to another historical irony: for just as Ireland was the first English colony, so too it would be the last in which an indigenous armed movement would fight what Republicans constructed as an anti-colonial war. Others would construct it differently, seeing the conflict in the north of Ireland as a sectarian civil war, or simply an explosion of anarchic and criminal violence carried out under the convenient banner of Republican or Unionist ideologies. Whatever one's perspective, the Troubles was one of the most protracted, traumatic and complex insurgencies in twentieth-century European history. It began in 1969, and ended with the Good Friday Agreement of 1998. Like all wars it brought terrible suffering, death, bereavement and individual and communal trauma. Like all wars again, most of those who suffered did not bear arms. It was primarily an urban war, and urban warfare is more terrible still because it has no boundaries; or rather because it dissolves all boundaries, invades all social relationships, from the most intimate and familial to the most public.

One narrative in the history of the Troubles, and the subject of this study, is the narrative of the community theatres which developed within working-class Republican and Loyalist communities during the war, and in the first decade of the Peace Process, 1997–2007. And while some of the texts and performances I document were created by Irish Republican Army (IRA) prisoners of war, and others by leading figures within the Ulster Defence Association (UDA), most were created by community activists. For the most part participants were non-professionals, who saw theatre as one of a range of cultural actions through which communities, silenced by the apparatus of state occupation, could speak. The theatre space was part of the battleground, both literally as a potential space of warfare and actual violence, and symbolically as a space of resistance and as the ground of cultural action. What also defines these theatres, and separates them from the left-wing theatres of the British mainland in the same period, is that they developed from *within* the working-class communities of the north where the war was primarily fought. Seeking to distinguish forms of interventionary theatre, Marxist critic and writer Himani Bannerji has differentiated between what we might term *organic* and *facilitated* theatres: between activist theatres which arise spontaneously from within situations of war, insurgency, and political and civil crises, and those which are interventions from outside.[4] The groups in this study, then, share three qualities: they were organic activist theatres, they were allied to a specific political or ideological formation, and, finally, they had a certain longevity. I have consequently excluded work which was carried out by professional theatre workers as part of state-funded initiatives to build cross-community links, as well as some of the ad-hoc productions which were created as part, for example, of the West Belfast Festival from 1987 onwards. My interest here is not in single productions or short-term interventions, but in how theatre became embedded within a community or movement, and the ways in which the rhythms and imperatives of the conflict determined the content, form and the contexts of performance. I have also excluded theatres from the post-1994 period except where the work is a continuation of theatre activity begun during the Troubles, as for example with Laurence McKeown and Brian Campbell, whose post-ceasefire plays are a continuation of an engagement begun in the H-Blocks in the 1980s. As a consequence the important work of companies such as Derry's Sole Purpose is not covered.[5]

Organization of material

In this section I have set out the research and historical contexts for the study. Part Two offers a series of casebooks on the work of community theatres active during the conflict, between 1969 and 1994. These are organized according to a rough chronology, a qualification necessitated by the difficulty in establishing with precision when companies were founded. This is due in part to the absence of documentation, in part to the intense pressure of a war in which events piled one upon another, and in part also because some theatres took place within prisons, or state holding centres. It is similarly difficult to fix the precise date of all performances, with accuracy varying from group to group depending on both their historical position (later work is better documented), and the existence of ephemera such as videos, programmes or fliers.

The first casebook considers the work of Belfast People's Theatre (1973–93), founded by Father Des Wilson, who is a central figure across all these histories. In particular I am interested in the intersection in his work of radical education practices, community activism and liberation theology. The second casebook focuses on the work of Belfast Community Theatre (1983–90), which shared both personnel and space with the People's Theatre. The most aesthetically innovative of the all the groups, Belfast Community Theatre, drew on the Irish theatre patrimony of Yeats, Synge, Gregory and Beckett, but also the European tradition of socialist theatre exemplified by the Workers' Theatre Movement, Piscator, Brecht and Littlewood's Theatre Workshop. Here theatre was part of a wider nexus of radical educational practice and cultural activism. The theatre created by IRA/Republican prisoners of war, from the early 'commemorations', through the development of pageant dramas in the 1980s, to the work of the mid-nineties, is described in the third casebook. These prison theatres are considered as part of the broader development of a theory and praxis of cultural struggle within the Republican movement in the period from

1981 to 1997. The intervention of Derry Frontline (1988–92) is considered next. Their work was defined by a culture-for-liberation template evolved by its founder, Dan Baron Cohen. Derry Frontline was the only company which claimed a foundational methodology, or which attempted to instigate a systematic process of radical culturalization. Loyalist communities did not produce political community theatres, for reasons I set out in the final casebook of this section. However, there were significant initiatives in 1984–85, and again in the mid-nineties, which deserve attention. Part Three then considers the evolution of Republican theatre in the post-1994 Peace Process period, and focuses on the work of DubbelJoint Theatre. Founded by Pam Brighton and Maria Jones, DubbelJoint is the only professional theatre company in the study. An important aspect of its work has been its support for community-led theatres, and its use of mixed companies of professional and non-professional performers. Two aspects of this work are considered, namely the production of scripts by JustUs, the Republican women's theatre group (1996–2000), and the plays of former IRA volunteers Brian Campbell and Laurence McKeown. Campbell and McKeown's work in particular offers important examples of theatre being used as part of Republicanism's broader ideological and political struggle to secure a united Ireland through democratic means. In Part Four I offer a summative analysis of Republican and Loyalist community theatres, and of their role in the conflict, and in the post-conflict period.

The Critical Context

The past decade has seen an increased academic focus on the Troubles and its theatres. Lionel Pilkington's study, *Theatre and State in Twentieth-Century Ireland* is a cultural materialist reading of aspects of the complex intersection of theatre and politics in the evolution of first the Free State and, from 1946, the Republic of Ireland.[6] The book devotes two chapters to the north of Ireland, one dealing with the relationship between theatre and state between 1922 and 1972, and the second focusing on the mediation of the conflict in selected works by playwrights such as Brian Friel, Frank McGuinness, Martyn Lynch, and Maria Jones. There is no treatment in the book of the community-based theatres which he had examined in journal articles, and which included an extended dialogue with Derry Frontline's Dan Baron Cohen.[7] Pilkington deserves credit as the first academic to recognize the importance of these theatres, and to locate them within the broader frame of the conflict. Dan Baron Cohen has edited a collection of plays by Derry Frontline, which includes a brief historiography and an account of working methods, and he has also written a series of essays analyzing and theorizing the company's work.[8] As a consequence, Derry Frontline's work has, to date, been the most comprehensively documented within academic writing. The essays are notable both for their focus on methods, and for the absence of any reference to the Irish members of the company. By drawing on other sources, including the company's archive at the Working Class Movement Library in Salford, I hope to offer a more complete history of the group. In 1993 David Grant of Queen's University carried out a survey of community theatre for the Community Relations Council. The result was *Playing the Wild Card*, a valuable overview of the field, which includes, amid the roster of amateur, semi-professional and professional community theatres, brief biographies of Derry Frontline, Belfast People's Theatre and DubbelJoint. Reflecting its funding constituency, the survey focuses on the potential of community drama for improving cross community relations. It is therefore necessarily circumspect in its assessment that the distinctiveness of community arts in the north exists 'despite not because of the Troubles'.[9] While I am sure that this is true of professional cross-community interventions, it is not true of the Republican and Loyalist theatres. Tom Magill's accounts of his work with Republican prisoners in the H-Blocks of the Maze prison, and with the Loyalist community of the Shankill Road, offer invaluable insights into two of the most important initiatives of the period, particularly in relation to our understanding of rehearsal methods and the politics of the performance context.[10]

The most recent monograph is Tom Maguire's landmark study, *Making Theatre in Northern Ireland: through and beyond the Troubles*.[11] Maguire's book is the first to offer a systematic critical and theoretical analysis of theatrical representations of the Troubles. His aim, he writes, is to 'compare the strategies by which different productions have engaged with specific elements of the political crises and the responses at play in their reception'.[12] Our interests overlap at certain points, for example in relation to the work of Derry Frontline and DubbelJoint. However, whereas Maguire's focus is on a politics of performance, mine is on a politics of process, embracing group history, organizational politics, rehearsal methods, texts and performance contexts, and, finally and decisively, the relation between these and the day-to-day unfolding of the conflict. This is possibly too crude a division of interests, but it suggests the fundamental differences between, or complementarities of, our separate approaches. These differences are expressive also of our different relationship, as writers and academics, to the Troubles.

Origins of the Study

My first encounter with the community theatres of the Troubles came not as a researcher but as a practitioner, and this fact has determined the history, ethos and purposes of this study. Between 1979 and 2000, I had worked as an actor and writer with left-wing theatres in Britain. The first of these groups, the socialist theatre group Cartoon Archetypical Slogan Theatre (CAST) was founded in 1965, and declared its work to be at an end in May 1986, following an Arts Council decision to cease grant aid. CAST's was a paradigmatic history. In its development from cultural 'street gang' to subsidized professional *ensemble*, the group was to exemplify the contradictions and crisis of left oppositional theatres in the period. I was a member of the company from 1980 to 1983.[13] In 1983, I co-founded Sheffield Popular Theatre (1983–90) with Warren Lakin, formerly the administrator of CAST.[14] In 1984 I left the company to set up Theatreworks with John Goodchild. Goodchild had made contact in response to an article I had written in the local alternative magazine calling for a 'common stage, accessible to all, through which a new theatre could evolve to provide a focus and a voice for political resistance.'[15] We shared a practical knowledge of Brecht, and of his theoretical writings, and we had read Augusto Boal's *Theatre of the Oppressed*, and the pedagogic works of Brazilian educationalist Paulo Freire. These influences were the theoretical and methodological underpinning of the theatre praxis which we developed over the following years. Theatreworks (1984–2000), concentrated its work in the inner-city communities of Sheffield, and in a range of campaigns, focused on local and national issues. We were not a theatre group in a conventional sense, but worked with local residents and activists to create groups *within* campaigns and community actions. Over the seventeen years of its existence, Theatreworks would develop theatre groups with, among others, the Sheffield and District Afro-Caribbean Association, the Black Justice Campaign, Sheffield Tenants Federation, Sheffield Centres Against Unemployment, Sheffield Credit Union Development Agency, Heart of Our City Campaign, the Anti-Poll Tax Campaign, Sheffield Advice Centres Group, Sheffield Troops Out Movement, Healthy Sheffield, the Child Poverty Action Group, the Sheffield Disability Forum, the Community Health Forum, the Anti Racist network, the Nicaraguan Solidarity Group, and the Stop Clause 28 Campaign. The first organisation to support the work in 1984 was the Workers' Education Association, and our partnership with community-based educationalists was critical to the development of these interventionary theatres. It was as a consequence of these links that Goodchild and I were invited to join a community education delegation to the north of Ireland in 1985. The purpose of the visit was to research the grass-roots community education networks which had developed in Republican and Nationalist areas during the Troubles. On our first evening we were taken through driving rain to a small council house in the Andersontown estate, where we met members of Belfast Community Theatre. Seated around a gas fire, they gave a rehearsed reading of a short play, *Focailin* by Fr Des Wilson, co-founder of the Belfast People's Theatre. As they rehearsed and then spoke about their work, I recorded the event on a camcorder. This reflexive urge to document (I was not sure then to what end) characterized my relationship with the Belfast groups. My and Goodchild's theatre background, and our work in Sheffield, provided the basis for a political and practical relationship that would develop over the following years. The process of writing this book, then, has been the process of locating those relationships in a wider, and largely undocumented, history.[16] The relationships with Belfast Community Theatre and Belfast People's Theatre were constitutive of a political commitment, and they have shaped the knowledge, analysis and the transparent ideological perspective of this history. Historian Ludmilla Jordanova has stressed the need for historians to acknowledge the effect on History of

> The emotional responses historians experience when working with their sources, and especially those upon whom they rely most heavily. These responses are complex and certainly cannot be summed up in a few words, and yet they infuse everything historians do.[17]

Such emotions do not invalidate historical narratives, but complicate them. My relationship with members of Belfast Community Theatre and the People's Theatre also provided me with significant primary sources, which include unpublished play texts, interviews with participants, correspondence with key figures, production papers, videos of performances, and rehearsal notes. I have also drawn on other and more recent dialogues with cultural activists, writers, actors and directors, including former IRA prisoners of war. I have foregrounded these voices, allowing witnesses to define as much as possible the terms on which their work, and their view of it, is received. Their narratives underscore what Franz Fanon's biographer Hussein Bulhan has called 'the necessary continuity between individual biographies and collective histories'.[18]

My aim has been to find a proper balance between the knowledge which has come from engagement, and the knowledge which has been derived from more traditional forms of research: to avoid polemic while making transparent my political perspective on the central issue of a united Ireland. And while there are differences in the balance in each casebook between these forms of knowledge, all share a focus on process, and on the relations of production mediated through a representative, witnessed performance. The result is a historiographical *bricolage*, the making from these sources of one possible version of this history. Another feature of these theatres and their work is that they cannot presume upon a critical hinterland as one might in a study of, say, Samuel Beckett or Brian Friel. The emphasis on the specific political and cultural context within each casebook reflects this absence.

I have followed the advice of the series editors in privileging documentation over interpretation, narrative and context over theoretical or conceptual analysis, though all are present in some measure. The Troubles were too long in duration, too recent and too complex, for any single study to presume to offer 'a history' of even this small field of theatre making. I have therefore allowed each casebook to generate its own context. I am in agreement with the Indian Marxist critic and poet Himani Bannerji, an exponent of a form of 'deep description', who argues that it is only through an understanding of the specific social and political relations which shape and contain popular theatres that we can understand the critical intersection in these forms of politics and methods, ideology and creative processes. She writes:

> The experience of theatre starts long before the curtain rises and the play begins. Our theatre exists in the world in which we live, and our theatre experience, shaped by that world, rises from it and returns to it. The world of theatre is not sufficient unto itself.[19]

Other important formal influences include the historiographical and critical writings of Eugene Van Erven and Rustom Barucha, whose works offer a rich and evocative coming together of personal encounter, political context, performance analysis, documentation and reception. Barucha's work is distinguished in part by its detailed accounts of performances. How to convey the immediacy of performance, and how to read it usefully into its socio-political context, is an ongoing challenge to all theatre historians.[20]

Definitions and Key Terms

I am indebted in this section to Stephen Howe's stimulating study, *Ireland and Empire*, in which he identifies the dominant post-war political perspectives on Ireland's history. The perspective shared by the IRA, Sinn Féin and Republican Marxists, and the one which dominates this study, sees Britain as having played 'an unbroken, direct and consistent role' in the colonial development of Ireland, latterly through the act of partition, which created a 'pseudo-sovereign neo-colonial state' in the Republic and a 'colonial enclave' in the north. Revolutionary action to supplant both was therefore considered legitimate.[21] Consequently, when I talk of the Republican Movement, or the Movement, I am referring to those who share, or shared, this ideological position. While the Nationalist community contains the Republican Movement, it also includes many social democrats who rejected armed force as a means to securing Irish unity, and who believed in using constitutional means to achieve all political ends. It is one of the complications brought by the peace that Sinn Féin has effectively created a new formation, a constitutional Republican party. Another perspective, often associated with revisionist historiography, saw colonialism as irrelevant to an understanding of Ireland's recent history, and only partially useful for accounting for its historic development. Just as important, in this view, were the internal dynamics of Irish society, Ireland's relation to Europe, and its place within the North Atlantic archipelago. This perspective would be intriguingly reframed in one of the few Loyalist theatre interventions. Unionists wish to maintain existing constitutional and institutional relationship between Ireland and Great Britain, which are founded upon the 1800 Act of Union and which Partition was intended to maintain. In Unionist historiography Britain is presented as a civilizing force within Irish history, and the north as an integral part of the United Kingdom. The true colonialists in the Unionist analysis are/were Republicans, who wished to occupy the land of a 'distinct national community'. Further distinctions need to be made. All Loyalists are also Unionists, but can be distinguished from them in three critical ways: they come primarily from working-class communities, they are/were committed to physical force, and their communities were part of the war zone. Gusty Spence, who reformed the Ulster Volunteer Force (UVF) in 1965, is clear about the class distinctions which inflect the Unionist/Loyalist relationship:

> The working class have always been on the cutting edge, you know, they've lived cheek by jowl, the Catholic working class and the Protestant working class. And inevitably the interface areas which are now the peace lines became the battlegrounds. The Unionists always live in a nice leafy suburbia. And if there was any threat to them, they have their police body guards, and so on and so forth ... so they were absolutely and completely out of touch with what was and is the thinking within the Loyalist working class. They never really considered the working class except at election time.[22]

Many Nationalists, especially those who supported the Social Democratic and Labour Party (SDLP), were middle-class professionals who had prospered, and there was consequently an important class dimension to relations within both Republicanism and Loyalism. Maguire has commented on this in his study, noting that 'the Republican movement has been strongly rooted within the Nationalist working class.'[23] In both movements progressive voices would argue for a unity based on class interests, and this is articulated in the theatres.

The Historical Context

When, on 28 July 2005, the Provisional Irish Republican Army (IRA) announced the end of its armed campaign to establish a united Ireland, it was the endgame of a four-hundred-year struggle by successive Nationalist movements to free Ireland from control by first the English, and later the British, colonial power. The Troubles were sourced in a history whose lineaments were defined during the period between 1606 and 1660, when the Plantation of Ulster by Scottish settlers began in the Ards peninsula of Ulster. In the words of historian R.F. Foster, 'The history of Ulster from that time to this was dictated by the fact that these proposals did not work out as intended.'[1] Certainly the central themes of Ireland's colonial experience were defined in that period, and the Troubles were, for both sides, the latest phase of historical forces set in motion by Elizabeth I and consolidated by the decisive Cromwellian campaigns of 1648–51. The economic exploitation of the majority Catholic Irish by a minority of Protestant Planters meant that from the beginning religion and land, faith and power, Catholicism and poverty, were fatally linked.

Successive Irish Nationalist movements would oscillate between democratic gradualism (O'Connell's Catholic Association, 1820s) and insurgency (Young Irelanders, 1840s), between secular radicalism (United Irishmen, 1798) and parliamentary gradualism (Parnell and the Land League, 1880s). From the 1690 Battle of the Boyne onwards, Protestants would see themselves as an embattled but anointed minority, Catholics as a disenfranchised and repressed majority.

Home Rule for Ireland remained the goal of Nationalist and Republican parliamentary activity and extra-parliamentary agitation and violence throughout the eighteenth and nineteenth centuries. Home Rule had been promised, and might well have been implemented in 1914, had war not broken out.[2] Far from bringing a united Ireland closer, the First World War, 1914–18, would powerfully cement the historic ties between Ulster Unionism and the British Crown and, in so doing, further entrench political divisions. A critical moment came on 1 July 1916 when some 5,500 soldiers from the 36th Ulster Division were slaughtered in the space of two hours at the Battle of the Somme, an event which was deeply imprinted into the consciousness of the Unionist people.[3] The terrible losses helped to galvanize resistance by the northern Protestants to Home Rule, a resistance already well established at the war's outbreak. Historian Michael Farrell:

> As the Home Rule Bill loomed nearer and nearer the Unionists prepared to resist. Although they were opposed to Home Rule for any part of Ireland, in practice they now concentrated their preparation in Ulster. Already they had established a separate Ulster Unionist Council (UUC). In 1910 they selected Edward Carson MP, a Dublin lawyer and former Solicitor General in a Conservative Government at Westminster, as their leader. In 1911 Carson threatened to establish a Provisional Government in Ulster if the Home Rule Bill was passed, and the Unionists began organizing and drilling a private army recruited through the Orange Order. In 1912 400,000 people signed a 'Solemn League and Covenant' to resist Home Rule.[4]

The Covenant became central to Unionist self-conception in the twentieth century. Home Rule, it declared, was a 'conspiracy' which would be 'subversive of our civil and religious freedom, destructive of our citizenship, and perilous to the unity of the Empire'. The duty of a Unionist was to defend by whatever means 'for ourselves and our children our cherished position of equal citizenship in the United Kingdom'.[5] To which end a retired British General, Sir George Richardson, set about organizing a growing citizen's army into the Ulster Volunteer Force. The reaction of Padraic Pearse, who was to lead the 1916 Easter Rising, to the sight of Orangemen armed and drilling with the British Army's connivance was, says R.F. Foster, a 'curious blend of approval and wishful thinking'.[6] Writing in the journal *Irish Freedom*, Pearse 'applauded the sight of Irishmen with rifles', and continued:

> Negotiations with the Orangemen might be opened on these lines: You are creating a Provisional Government of Ulster – make it a Provisional Government of Ireland and we will recognise it and obey it ... Hitherto England has governed Ireland through the Orange Lodge: now she proposes to govern Ireland through the AOH. You object: so do we. Why not unite and get rid of the English? They are the real difficulty; their presence here the real incongruity.[7]

It was not a likely scenario, as Pearse must have known. But the formation of the UVF did validate in Irish Nationalist eyes the right of resistance to parliamentary government. If Unionists could arm, then so too could Republicans, and in 1914 the Irish Volunteers, the precursors of the Irish Republican Army, were formed.

The Easter Rising of 1916 brought to an historical confluence the forces of mystic patriotism, constitutional nationalism, physical-force

Republicanism and Ulster rejectionism; forces which would later be played out in the Troubles. It was prosecuted by the Irish Volunteers led by Padraic Pearse, and the Irish Citizen Army, led by James Connolly, though the historical energy which drove it forward belonged to the Irish Republican Brotherhood, who had carried out periodic guerrilla attacks on the British occupiers since the mid-1850s.[8] On Monday 24 April 1916 a hundred or so Irish Volunteers and members of the Citizen's Army took over the General Post Office on O'Connell Street, Dublin, and declared it the centre of a new Irish Republic. It was Padraic Pearse who stood in front of the General Post Office in order to read out a Proclamation on behalf of the self-appointed 'Provisional government' to bemused, and largely indifferent, bystanders. Its central section ran:

> We declare the right of the people of Ireland to the ownership of Ireland, and to the unfettered control of Irish destinies, to be sovereign and indefeasible. The long usurpation of that right by a foreign people and government has not extinguished the right, nor can it ever be extinguished except by the destruction of the Irish people. In every generation the Irish people have asserted their right to national freedom and sovereignty; six times during the last three hundred years they have asserted it to arms. Standing on that fundamental right and again asserting it in arms in the face of the world, we hereby proclaim the Irish Republic as a Sovereign Independent State, and we pledge our lives and the lives of our comrades-in-arms to the cause of its freedom, of its welfare, and of its exaltation among the nations.

A military failure, crushed by the British after a week of fighting in the centre of Dublin, and condemned in the moment by the vast majority of the Irish people, the Rising was nonetheless turned into a success by the political response of the British state. The execution of its leaders, whom many saw as prisoners of war, awakened national sentiment. The most important impact of the Rising, according to historian Charles Townshend, was that it validated physical-force Republicanism:

> The Rising was certainly a manifestation of political violence, but it was more than this: it was, to a large extent a manifestation of violence as politics ... the armed propaganda of a self-appointed vanguard which claimed the power to interpret the general will ... cathartic action was substituted for methodological debate; ideal types replaced reality; symbols took on real powers.[9]

Such arguments would later be used to criticise the IRA during the Troubles, and, in 1916 as later, they would be blamed not for their failure to bring

Irish unity closer, but for deepening divisions, and by-passing the democratic will of the people.

As it would in the 1950s, and again during the Troubles, the British state used internment without trial and martial law as a means to quell further rebellion in the post-Rising period. Each time, however, these actions simply radicalized a new generation of Irish patriots. In 1916 internment helped to create a future IRA leadership under Michael Collins, who used his time in the detention camps to develop the guerrilla tactics which would prove so successful in the war of independence which followed Sinn Féin's all-Ireland victory in the 1918 elections, and the establishment of the first (illegal) Irish Dail in 1919. The war of independence was brought to an end by the Treaty of December 1921, which created two incomplete states, a Free State in the South (which became the Republic of Ireland in 1949), and the statelet of Ulster or Northern Ireland, still part of the United Kingdom, in the north-east of the country. The South, dominated by an authoritarian Church and a conservative and corrupt polity, was hardly the Republic dreamt of by those who had died in the 1916 Rising, of visionaries such as Padraic Pearse, or internationalists and socialists like James Connolly, even though it was dominated for much of that time by the Fianna Fail Party of Eamonn de Valera, who had led the Republican dissidents in the civil war. It would take until the late twentieth century for Eire to modernize its economy, first, and then, and more slowly, its social and political institutions. During that time the north remained to most in the South as distant as it did to those in England, when they bothered to think about it at all.

Periodic IRA campaigns to eject the British, most notably the Border Campaign of 1956–62, ended for lack of popular support, and both parliaments on the island of Ireland introduced internment for suspected IRA members. The organization survived north and south as a rump, generally confined to blue blood Republican families, such as the Hannaways and Adams of Belfast; the lineage which shaped current Sinn Féin president Gerry Adams, whose father was imprisoned for IRA activity, and who could trace his forebears back to the Fenian movements of the nineteenth century.

Indifference defined the British state's attitude to the north of Ireland as much as, or perhaps more than, active encouragement of what seemed a quasi apartheid state, with discrimination against Catholics enshrined in successive government acts. However, this situation, in which to all intents and purposes a single party or political bloc maintained uninterrupted power over many decades could be found, argues Simon Prince, in other states, for example Germany in the post-Nazi era in Germany.[10] In the same period Portugal and Spain were ruled by fascist parties, and the eastern bloc was an amalgamation of single party states maintained by state repression. What was particular about the Northern Ireland state was not that it was dominated by a single party, but that it was part of the United Kingdom, a parliamentary democracy.

It was a modern state which denied a significant minority of its people equal status within its political, economic and civic institutions. The Orange State was founded on the Special Powers Act of 1922, which gave the state's security forces the powers to arrest people without warrant, to detain them without trial and to ban all meetings and processions. It was a state created within an internal border drawn to ensure a Protestant majority. Where, as in the second city of Londonderry, Catholics were in a majority, gerrymandering ensured that Unionists remained in control of the city council. Catholics were disenfranchised by laws which restricted access to home ownership, while allowing only rate-payers to vote. Many would argue with the conception of Nationalists as a colonized people, and a more useful analysis is perhaps to be found in the concept of internal colonization: that is to say of the reproduction, within a political state with claims to democratic authority, of the relations and apparatus of colonization through the internal repression of one people by another, or one ethnic grouping by another.

The Civil Rights Movement

Discrimination against Catholics in the allocation of housing and employment were two of the central issues which gave rise to the Northern Ireland Civil Rights Association (NICRA) in 1967. Founded on 29 January 1967, NICRA initially included representatives from every political party in the north, as well as activists from the Campaign for Social Justice, The Wolfe Tone Societies, Belfast Trades Council and the wider trade union movement. Among the demands made by the new broad front organization were: the repeal of the Special Powers Act and the disbandment of the 'B' Special paramilitary police force; a universal franchise for local government elections; an end to gerrymandering of election boundaries; and the removal of legalized discrimination in civic institutions, including education, housing, employment and health. The demand from the majority of Nationalists and progressive voices at this time therefore was not for a united Ireland, but for the reform of the existing state. Gerry Adams has argued that the Civil Rights movement of 1968–69 had no agenda beyond the ending of discrimination in employment, and the securing of universal suffrage in local elections.[11] In that sense the movement was, says Adams, part of an international juncture, which linked Belfast and Derry to Prague and Paris, to Saigon and Berkeley. This was also how leading socialists and Marxists within the NICRA saw the situation. Simon Prince:

> [Michael] Farrell remembered the Derry protests as 'our Chicago', but it was also 'our Paris, our Prague'. 'One world, one struggle' – that was the motto of '68 according to [Eamonn] McCann. The leftists saw themselves as part of a global revolt against imperialism, capitalism and bureaucracy.[12]

The late 1950s had seen a fundamental shift in Republican thinking about the road to a united Ireland. Leading figures such as the Communist Roy Johnston, a Cambridge graduate, and Cathal Goulding, had set out a blue-print which proposed the building of a non-sectarian, mass working-class movement. IRA volunteers were encouraged to get involved in local campaigns and single issue struggles. So, while there were from the beginning real tensions between Republicans and NICRA's non-republican membership over tactics and goals, it was the violence of the sectarian state's response to the campaign for civil rights which ignited latent Republican aspirations, and brought the fact of partition into sharp focus. The brutal attacks on the People's Democracy marches, the most famous being at Burntollet Bridge, eight miles outside Derry, on 4 January 1969, when Loyalists, including many off-duty members of the B-Specials, assaulted the marchers with clubs, wooden batons and fists, were televised across the world. That night the RUC and B-Specials invaded the Catholic Bogside and Creggan estates in Derry, firing indiscriminately at civilians and destroying property. For many on both sides the event was decisive. What followed became known as the Battle of the Bogside, as local people barricaded the ghettos, and kept the police at bay with improvised weapons, creating no-go areas for state forces which would stay in place for the next three years.[13]

While there were moderate factions within Unionism willing to concede reforms, the majority set their face against accommodation. Consequently, the attempts by Prime Minister Terence O'Neill and his successor James Chichester Clark to begin a process of moderate reform, and the 1969 Downing Street Declaration, which affirmed the right of Catholics to civic equality and freedom from discrimination, simply inflamed Loyalist and radical Unionist opinion, and there was an intensification of attacks on Catholic areas across the north.[14] Belfast saw the largest movement of civilian population since the Second World War as families were burned out of their homes on the Lower Falls, and thousands streamed across the border. The Republic set up refugee centres for the displaced Nationalists, and placed its army on alert. On 16 August 1969, the British government sent in troops, but by then it was too late. Events had demonstrated to many Republicans that the state was not reformable. The Bloody Sunday events of January 1972, when British soldiers killed fourteen unarmed civilians, marked a point of no return. These, and many other events, are the subject of the theatres, and I will return to them.

A People's Army

Resistance to the British state was led by the Irish Republican Army. While the smaller Irish National Liberation Army (INLA) would play a tactically significant role during periods of the conflict, it was the IRA which overwhelmingly determined and dominated both military and political resistance from within the Republican and Nationalist communities. In 1969 the IRA was, as I have noted, a rump, with few arms and fewer volunteers. Indeed, many future leaders of the Provisional IRA, such as Derry's Martin McGuinness, were raised in deeply conservative Catholic homes where the political situation was never spoken about. Brendan Hughes, a leading 'Provo', and who was to take part in the first hunger strike in 1980, has spoken of the impact of seeing his relatives burned out of their homes:

> I was a Catholic, and I seen the Catholic community under attack. My whole reason for joining the Provisionals at that time was not to bring about a thirty-two county democratic socialist republic, and I had no ideology at that time. We were a reactionary force. Here we are being attacked by Loyalists, by B-Specials, by the RUC, by the British Army.[15]

Hughes's stress on communal loyalties rather than political ideology is echoed by Ron McMurray of the UVF, who notes that, 'one of the main motives for a lot of people was that you were doing something for your community, in that we perceived an attack on our community or on our identity'.[16] This insistence on the lack of ideological and political coherence in the early phase has been well documented.[17] It was only after the IRA split into Provisional (PIRA) and Official (OIRA) wings in 1970, that the achievement of an all-Ireland socialist republic became a stated aim of the IRA.[18] Eamonn McDermott, a former IRA volunteer from Derry:

> It's a cliché now, but the British Army created the IRA … They brought the national question into it, before then it wasn't really an issue. Republicans would argue that it was there from the start, but that's a load of rubbish. Initially we were trying to reform the state; the national question and partition came later.[19]

Bernard Fox, who would later become a leading figure in the IRA, recalls asking to join up after he had been shot at in the street. Asked if he was capable of killing a British soldier, he remembers his surprise, as 'at that time I hadn't the idea that it was the British government's fault'.[20] Ed Maloney writes that 'the story of the growth and development of the Provisional IRA in Derry is the tale not about how ideology triumphed, but about how police and military violence created and nourished the need to retaliate'.[21] The violence of the state's response generated its own historical logic and momentum, and gathered in its wake eight hundred years of colonial oppression, and resistance to it. From a negligible presence in 1969, by the end of 1970 the IRA had become a formidable force, though vulnerable to infiltration. The Troubles were long enough for the movement to move, or at least important fragments within it, from a Defender mentality defined by a political and theological conservatism, to neo-Marxists who projected as their aim a united socialist Ireland. There is a consensus that it has been the most effective guerrilla army produced in modern European history. It saw itself as a community army, 'a People's Army', which was resurrected in 1970 as a defence force against Loyalist and state-sponsored attacks on the Catholic community.[22] Republicans and many Nationalists viewed the British army as an army of occupation, and it was upon this analysis that the IRA based the legitimacy of their actions.

According to Foster, at the core of Irish economic and social organization in the modern period has been the concept of *meitheal* – of social relations defined by mutual aid.[23] It is a central concept in this study. It was this *meitheal* solidarity, a practical class-consciousness, which was the key to the IRA's ability to engage the British army for some thirty years. After the 1970 split in the movement, a split caused by fundamental differences over whether a united Ireland was to be achieved by force of arms or through the building of a mass working-class movement, the Provisional IRA had criticised the Officials for seeking to impose an alien and 'totalitarian dictatorship' upon the people of Ireland. Instead they proposed an indigenous form of mutual aid, saying: 'Ours is a socialism based on the native Irish tradition of Comhar na gComharsan [Neighbourly Co-operative] which is founded on the right of worker ownership, and on our Irish and Christian values.'[24] For some in the Nationalist community, however, the IRA was a semi-fascist organization, a self-appointed militia which perpetuated sectarianism, or fed off it, and was a greater barrier to political progress than the British. Certainly the atrocities which defined parts of their campaign alienated and horrified those close to them, as well as those predisposed to dismiss them as criminal thugs. Father Des Wilson, a priest from Ballymurphy, called for a focus on causes:

> I have made no secret of my own view, a view much changed from what I believed in 1965. The British government has oppressed and degraded our people, set them at each other's throats, offered the Protestants of Northern Ireland small gifts and the Catholics kicks, but by doing these things controlled them both. It has been an unjust regime, and if it ceased to be so it would cease to rule ... I also believe that war is the worst of all ways to have to solve problems, but that if good people go to war we have to ask why it is that good people do such things.[25]

One cause was imperialism and its bedrock of reflexive racism. The Tudors inaugurated the tradition, marking the Irish as savages and pagans, and the land itself as a 'wild beast's cave' which should be 'razed' of life.[26] Racism was to play a key role in preparing the British public for counter-insurgency excesses.[27] The projection of the Irish as sub-human had been a theme of political commentary and, in particular, of cartoons, since the rebellion of the United Irishmen in 1798. Contemporaneous illustrations showed them as aggressive, unkempt and simian-like figures, a template which was to persist with little real variation for two hundred years. The objectification of the 'Other' as less than human is part of the narrative of colonialism and totalitarianism. The media played a strategic role in stripping the conflict of its historical and political character and replacing it with a racist fiction, in which the Irish were presented as drunken killers, while the British were altruistic arbiters of an internecine bloodbath. Journalist Milton Shulman declared in 1980 that the Irish enjoyed the 'senseless pastime of murdering each other',[28] while right-wing commentator John Junor opined, when hearing that Ronald Reagan was to visit Ireland, that he personally would 'prefer to spend three days in June looking for worms in a dung heap'.[29] This racist narrative was to become especially vital at times when the British State breached the human rights of Irish men and women. When evidence emerged in the late 1970s of the systematic use of torture in the interrogation of suspects, the *Sunday Times* framed the ethical dilemma faced by the British people thus: 'The notorious problem is how a civilized country can overpower uncivilized people without becoming less civilized in the process.'[30] In her analysis of the return of torture as a tool of inter-state and intra-state policy in the twentieth century, Kate Millet writes:

> With the British public, [the state] can depend on a long history of an attitude which, on examination, is distinctly racist. Though both groups are Caucasian, even Christian, British contempt for the Irish is ancient and entire, a racial hatred in fact … Torture is introduced into this situation through a long habit of malice.[31]

The majority of those to suffer in the war did not bear arms, including the majority of those who were tortured by members of the state's intelligence forces. It is therefore proper to talk of the British state's counter insurgency policies in the north of Ireland as constituting the collective punishment of a people, a punishment outlawed under Article 33 of the Geneva Convention. Collective punishment under the Convention includes holding individual persons responsible for actions which they did not commit, or over which they have no power, simply because they belong to a community or peoples, members of which have committed violence against the state or another power. The convention specifically forbids torture and extra-judicial killings, as well as 'outrages upon personal dignity, in particular humiliating and degrading treatment'.[32] All were used against Nationalist and Republican communities regardless of individual affiliation or belief. As in all wars, civilian deaths accounted for the greater part of those killed. Over the thirty years 3,638 people died, and 40,000 were injured from a population of some one and a half millions. Historian Marc Mulholland:

If one extrapolates those figures to Britain, some 110,000 people would have died, with 1.4 million injured, equivalent to just under half of the British deaths during the Second World War. By 1998, about one in seven of the adult population, disproportionately Catholic, had been a victim of a violent incident.[33]

The war brought death and deep trauma, injury and arbitrary violence to the working-class communities of the north, and these realities determined the totality of the theatres' processes.[34] They were political theatres, but they were political theatres of a kind not found elsewhere on the mainland of Britain in the post-war period.

PART TWO

CASEBOOKS (1)
COMMUNITY THEATRES
OF THE TROUBLES

'Gentle Fury'

Father Des and the People's Theatre

God rules in Heaven/And only in Heaven does he rule/In this land of ours must rule/The Colombian People.[1]

Introduction

On 15 February 1966, in the province of Santander, Colombia, Camilo Torres, former priest, now a soldier of the Army of National Liberation (ANL), was shot dead by government soldiers during a failed ambush. In 1965 Torres had asked for, and been granted, laicization, so that he could commit to the revolutionary struggle being waged by the armed wing of the opposition Frente Unido. 'I took off my cassock to be more truly a priest,' he famously declared, and, more provocatively, 'The Catholic who is not a revolutionary is living in mortal sin.'[2] In the period leading up to his laicization, Torres had called for the expropriation of Church lands and their distribution among the people, and for greater links with the Communists. To Fabio Vasquez, an ANL commander, Torres had

> United the scientific conception of revolutionary war, considering it the only effective way to develop the fight for freedom, with a profound Christianity, which he extended and practised as a limitless love for the poor, the exploited, and the oppressed and as a complete dedication to the battle for their liberation.[3]

Ten years later, in Belfast, another priest, Father Des Wilson, also sought to free himself to work among his people. He requested not laicization, but a form of 'retirement', an action which caused his superior, Bishop Philbin, to accuse him of 'threatening to destroy the Church'.[4] The 'retirement' was granted, but Fr Wilson was denied any further use of Church property, and cast into an economic, legal and institutional limbo. He was ostracized by his former colleagues on the Priests' Council, a response which caused him great hurt. As he notes in his autobiography: 'A priest denied the use of churches is made to look like a criminal. People do not know what it is all about.'[5] The Catholic media began a concerted smear campaign in which Fr Wilson was said, variously, to have had a nervous breakdown, or run off with a woman, or taken up with 'lapsed Catholics and communists'.[6] The truth was that he had simply decided to place himself at the disposal of a people fighting what he saw as a revolution against an oppressive state. Both Torres and Fr Wilson belonged to an historical moment in which the revolutionary forces unleashed by twentieth-century liberation struggles in Africa and particularly Latin America, radicalized the Roman Catholic Church. John Gerassi:

> In Sao Paulo Dominican monks work with urban guerrillas. In Montevideo a priest heads an underground revolutionary network. In Bolivia fifty Catholic clergymen openly espouse armed rebellion. In Lima a priest co-directs the National Liberation Front. In Buenos Aires another identifies the love of Christ with the violent struggle of the poor. In the mountains of Colombia a priest fights, gun in hand, with the guerrilla Army of National Liberation. Seemingly everywhere in Latin America, Catholic Churchmen are committed to violent social revolution. Well, not quite.[7]

Gerassi's qualification is important. However, although it was only a small minority of priests who engaged in revolutionary activity, their influence on the Roman Catholic polity was considerable. The Second Vatican Council (1962–65), heralded as a sign of liberalization and modernization within the Roman Catholic Church, had been an attempt, mostly successful, to contain these forces, which would find alternative expression and profound global influence through the theories and practices of liberation pedagogy, culture and theology. While Fr Wilson did not join the armed struggle against the British occupation of the north (some priests did), he nonetheless believed that it met the theological conditions for a Just War, writing that, in this sense 'the Republicans were more theologically correct than the bishops'. The Vatican's ritual condemnations of violence were felt to be irrelevant to the reality on the streets of Belfast, where Fr Wilson himself was beaten up by paratroopers, and where two priests would be killed by British troops as they ministered to dying parishioners.[8] In 1979 he wrote of the Pope's visit to Ireland, 'People had already discussed the moral problems of war and revolution and had solved them one way or another. Either it was morally acceptable to fight a bad government or it was not, and the Pope's visit was not going to make much difference.'[9] Renewal and hope, he firmly believed, would come from the laity, including from those who had taken up arms to defend their community. 'The Republican movement has the potential for good, like all movements of people from below, if we could recognize it,' he wrote, continuing, 'a combination of their idealism and the Christian idealism of sharing would be a powerful thing.'[10] Like Torres, Fr Wilson was also a writer of distinction. Torres' essays, collected by Gerassi, reflect his sociological training. Their breadth of interest, taking in economics, science, trade unionism, problems of popular organization, the dignity of work, the crisis of the relation of priest and people, and so on, are mirrored in the writings of the Irish priest, whose monographs, pamphlets and journalism constituted a discourse of dissent of which the theatre was just one part.[11]

A Quarrelsome Prelate

Fr Des Wilson was born in 1925 at the Antrim House nursing home on Cliftonville Road, Belfast, and has lived and worked in the city ever since. After ordination, he served for eighteen months as chaplain to the Mater Infirmorum Hospital, which included the role of spiritual director to a Legion of Mary group which worked with prostitutes in the city's dockland areas. These experiences, which brought him into contact with the most destitute, marginalized and poor of the Nationalist people, made a lasting impression on the young priest. In 1951, he was appointed as the spiritual director to trainee priests at St Malachy's College, and seemed destined for an illustrious career within the Roman Catholic hierarchy. However, in 1963 he wrote a critique of a theological work by the then Bishop Cahal Daly, later a Cardinal, which drew national attention. He was given to understand that, when a vacancy arose, he would be moved for his temerity, and in 1966 he was duly sent to St John's Parish on the Whiterock, in Greater Ballymurphy. Blighted by endemic poverty and poor housing, Ballymurphy also lacked the most basic community amenities, including open spaces, education centres and community meeting places. It was through an attempt to meet this need that Fr Wilson laid the foundations for one of the most remarkable and radical community education ventures in Western Europe, Springhill Community House. Determined to find spaces where people could come together to talk, in 1972 Fr Wilson rented a narrow, three-storey terraced house on the then new Springfield estate. The house next door was taken over by Ballymurphy Enterprises, one of many community-led responses to the area's 'appalling unemployment'.[12] Springhill was not founded as an education centre: it became one because the people wanted it to be one. Fr Wilson:

> One way to understand what happened in the north of Ireland is to think of a constant creation of alternatives by people in crisis. They created alternative education, alternative welfare, alternative theatre, broadcasting, theological and political discussion, public inquiries and much else. They also created at various times alternative police and alternative armies.[13]

One of those alternative armies, the Provisional IRA, had grown exponentially since 1970. With 479 deaths, of which 267 were Republicans, 1972 witnessed the greatest number of annual mortalities in the whole of the Troubles. Some 86 soldiers were killed, the most the army would ever lose in a single year. The massacre of fourteen civilians on Bloody Sunday in Derry on 31 January 1972 was only one of many deadly military attacks on non-combatants.[14] Bloody Sunday marked a watershed, and convinced many moderate Nationalists that the British Army was essentially an army of occupation whose sole aim was to crush the insurgency, regardless of the consequences for the human rights and civil liberties of non-combatants. On 21 July, the IRA set off twenty-one bombs in Belfast city centre. Although warnings were given and acted on in nineteen cases, two of the bombs exploded, killing nine civilians and horribly wounding dozens more. Most of those killed were Protestants. It was an horrific event, and was quickly dubbed 'Bloody Friday' by the media, so equating it with Bloody Sunday. The deaths, and the televised images of police shovelling human body parts into bin liners, caused revulsion within the Nationalist communities, as well as nationally and internationally. Bloody Friday gave the British state the excuse it had been waiting for to reoccupy Republican no-go areas. The outcome was Operation Motorman, which began in Derry on 31 July, and involved the application of overwhelming and systematic force with the aim of terrorizing Nationalist communities and immobilizing their economic, political, civic and communal structures. The means employed to achieve this aim: torture, arbitrary arrest, beatings, sexual assault, destruction of property, burning out of homes, humiliation and degradation through systematic and continuous persecution, racist abuse, disappearances, extrajudicial killings and the occupation or destruction of schools, shops, community centres, economic units and Church property, was unprecedented in its scale and ferocity. Operation Motorman represented the largest mobilization of British military power since Suez and involved an unprecedented peace-time violation of human rights and of the judicial process.[15] For the most part, its victims were not those who had taken up arms. Called upon to condemn the brutality, Cardinal William Conway turned away a community delegation with the remark, 'I know of far worse cases in other places'.[16] He may have been thinking of Colombia. It was in direct response to Operation Motorman that, on 20 November 1972, sixty-five parish priests, including Fr Wilson, wrote an open letter to the media:

> We are Catholic priests working in Belfast. We have condemned violence when carried out in the past by private citizens. We cannot remain silent in the face of the violence now being used by the British army, particularly in the poorer Catholic areas. No military victory could justify this campaign of attacking a civilian population. Innocent and unarmed civilians, regardless of sex or age, are being

shot by soldiers in and out of uniform. Homes are raided over and over again at all hours of the day and night. People are arrested daily in their homes, places of work, social clubs and on the streets. Many of those arrested are subjected to beatings and inhuman and degrading treatment.[17]

The Army's response was to brand the priests as 'IRA propagandists', an action Fr Wilson describes as 'clever and vicious'.[18] Clever because it undermined cross-community dialogue, vicious because it rendered him and the other so-called 'Provo Priests' targets for Loyalist assassination. On one occasion when he protested to a British Army Major about the harassment of his congregation, whom the Army claimed were smuggling weapons during mass, he was told, 'But you know, Father, this is the way we did it with the Arabs'.[19] The comment was profoundly revealing. To the army, its reflexes honed in Malaysia, Kenya and Aden, the Irish were not rebellious subjects, but rebellious natives. The Major's comment made it clear that the IRA and the British Army agreed on one thing at least, that it was not a civil war, but a war fought between colonizers and colonized. It was following one such encounter that Fr Wilson wrote in his diary that he had been, 'Silenced in my own country. Or perhaps I am just slow to learn that it is not my country after all.'[20]

As the counter-insurgency intensified, so also did his re-evaluation of the nature of the priesthood. The priest's role, he decided, was to 'be here and do quietly what is necessary to serve the poor people in a way that will help them have a good life. Not to dominate ... A boy comes in to ask can we get a doctor for his mother. A priest's function? A human person's function.'[21] He notes of the response of the Church to the state repression that it is 'binding the people's burdens, not lifting a finger to remove them'.[22] By 1975 his relationship with the Church had reached crisis point, and his 'retirement' was agreed. His treatment, and especially his exclusion from Church property, caused widespread anger among the Ballymurphy laity, and 1,500 of them occupied St Thomas's School on 18 June, and formed a Parish Council Steering Committee with the intent of laicizing control of the local church. Representatives were sent to the diocese and to the Papal Nuncio, who refused to see them, and churches and Catholic centres were picketed. The incidents marked, says historian Ciaran de Baroid, the point at which 'the trenches were dug between people and their priest – and the establishment'.[23] For the next three decades Springhill House became both the priest's home and his church.

Springhill House

When I first visited in 1985, Springhill Community House was surrounded by burnt-out buildings (the area was known locally as Little Beirut), and approached across a debris of concrete and glass. In the decade since its inception, this small council house had become a centre of education and healing for the war-torn community.[24] My first night in Belfast was spent on the floor of the Springhill House living room. In the small living areas some 300 adults and children a week came to attend formal and informal education classes. 'The biggest room in the house could hold about 15 people comfortably,' Fr Wilson wrote, 'and a few more uncomfortably.'[25] This was the front room where visitors slept during visits, where education classes took place; where mass was celebrated and impromptu jazz sessions held, and where theatre was performed. It was here also that John Goodchild and I would perform sketches on our visits, our stage the narrow space between fireplace and sofa, our audience whoever happened to be there at the time. These were conditions we were used to, having performed many times in tenants' rooms in Sheffield, or in small crèches and meeting rooms. These impromptu performances were an important expression of our social and political relationship with Springhill.

In the tiny kitchen a stream of visitors from across the world would cram around a small table to eat, drink tea, talk, argue, and plan. The small bedrooms upstairs would be used during the day as classrooms and meeting rooms. In a pamphlet, Fr Wilson talked of Springhill as offering 'an empty space' where people could 'create their own discussion around their concerns, and determine possible remedies for them'.[26] The concept of the 'empty space' underpinned Springhill's political philosophy, and guaranteed its longevity: 'One of the strengths we had – and we often reflected on this – was that even if all the sources of money dried up we would still have a house, a space, and that was the important thing. And you could start all over again because as long as the space belonged to you … what could they do?'[27] Fr Wilson talked a great deal about the damaging separation of human activities such as work, education, culture, politics, into specialized buildings. The mind was also kept uncluttered; not for reasons of intellectual or aesthetic purity, but because of the threat of torture. Talking of a decision to keep as little information as possible on paper 'or in my head', he notes:

> Many of our neighbours were tortured for information. Any of us could break down if we were tortured and anybody could be tortured, some of the most uninvolved of our neighbours were. To say nothing, the best way is to know nothing and hence came cultivated forgetfulness. You keep things in your head as long as you need them, then forget them.[28]

The rich resistance culture embodied in Springhill House was based on these twin forms of 'emptiness'. It would find one of its most eloquent expressions in the work of the People's Theatre, founded in 1973 by Des Wilson and local amateur dramatics enthusiast Michael Hilton.

The People's Theatre

Joseph Sheehy describes the People's Theatre as the 'most successful and enduring of all the Springhill experiments'.[29] In its twenty-plus years it would pass through a number of phases, with Fr Wilson as the consistent presence. Michael Hilton's reflections on its early period are worth citing in full:

> When Des moved into Ballymurphy, we set up play readings. The first one took place in a tin hut just up the road from 123. Des and Brian Smeaton took part; it also marked the debut of Angela Feeney who sang for us and went on to great things in opera circles. We invited a number of people from Des' discussion groups to see for themselves that all that was required was a little confidence. And instead of relying on people from my amateur dramatic group, more and more locals were included – until in the end they were doing the whole thing. Local writing talent had never been tapped; we decided to encourage one of the English classes to take up creative writing … this is how the first short stories, the first poetry, the first drama extracts came about and were then performed; first reading and then acting them out. Visitors kept turning up to witness the revival of what theatre was meant to be. Among them was Dan Berrigan, the famous American peace activist: he and I read extracts from his play about Vietnam (*The Trial of the Cantonsville Nine*, March 1974). There were basically three writers back then: Des, Pat Burns and myself … These were the originals: Des, myself, Peggy Hayes, Margaret Loughhead, Alice Hesketh, Susie Davidson, Angela Thompson, Ethel Moan, Liam Andrews (more an associate than an actor), Seamus McCabe, Liam Molloy, and of course Pauline, my wife. At that time there was tremendous conflict in the streets, rioting, harassment from the security forces, etc. The material reflected these issues; it really motivated people to write. No individual dictated the direction we would take; the people themselves decided – by the kind of material they created: for example, you might end up with a number of pieces on the health service, on harassment, money lenders etc; and the show would be built around these themes.[30]

The majority of those who became involved had no experience of theatre, so the group was also a training ground, a place for collective experiential learning. Before the prohibition on using church premises, productions had been presented in local schools, such as St Thomas's and St Bernadette's, or in church halls such as St Kevin's. The group's first production was *Passion Play*, written by Pat Burns, and performed at Christmas 1973. It offered a radical re-reading of the New Testament, writes Sheehy:

They took the drama of the crucifixion and saw in Christ's cry of 'Why have you forsaken me?' a decisive act of solidarity with the victims of injustice down the ages. Their Jesus was a Jesus who had suffered army harassment and internment like themselves, who had been interrogated, beaten and abused. Suddenly, before my eyes, the Roman soldiers became Brit troops; and Jesus, dazed and bloodied after His session in Castlereagh was led away to a lonely place to be machine-gunned.[31]

Such interpretations had to be argued for within the group, which contained people with a more conservative view of the Catholic Church. Although they all recognized Des Wilson's profound commitment to the priesthood, there were important divisions over the political and theological direction Springhill was taking in the period. A less controversial production was the wonderfully named *Holy Show*, where local clergy were invited to come together and perform in short revues for their parishioners. Irish mythology was gently parodied in these sketches, with Fr Wilson playing the role of Cuchullain in the skit *Thompson in Tir na nOg*. Local performances were supplemented with Arts Council funded visits from the likes of the actor Harold Goldblatt, and Margaret D'Arcy, a local actress and theatre enthusiast. They gave readings from Irish plays and poetry at the 1974 and 1975 Easter Shows, which were staged at St Bernadette's school, and also included topical sketches, folk songs, and traditional Irish music. The People's Theatre was an organic community theatre, which drew on an appropriately catholic range of dramatic forms. Hilton again: 'We encouraged audience participation as much as possible. We were the first to revive the tradition of the old music hall, planting people in the audience to stir them up.'[32] Fr Wilson, says Hilton, was the first to recognize the therapeutic value of involvement in the theatre amid the relentless attrition of the war. It was a *meitheal* theatre, with whole families, such as the Donnellys and Davidsons, involved as writers, actors, musicians and producers.

An important figure in this early period was Lelia Doolan, later President of the Irish Film Board. In 1972 she was appointed artistic director of the Abbey Theatre, Dublin, and visited Belfast regularly to cast an eye over new works at the city's Lyric Theatre. She had met Fr Des Wilson when writing articles for the Irish Press, and visited Springhill House during her visits to the Lyric. She remembers that the People's Theatre were at that time reading Synge and Lady Gregory, and that she thought that this was 'very old hat'. Doolan had been involved in political theatre with the Dublin Pike Theatre in the late 1960s, and suggested that the embryonic company should 'get in touch with what was real to them and of interest to their audience' by writing material based on their experiences, 'a kind of political cabaret'.[33] She says that Des Wilson was 'already thinking along these lines', and in the following year new and more topical material began to emerge from the writing classes. One of the writers produced through the classes was Theresa Donnelly, who would later achieve fame, if not fortune, as the author of *Put Out That Light!*, which Sheehy describes as 'a beautiful evocation of life during World War Two'.[34] The play was first produced at the Conway Mill theatre and then later at the Lyric Theatre, Belfast in 1993, where it was directed by Joe Devlin. Donnelly wrote a series of comic monologues for the People's Theatre, including pieces such as *If I Was Private* about poverty and health care, and *The Phone Call* about welfare benefits. She also contributed, like Fr Wilson, song pastiches on topical issues. The monologues are notable for their wonderful comic energy and their evocative demotic poetry. Here is the speaker in *If I Was Private*, who, while she is sitting in her doctor's waiting room, regales the audience with her reflections on class, poverty, health and Valium.

> Dr. Mc Coubroy. He used to keep this big, big basin of disinfectant – made all his patients put their coppers or half crowns in to it. That was so he wudn't get con … contam … so he wudn't get a disease. This aule creator used to do odd jobs for him. Name of 'Nose-On-The-Plate'. I don't think that was his real name, but it was what I knew him by. Wasn't the fule shilling, like. The doctor tuk pity on him. Had him around for years. Well anyway one day he was washing the windys outside and when he wasn't luking, here dear, didn't some wit put a brick in his bucket of water. The auld creator lifted the bucket and pitched it up round the big green windy with gold letters on it. Brick, glass and water all showered into the waiting room. It was a mercy nobody was in it at the time […] They've great faith in nerve tablets, haven't they? They're handing them out like Dolly Mixtures. Personally I prefer Dolly Mixtures – there's no side effects. They put everything down to (*Changes voice politely*) 'It's only your nerves, dear', or 'I'm sorry but it's your age, you know'. If only they'd realize that for some people it's sheer loneliness. It can destroy their will to live, ye know. Just needing someone to talk to. I doubt if they'll ever find a medicine that can take the place of people. Thank God I'm not like that. I'm one of the lucky ones. I have my cat, my plants … (*Pauses and points at audience*) and you.[35]

One trope of these sketches is the Kafka-esque bureaucracy in which the poor are trapped as they attempt to access their right to health or basic sustenance. Another, explored in a sketch by Tony McCabe, *The Merry Go Round* is the way in which the funding pumped into the north in order to provide work and so address structural inequalities, finds its way into the hands of consultants, planners, designers and officials.

In 1974 Doolan received a commission from Barrow–Cadbury to facilitate cross-community film and theatre work, and set up a series of weekend workshops for the Ballymurphy group at the Benburb Retreat Centre in rural East Tyrone. The first of these was on Mumming, and involved improvisation workshops leading to an impromptu performance of a version of St George and the Dragon in the evening. In September 1975 the group took temporary possession of a room above a disused pool centre on the Whiterock Road, converting it into a small forty-seat theatre, where they performed the revue *Grandmother for Sale*. It was at this time that company resistance to Fr Wilson's and Doolan's focus on topical material manifested itself. Some felt that the war already defined too much of their lives, writes Hilton, and that they had 'became sickened by it'. They were, consequently, 'fed up with drama that always has to have a message', and wanted theatre which was 'a bit of fun – a pantomime or something – a "utopian experience", like the old Hollywood movies; let's be entertained. That was definitely a mood in the theatre at that time.' For Doolan the two were not incompatible, and on 22 February 1976, Ballymurphy Community Centre hosted a new pantomime, *Proddy O'Taig and the Golden Pot*. The pantomime was, she told Hilton, an attempt 'to create a modern Odyssey in which a fella, half Protestant and half Catholic, goes through history looking for his golden pot. It was ridiculous, it was idiotic and it was very funny in its way. It worked rather well.' By the time the group moved to the community centre in late 1975, it had some sixty members and a developing Young People's Theatre. In the following year the People's Theatre toured to centres in Belfast, Derry, and Kilkenny.[36] One typical revue was given at a Social Studies Conference in Kilkenny on Friday 6 August 1976. The sketches included:

> *The Fishmonger and the Ragman*
> *The Fishmonger's Wife and the Ragman's Wife meet in hospital*
> *That's Something*
> *The Park Bench*
> *The Soldier*
> *Margaret*
> *Reading of Internment script*[37]

As well as writing material, Des Wilson also acted, as did Noelle Ryan, a former nun, who had arrived at Springhill in 1971. Des Wilson writes: 'Noelle was a member of a contemplative religious order and left it because life of that kind turned out not to be suitable after all. That was our good fortune. She had left the order and worked in Liverpool and other places in various charities. She came to Belfast thinking she might be able to help. She was right!'

Thirty-five years later she is still there. Although the theatre included writers with a gift for comedy and satire, such as Paul Walker, Theresa Donnelly, Tony McCabe, Kathleen Davidson and Hilton himself, Doolan had no doubt who was the most gifted, telling Sheehy that 'Des was the one with the real talent'.

> The Money Lender was a very good sketch – that was Des. One of the best sketches he ever wrote was *That's Something* – about labelling people. A Provo and a Sticky (opposing wings of the IRA) sit on either side of a nervous Des. He asks them to explain their differences and they hurl slogans at each other. They are still arguing as they leave. A Loyalist paramilitary arrives.
>
> 'Are you a Prod?' he demands, 'I'm a Prod.'
>
> 'Not really'
>
> 'A Fenian?' He curls his fist.
>
> 'Not really.'
>
> Total disbelief: 'What else is there?'
>
> 'Well, my father was a Catholic and my mother was Protestant. I have two aunts that were Quaker.'
>
> 'So you're a nothing?'
>
> 'In a way, yes,' he says apologetically.
>
> 'But you must be a Catholic nothing or a Protestant nothing. You can't be a Nothing nothing!' He heads off after the IRA men.
>
> Des addresses the audience. 'A Catholic father and a Protestant mother ... so I'm a religious nothing.' A shot is heard. 'A Brit for a father and a Scot for a mother ... so I'm a political nothing.' Another shot. Then a third. 'But I'm still alive, and that's something – I think.'

Another of Fr Wilson's early pieces praised by Doolan was *The Soldier's Synge*, which was still in the People's Theatre's repertoire in the 1990s.

The Soldier's Synge

A British Army Major is preparing a unit for a new hearts and minds campaign, or, as he puts it to his troops: 'We have to stop bashing the natives and start trying to win them over to our side ... Get friendly with them and all that ... speak English the way the best of the natives – I mean the people – speak it.'[38] To this end Operation Libraryman was being launched. Libraries had been raided for copies of Yeats and Synge, and a script of 'authentic' Irish dialogue created. The result is a delight of absurd inflation that succeeds in out Synge-ing Synge. Before they go on their first raid the soldiers rehearse their absurd 'roles':

SOLDIER ONE: It is yourself that would be putting a curse on an old woman and she peeling the potatoes that we wrested from the soil of the fields with our own bare hands and bent backs with

Figure 1. Des Wilson, second from the right, at a performance of Belfast People's
Theatre sketches, Conway Mill, Belfast, 1999.

	all the pains and distresses of the world at us day and night? Begob and begorrah 'tis ourselves will eat before ye this blessed night, or have the curse of Balor the evil eye on the white locks of your hair. Arra and wisha. [...]
MAJOR	'Tis the playboy of the Western World himself that's in it. That killed his father before him and will kill a thousand more, like Cuchullain of Uls, and he tied hand and foot to the hulk of a tree. Arrah and Wirrah.

Here, in a deadly game, the imagined Irish are invoked as a weapon against
the real, and a poetic language, inflected with liberationary impulses, is used
as a tool of counter-insurgency. Fr Wilson returns the colonizer's caricature
of the native with interest. When the soldiers raid the O'Shaughnessys' home
looking for weapons, the writer plays with different performative frames in
order to subvert any realistic reading. The section is worth quoting at length
as it reveals the comic and serious purposes which are at work:

Scene 2

> *(The O'Shaughnessys' home. Mrs O'Shaughnessy is ironing.*
> *Mr O'Shaughnessy is reading a newspaper. Three loud*
> *knocks on the door.)*

Mr O'Shaughnessy:
> Who's that? (*Makes to get up and see*)

Mrs O'Shaughnessy:
> Never mind. If it's someone we want in, he'll come in. If it isn't he'll knock again. (*Three more loud knocks*)

Mrs O'Shaughnessy:
> There, what did I tell you? (*Enter Major with a gun in his hand*)

Major:
> Begob and begorrah, woman of the house. The top of the morning to you. (*Mr and Mrs look at each other in amazement*) 'Tis the fine soft day that does be in it, woman of the house. And man of the house too, of course. Arrah!

Mrs O'Shaughnessy:
> Bless us and save us! What's this?

Mr O'Shaughnessy:
> Never mind him, Mary. It's one of them fellas from the People's Theatre dressed up. They're doing it for a show tonight up the road. Probably looking for money.

Mrs O'Shaughnessy:
> Oh, is that all. How much?

Major:
> No, good woman of the house. It's not your money I'd be after being after, if you see what I mean. 'Tis Major McLaughlin O'Teabags that does be in it this blessed night.

Mrs O'Shaughnessy:
> More like Larry O'Hooligan with all that silly talk.

Major:
> 'Tis the major himself from the barracks above at Fort MacTaggart that's in it. Arrah and begob. And 200 brave men in the Queen's bright uniform like 2,000 Cuchullains ready to do battle – if you'll pardon the expression. But why talk of battle itself? Sure, 'tis not Mrs O'Shaughnessy I see before me this blessed minute. 'Tis like Queen Maeve herself you are, and she ironing her shift before appearing at the court of the High King himself. Begob and Arrah!

Mrs O'Shaughnessy:
> Will I hit him with the iron?

Mr O'Shaughnessy:
> No, leave him alone the poor demented creature. Humour him, Mary, humour him, for goodness sake, or he'll wreck the house.

The soldiers are fools, but, in the Wilson lexicon, they are dangerous fools: dangerous fools are fools with an army and torture cells, fools who wreck homes and break heads. The stereotyping is implicit: the Irish at their best are projected as poetic primitives: rebellious dreamers: open-hearted subversives: amoral anarchists: what they are not is historical subjects. Unable to communicate with the O'Shaughnessy family, the Major hands over his gun in order to consult his 'script'. The bemused couple now have him at their mercy, though they are convinced he is mad and harmless. At this point their daughter, Rose, enters, and, realizing what the soldiers are up to, asks innocently if they want the 'arms from the cellar'. The major is suitably delighted: 'I should jolly well say so! What I mean is begob and begorrah, yes!' An assortment of eighteenth-century pikes is brought up from beneath the cottage. When a bemused Major asks to be shown how this ancient Irish weaponry works, Rose grabs a pike and chases him and the troops out of the house. In his panic, the Major leaves the real gun behind, and Rose stores it away for the future.

The pikes' symbolism is central to the play's meaning. At one level they are simply offered as a neat joke against the British, representing weapons that were not found in earlier raids in the long history of occupation. They point to the continuity of the anti-colonial struggle, a struggle which has always been fought between unequal forces and with unequal weaponry. They also remind their audience of a tradition where rebellion did not end, but simply paused; where guns were silenced, but never surrendered (thus the profound historical significance of decommissioning by the current IRA). The theatre script parodies the social script in order to reveal that it is a script. Theatre, it is suggested (very lightly), is a resource of hope, because it offers a means to reveal the social construction of reality. The fact that Wilson chooses to challenge the violence and racist energies of the occupation through a playful parody of Synge's hybrid language is interesting. According to Kiberd, Synge wanted to create a language which provided a meeting place for the two cultures: a 'bilingual weave' which would demonstrate the 'continuing power of the radical Gaelic past' to 'disrupt the revivalist present'. Kiberd's analysis rescues Synge from accusations of creating a vulgar stage Irishness, and instead sees him anticipating in *The Playboy of the Western World* Fanon's three-stage theory of artistic decolonization.[39] Wilson's analysis is equally subtle. He plays both sides against the middle in order to demonstrate that no language can provide a meeting ground based on structural injustices and occupation: that what we have in Synge is not hybridity but linguistic occupation. Northern Ireland is also a hybrid: an English state inside an Irish land.[40] The comic possibilities of language are explored again in a shorter piece, *Ag Foghlain Gaelige*. The Army Officer asks a member of the Irish Language Association, Glor na nGael, to teach him some phrases of Irish: he confides that the imperatives of counter-insurgency mean that he needs to be able to eavesdrop on Republicans' phone calls. Naturally he is taught phrases which either reveal his role, or are scatological and abusive, with predictable consequences. The vagaries of phonemes are used to play with the idea that language is itself a weapon: as he interprets 'fam bomaite' (wait a moment) as 'fine bomb'. In a typical dig at the hierarchy, he is advised that he should only use these phrases when talking to bishops, which he does. It is a bishop who explains his error, and then tortures him for his chutzpah by making him listen to 15 pages of Archbishop Cahal Daly's writing.

Theatre, Liberation Theology and Politics

In 1978, when Lelia Doolan moved back to Dublin, an important phase in the People's Theatre's history came to a close. There had been many clashes with Hilton and others over her approach to theatre. In the early days Hilton and Fr Wilson had worked consciously to empower a group for whom priests were automatically seen as authority figures, and had largely succeeded. When Doolan arrived, this egalitarian ethos was challenged. 'Instead of people making their own decisions, now they were being directed: their writing was being directed, the theatre was being directed in a certain way,' Hilton told Sheehy. Doolan agrees, confessing to Sheehy later that, 'I just directed and terrorized the living daylights out of them, trying to give the thing some coherence, a professional look ... very often there was a lot of shouting and carrying on, which I was part of.'[41] Overall, however, it had been a largely fruitful collision between a committed but hierarchical professionalism and a popular, democratic ethos, and she was much missed.

As the decade drew to a close there was a constant flow of people in and out of the group. Attempts by more confident individuals to steer the company in a more commercial direction were resisted by Hilton and Fr Wilson, who encouraged them to form separate companies. However, Fr Wilson was very clear-sighted about the need for a more radical renewal of the kind represented by Belfast Community Theatre, which developed alongside the People's Theatre in the eighties:

> I was very excited by the possibilities of The People's Theatre; but we found that you'd start off with a fairly radical outlook, and the writing would be fairly critical, maybe not radical, but certainly critical. As time went on however, it tended to become more and more like an amateur dramatics' society. So you'd finish up with people doing a pantomime or a play like 'The Far Off Hills'. And then somebody would have to step aside and radicalize it again.[42]

Belfast Community Theatre was one such moment of renewal, and its work, covered below, can be seen in one sense as a development from, and amplification of, the politically committed work of the People's Theatre. What Belfast Community Theatre did not offer, and this was Fr Wilson's unique contribution to the field of resistance theatre, was writing that presented a revolutionary reading of Roman Catholic theology and history.

While Fr Wilson was, according to Joseph Sheehy, uncomfortable with the term, his ministry is seen as the moment when liberation theology entered Ireland. It was certainly the moment when it entered Irish theatre history.

Liberation Theology, Popular Theatre and the Salvific Path

Liberation theology was inaugurated at the Medellin Bishops' Conference in 1968, when Latin American bishops took a stance of solidarity with the poor, and against colonial and neo-colonial repression. Institutional violence was condemned as 'a situation of sin'.[43] This was iterated in 1972 at La Puebla, when the bishops declared that the 'Love of God is a labour of justice on behalf of the oppressed'.[44] The dominant voices within the liberation theology movement were those of priests, such as the Brazilian Leonardo Boff, and the Guatemalan Gustavo Gutierrez. In his writings Gutierrez stressed the historicity of theology. Theological ideas arose from specific human realities, and it was the job of theology to reflect upon those realities, and to see them and the human suffering to which they gave rise not as a distraction from meditation, but as its ground. For Boff, liberation theology was expressed only through 'human work towards a just society as part of a salvific process … liberation and salvation were not alternative paths but alternative terminology'.[45]

In an influential monograph, Father Joe McVeigh, another of the 'people's priests', who was a tireless activist and skilled polemicist, called for an Irish liberation theology founded on the ancient concept of the *meitheal*, or community, noting that it would be a '*meitheal* theology since it is a theology of the people'.[46] His eloquent text begins from the premise of the Church's historicity, and of the British occupation of Ireland. 'The Church' he writes, 'is a movement within history and therefore part of history', just as the Bible is 'God's word on the poor in history'.[47] An Irish liberation theology must 'reflect the experience of the Irish people as an oppressed and colonized nation which has not yet achieved full political and economic freedom … it will deal with the causes, not the symptoms of violence, poverty and inequality'. Consequently, the role of the priest was to 'bear prophetic witness, which aimed at empowering the poor while also engaging in constant criticism of the political process'.[48]

The revues which the People's Theatre presented periodically throughout the eighties embodied this philosophy. Commentaries on the Church and theology were interleaved with more obviously political sketches. With provocative titles such as *You're Not Going To Like This!* the revues incorporated theatre, poetry, music, song and dance into an evening's popular entertainment, and acted as a commentary on immediate communal or political events, such as the latest inter-governmental talks, the vacuities of ecumenism, the collusion between Church and state, and the violation of human rights. The protagonists of Fr Wilson's theatre are always the 'little people', for they are the locus of hope in a corrupted polity. 'It doesn't matter how small the group may be, or how small the person,' he wrote, 'they are important, and they could be the beginning of a new kind of society.'[49]

A representative sequence from the review *You're Not Going to Like This! No. 2* opens with Man standing at the top of a ladder in the centre of the bare stage. Man is talking to God, and trying to persuade Him to come back to earth, to intervene in the Troubles, and to work 'a few wee miracles and that'.[50] Another crucifixion would follow, he admits, but, after the necessary suffering, the resurrected Christ could, in this vision, 'Come again, large as life, and start a new Church'. There is thunder and lightning and Man retreats. He waits, and moves forward to try again. A priest enters and, appalled at this usurpation of his sacred intercessionary role, demands that the supplicant let him intercede with God. He explains to Man how the salvific hierarchy works, and the humour is wonderfully sly: 'You tell me what you want, and I put on this big hat here, and talk to God for you.' Man agrees, asking that the Church intercede so that God might help him overcome poverty and the violence of the occupation. In the priest's response Fr Wilson articulates the collusion of the Catholic hierarchy in the collective punishment of a people:

> P   (*in a kind of chant*):   Oh Lord, we do humbly pray and
>   beseech you that you would in your great mercy vouchsafe
>   to reward your humble servants the managers of banks, the
>   lenders of money, the owners of big business and other Godly
>   persons, and protect them from the evil and wicked folk who
>   would refuse them their proper payments with interest.
>
> M: and the police and soldiers came in and beat my family up
>   last night.
>
> P: and thou wouldst deign to grant safety and protection to the
>   forces of law and order in their fight against terrorism and
>   wickedness.

The priest now turns the conversation with God into a competition. He challenges Man to a test to see whom God favours: his anointed representatives, or the unwashed laity. Each will ask a favour. Man agrees and asks that God help him cope with his life. There is thunder and lightning and a huge tablet of Valium descends (to much laughter when I watched the piece). The priest now comes forward, asking God to help him 'confound this miserable sinner'. Another huge tablet descends: on it is written: 'Get Lost Goofball!' More laughter. Enraged the priest rushes up the ladder screaming. The last few lines are quite startling in the context of audience and writer:

> MAN: Don't come down here again, Lord, for God's sake don't you come down here again!
>   P: If ever you come down here again …
>   M: He'll bloody crucify you!
>   P: I'll bloody crucify you!

The priest storms off. The scene's final image is important: 'Man: Hey Lord? (*Goes up ladder*) I think you know rightly which of us to listen to.' Just as the Christ of the Gospels chose his disciples from among the labouring people, so the protagonists in Fr Wilson's work are those most despised and feared by the hierarchy: the poor, Republicans, and women. 'I think maybe God is a woman,' says one character, 'Nobody but a woman could be as patient as that.' In another sketch a priest chastises Woman for daring to 'Make the Lord Jesus out to be like he was a low class character like yourself'. To which she replies, 'Well, I think maybe he was'. The God of the Poor, wrote Fr McVeigh, was also 'a member of a colonized race under occupation', one who was crucified as a rebel.[51]

In another sequence which pillories the Church's systemic misogyny, Fr Wilson focuses the contentious theological issue of female ordination. Woman enters a church just as the priest is finishing a sermon, and asks if she can preach from the pulpit. He allows her to only because the church is empty: 'If a woman is going to say anything in the church, make sure there's nobody there to hear what she says'. Woman is a mother and is poor: she is, or so it is intimated, not unlike Mary, the mother of God. Her improvised sermon is a reworking of the New Testament parable of the encounter between Jesus and the widow of Naim. In Fr Wilson's retelling, the experiences of the Nazarene and the mother from Ballymurphy are conflated; the rhetorical formality of the Bible is recast in the demotic of the ghetto: this is the Bible as Belfast craic:

> WOMAN: There was this day, and Jesus was strolling along the road, and all his disciples coming after him and the Scribes and Pharisees watching him like a hawk, and taking notes and doing head counts and road checks and body searches and all. You know, the sort of thing the same bunch of bastards would do the day if they were on the streets of Belfast.

In the original, Jesus is asked to help a widow whose son has died prematurely.

> Peter takes a look at the wee widow woman and her son lying dead there at the side of the street, and all the crowds round her crying their eyes out. And then he takes a wee gander at Jesus, and he's

crying his eyes out too. And Peter says, 'Hey Jesus – you wouldn't work a wee miracle, would you?' And Jesus says, 'Certainly, I was only waiting to be asked'.

And so the son is raised from the dead. When the people urge that the good news should be spread, Jesus warns them of the risk of supporting him. He is, after all, a revolutionary facing powerful enemies. Again the experiences of the women of Naim and of Ballymurphy are conflated. Like Christ's followers, this audience is also denied the right to enter their cities without fear: 'Woman: Jesus was afraid, you see, that the whole crowd of them, and especially the women, would form up in a procession and maybe march to City Hall. And as you know, the peelers wouldn't allow women to march on City Hall.' Here, as elsewhere in Fr Wilson's writings, women are presented as a revolutionary force. Springhill and later Conway Mill would be sustained by a number of remarkable women, such as Sister Noelle Ryan, Elsie Best, Theresa Donnelly, Pat McGlade, Marie McKnight and many more. Some, such as Donnelly, McGlade and McKnight, would act in the theatres, and all were committed activists, educators, and mothers. It was men, not women, who abandoned Christ; it was women who kept watch at the foot of the cross, and it was mothers who maintained family life in Ballymurphy, who gave birth and raised children in a war zone. The Nationalist enclaves of West Belfast contained widows whose sons had also died prematurely. These sketches reflected the radical revision of Catholic theology that was taking place within the community. A course entitled 'The People's Theology', facilitated by Des Wilson and Joseph Sheehy, set as its aim the creation of 'a real theology of the people' founded on the egalitarian practices of the early Church:

> Our monthly Agape [a-ga-pay] is the Eucharist of the early Church, predating clerical patriarchy and doctrinal division. The original Agape was an inclusive celebration in people's homes, the leader being the woman or man of the house [e.g. Priscilla and Aquila, Lydia] … We use a Celtic Agape to explore the People's tradition.[52]

Later in the same sequence, Woman asks a bishop if she can be ordained. Again humour is used to both reveal and subvert orthodoxy:

WOMAN: I want to be a priest.
BISHOP: You can't be a priest, you're a woman.
WOMAN: What's wrong with being a woman?
BISHOP: Well, look at the way you're dressed for a start.
WOMAN: What do you mean, the way I'm dressed?
BISHOP: Well, look at you; you've got a funny hat on.
WOMAN: So have you.

> BISHOP: Yes, but that's different. You've got a woman's funny hat on, whereas I've got a bishop's funny hat on.

As Woman leaves, Soldier enters, and she pauses. The exchange which follows has echoes of Brecht, and a similar bitter humour:

> B: He's going to be a priest you know.
> W: He's going to be a what?
> B: A priest. Fine upstanding young fellow. A good Catholic too. Never kills people on Fridays.
> W: That's nice.
> B: And his mother's a Protestant …
> W: Really?
> B: Yes. So he doesn't kill people on Sundays either.
> W: So, he's going to be a priest. Well, at least that will be one soldier less. Jesus will be pleased.
> B: Not at all. Private Thackerberry's going to be a soldier and a priest. An army chaplain you know. It's all arranged.

Woman decides to test the Soldier's knowledge of the Bible, and asks him to name one of St Paul's letters, to which he replies:

> SOLDIER: St Paul wrote … St Paul wrote … ah … ah St Paul wrote 'Take a Pistol to the Fenians'.
> BISHOP: No, no, Private, the Epistle to the Ephesians, the Epistle to the Ephesians.
> Soldier: That's correct, my Lord. 'Take a pistol to the Fenians.'
> WOMAN: He's a nice one to make a priest of.

The misreading denotes a deadly conflation of bible and counter-insurgency manual. All readings serve the same purpose, the elimination of the revolution. Church and state, says Fr McVeigh, were bound by a unitary purpose in which the Church was viewed, correctly, as a 'bulwark against the drift towards independence and Republicanism'.[53] Confused and agitated by the Woman's questioning, the soldier shoots her. The Bishop is less concerned with the morality of this action than with the negative publicity that might follow. How can Bishop and Soldier justify Woman's death? The Soldier's rehearsed defence is: 'Tried to escape by asking questions.' The audience laughs at this bitter joke – a joke because the deaths of so many innocents will be justified by false, sometimes absurd claims; bitter because the absurdity denotes a dehumanization. Those we do not recognize as fully human can be killed and the pain of their loss deepened by lies, misinformation and denial. Children who are carrying milk home to their families can have their heads caved in by baton rounds, grandmothers can be shot in their gardens,

Figure 2. The Ecumenical Tea Party, by Des Wilson, Belfast People's Theatre,
Conway Mill, Belfast, 1999.

priests murdered as they seek to protect their parishioners, and the state will
fabricate reasons for their deaths. The Woman dies because her questions
threaten the legitimacy of Church and state. Repeatedly in his writings Fr
Wilson notes how the political and economic power of the Roman Catholic
Church was not used to alleviate suffering but to reinforce repression. He
was clear-sighted about the economic and class interests which shaped
this collusion, and about the way in which the Roman Catholic Church
allowed itself to be co-opted into the repressive apparatus. Ecumenism
was consequently parodied in a number of sketches which showed how
the theological differences separating Catholicism and Protestantism were
transcended by a shared political commitment by the hierarchy of all
churches to keep the poor in their place. A rhetorical compassion for the
oppressed could be displaced onto more distant and safer causes. In the
Ecumenical Clergy Song two clergymen, one Catholic and one Protestant,
dressed in Aran sweaters and collars and wearing outsized mitres, celebrate
their commitment to the (distant) oppressed:

When anyone's rights are in danger
You'll find we will never say Nay
We're always a snip for good causes
As long as they're far far away ...

When Africa's causing a problem
We go out and march in the street
When the Arabs are getting beheaded
We show our great rage – with our feet

These themes of hypocrisy and pusillanimity were pursued in a wide range of satirical skits, including the *Ecumenical Tea Party* and the *Bishop Interview*.

'Drowning the Revolution in Baby's Milk'

In October 1986 a group of prominent and moderate Roman Catholics from Greater Ballymurphy, who had for years condemned the actions of the IRA, felt moved by the security forces' escalating attacks on community groups to write an open letter to the Irish Government and the Roman Catholic Primate of Ireland. Angered by a statement by the Irish Republic's Taoiseach, Garret Fitzgerald, to the effect that the 1985 Anglo-Irish agreement heralded the 'end of the Nationalist nightmare', they responded:

> We who know listen in stupefaction. We try to comfort the mother of three-year-old Paul Burns of Springhill who was tossed over a wall like a sack of spuds; we listen to 68-year-old Frank Hardie, who is deaf and had his skull split open for not responding quickly enough to a soldier's question; young Martin Morris who was asked if he had any problems and then was smashed in the face and told that 'Now you have one'; Ned Ryan who received eight stitches in his head [...] Gerry Daly who was kicked in the groin and smashed in the face with a rifle butt for the crime of walking down the street; the McManus children who had to be kept from school because they were beaten and threatened every day by the military; young Jimmy Lennon who had a rifle butt broken across his mouth as he gave his name and address to a soldier; and many many more. What do we tell young Irish women who are daily called 'whores' on their own streets? How do we reconcile their reality with the land of delusion currently occupied by the Irish political establishment? Can somebody somewhere please explain this new era, this 'ending of the Nationalist nightmare' of which we hear so much? [54]

They received no succour from the Roman Catholic hierarchy, which had repeatedly and cravenly insisted that to condemn the Army's violence would damage ecumenical unity. Not even the use of torture could bring them to condemn the British state and its counter-insurgency strategies. The Church authorities also worked to undermine all grass-roots community based initiatives, even those that tackled the endemic poverty and unemployment whose excoriating effects upon the community were masked by the war. These attacks were part of a significant shift in counter-insurgency strategy following the signing of the Anglo-Irish Agreement, and had been signalled in a speech to the House of Commons by the then Home Secretary, Douglas Hurd. The new strategy recommended targeting community groups, and 'persons prominent within them' who had 'sufficiently close links with paramilitary organizations to give rise to a grave risk that to give support to such people would have the effect of improving their standing and furthering the aims of paramilitary organizations'.[55] In the period this new policy was developing, Springhill had taken over one of the nine floors of Conway Mill, a massive former linen mill on the Lower Falls, which became home to the Conway Education Project. The other floors were taken up with a range of commercial, industrial and social enterprises. One of the former loom rooms housed a theatre, its former purpose reflected in the two rows of pillars which ran its length, creating a central audience area and two side sections. One end of this long rectangular room was occupied by a small stage, capable of being extended with the use of rostra, creating a thrust effect. At the other end, next to the toilet, was the lighting box, a tiny black room boarded off from the rest, with a glazed viewing panel facing the stage. The lighting rig when I first visited in 1985 was of the kind that you might still occasionally find in old school halls, with dimmer tracks fixed to the wall, and iron handles which had to be hauled up and down. It was on this stage, and by pure chance, that Goodchild and I would first perform in Belfast. Home to the People's Theatre and Belfast Community Theatre, it would host visiting companies such as Derry Frontline, and be a major venue for the West Belfast Festival (Féile an Phobail) from the festival's inception in 1987. Managed by a committee of activists, Conway Mill embodied Fr Wilson's vision of culture as a way of life. It was, he writes, 'an integrated site where work, enterprise, independence, culture, education would be in one place; where you could go to work in the same building as the theatre, where you could have education alongside people building up their enterprises'.[56] In the new security climate, however, Conway Mill became a prime target of the counter-insurgency. The Pound Loney Club, which was affiliated to Sinn Féin, owned the building, and this was enough to draw down upon all Mill users the weight of the new strategy. In his counter-insurgency manual, General Kitson had urged the use of 'compliant elements of the rebellious communities in the suppression of the revolution', a process which he rather bizarrely termed 'drowning the revolution in baby's milk'.[57] The strategy involved using economic aid as a means to enforce compliance. The Northern Ireland Office consequently mobilized its forces against Springhill House and Conway Mill: 'They boycotted it, refused financial help, sent the troops to harass people inside and outside the premises, created a propaganda campaign which dubbed the Mill, which was set to create more than 200 jobs, a front for the IRA.'[58]

SDLP councillor Brian Feeney accused the Mill's occupants of being 'fronts for the IRA, and of laundering government funds', an accusation repeated to devastating effect in an ITV Cook Report broadcast in November 1985. In order to further isolate Springhill House and Conway Mill, the Workers Education Association and the Ulster People's College were warned by the Northern Ireland Office that they would lose funding if their tutors taught at either centre. The community began legal proceedings against ITV which lasted for five years and which vindicated them, but the legal battle absorbed energy and resources which could have been fruitfully spent developing the centres. It was such experiences which led Fr Wilson to counsel activists against relying on external help or resources: 'Look, what you've got to aim for – as far as education is concerned – is how to assist learning without money and without teachers. Now, how do you do that? ... *because you're going to be driven back to that point some day.*'[59] (Italics in original.) Fr Wilson's activism sprang from a belief, analyzed with great acuity in his book *An End to Silence*, that the state had failed, and was no longer capable of delivering justice: that, on the contrary, it had became a negation of humane and democratic life, a perversion of it, and that a new polity could only be created through a process of popular grass-roots renewal.[60]

The Political Sketches

If I have focused to this point upon Fr Wilson's use of the stage to propose a people's liberation theology, it is because it was a unique contribution to the rich range of theatres produced here. However, I would not want to suggest a separation between liberation theology on the one hand, and the large number of other pieces he wrote on topical economic and political issues, on the other. Like his friend Fr McVeigh, Wilson believed that 'building the Kingdom' must be achieved first in the 'political sphere' through 'accompanying our people from within through the transformation of structures'.[61] This radical self-reliance defined all aspects of Springhill's and Conway Mill's work, including the numerous grass-roots initiatives to create employment. Evidence of the Unionist state's systemic discrimination against Catholics was found in the entrenched poverty and unemployment found in Nationalist areas. There was, of course, deprivation in Loyalist communities, but sectarianism rendered an unequal economic order doubly so for Nationalists. In a speech addressing the challenge of constructing a society without violence, Fr Wilson, noting the continuous connection between big business and war, observed 'that while the Church had enthusi-astically mobilized against godless communism, there was never a Church crusade against godless capitalism, which seems a pity'.[62] In sketches with titles such as *The Capitalist, The Moneylender, What Can Poor Rich People Do? The Department of Economic Devilment*, and *The Ordinary Folk*, he would wage his own crusade against economic exploitation and sectarian employment practices. *The Moneylender*, which excoriates those from within the community who exploited the poverty of their neighbours, is a good example of the genre. The plot is simple. A woman, C, desperate to feed her children, borrows £1 for a week from the moneylender, M, and agrees to repay £1.60. The sketch is structured in two parts. First we see the woman negotiating the loan. She exits. The moneylender, M, then turns to the audience and mocks them for working, for labouring in order to live: 'You earn money. I lend it. You make a little; I make a lot. Let me tell you how I do it.'[63] At this point another actor, N, appears, and takes M's place at the table, leaving the latter free to address the audience. The scene we have just witnessed is now re-enacted, but this time with the moneylender's commentary as he demonstrates his exploitation:

> C: I need help.
> M: I know what she wants but I don't let on. So I pretend I don't understand her. I say …
> N: Directions, advice or money? If directions, yes, if advice, yes; if money, no, unless of course …
> M: Unless of course she can pay through the nose. So, I say …
> N: Do you know that human beings can survive eight whole weeks without food?
> M: That humiliates her. Sometimes people cry at this stage.

Eventually C agrees to repay the exorbitant interest. N and C now freeze as M explains how, if C was not poor and had a proper bank account, she could borrow the same pound for a whole year for only eighteen pence, instead of paying the £31.20 which he charges. We then find out that M is the woman's neighbour: 'I live just down the street, I'm a friend. I'm a good guy, a friend in need.' Usury, the piece argues, destroys the ethic of the *meitheal*, and undermines working-class solidarity. *The Capitalist* is I think the most perfect example of this model, and is worth quoting in full.

The Capitalist

> (*Tree at back of stage. Enter Capitalist, with bag with Capitalist in large white letters on it. Walks by tree, then stops, looks back at and all around it. Then to right where he sits on bag and thinks. Gets up and opens case, takes out a number of notices, selects one, with hammer pins notice up on the tree: 'TREE FOR SALE'. Sits on case again and waits. Enter woman from left. Walks past tree, then stops and looks at it.*)

WOMAN: You selling that tree?

CAPITALIST: You need a tree?

WOMAN: I need a tree.

CAPITALIST: I'm selling a tree.

WOMAN: How much?

CAPITALIST: Two hundred pounds.

WOMAN: One hundred pounds.

CAPITALIST: We'll split the difference. One hundred and fifty.

WOMAN: All right. (*Gives out money from handbag, counting it out.*) I'll take it with me.

CAPITALIST (*gets up, all business*): No. Not at all. I can arrange to have it delivered. Cutting down and delivery is thirty pounds extra.

WOMAN: All right. It's more convenient that way. (*Counts out more money.*) Thirty pounds.

CAPITALIST: Where to.

WOMAN: 210 Malone Road.

CAPITALIST: First thing tomorrow morning.

WOMAN: Thank you. (*Going off.*) What a lovely tree. I like trees. They make good fire-wood. That will keep us in fire-wood all winter.

(*Capitalist takes notice off tree and sits waiting. Enter Owner who looks at tree. Owner puts his hand on the tree and is concerned about it.*)

CAPITALIST: You own that tree?

OWNER: Yes.

CAPITALIST: Worth a bit of money that tree.

OWNER: It's been here for a hundred years.

CAPITALIST: Then you need a new tree.

OWNER: I can't afford new trees. I like trees.

CAPITALIST: (*Opens bag*) I'll buy it. Then you can plant two trees for the money. Fifty pounds.

OWNER: Then I'd have two trees. I like trees.

CAPITALIST: Fifty pounds. (*Offers money.*) You could buy three new trees for that. You like trees.

OWNER: Three trees for one. All right.

CAPITALIST: Fifty for the tree (*Counts it out.*) And ten pounds if you cut it down for me and deliver it.

OWNER: Seventy pounds. That will buy four trees. I like trees.

CAPITALIST: Deliver it tomorrow morning.

OWNER: Where:

CAPITALIST: 210 Malone Road.

OWNER: That's a good bargain. I'll go and get an axe. I like trees. (*Exits*)

CAPITALIST: Dammit. I'm beginning to like trees myself.[64]

Songs also played an important role in the People's Theatre's work, often as pastiches of well-known ballads or light opera numbers. It was often through song that Fr Wilson satirized the self-pitying greed and hypocrisy of the conservative Catholic middle classes:

> We're sorry I'm sure
> For the ones that are poor
> And the folks that sign on the Buroo
> But the Boarding School fees
> And the high price of skis
> What can poor rich people do?
> And we're members all
> Of St. Vincent de Paul
> Of the Lions and Rotary too
> We've collections and dinners
> For workless poor sinners,
> What more can the middle class do? [65]

What the middle classes could and did do in the eyes of working-class Republicans and Nationalists was collude with the state to undermine community-led initiatives such as Springhill and Conway Mill. The conservative laity and the Church authorities were part of a civic and political bloc which allied itself with the British army in the ideological war being fought in the north. These forces constituted a formidable ideological and political force which, influential in commerce, education, and in the civil and financial institutions, was critical to the overall counter-insurgency strategy. Republicanism was not only a threat to the Orange State, but to the power and wealth of this bloc and that of their allies in the Irish Republic.

Questions, Hope and Renewal in *Focailin*

One of Wilson's most striking pieces, *Focailin*, an expressionistic meditation on obedience, fear and violence, was staged at Conway Mill in 1985 and 1986. The performance was given by Gerard McLaughlin, Marie McKnight and Tony Flynn, who also belonged to the Belfast Community Theatre. This short play has three characters, Clown, Focailin and Operator. Onstage we see Focailin, suited, clean, urbane, representing institutional authority, the Bankers, Business, the Church, the Army and Judiciary. Clown, garbed in stripes and colours, her face painted in the classic style, is the embodiment of conscience. Her voice is that of the community, Brecht's 'little people'. Operator is nondescript and his clothes tell you nothing of his affiliation (in Belfast death comes dressed like my neighbour). The stage is bare except for a low bench or table which serves as a pavement edge where Clown perches periodically. The drama centres on a series of elliptical conversations between the three. It is Beckett-like in its tersely allusive language and its circular dramatic structure, and in performance the relationships are registered through a series of precise and controlled physical movements. It is a play about institutionalized killing and systemic hatreds which are not incidental but constitutive of public life: a play which embodies in its simple choreography Raymond Williams' evocative summary of twentieth-century state barbarisms, of 'men reduced to objects and killed from lists'.[66] It is a play about fear. Fear drives collective hatreds and fuels the acts which drive the violence forward. The killers are themselves fearful:

> CLOWN: Look how you're trembling.
> FOCAILIN: Cold.
> CLOWN: Fear. Cold fear. How many did you kill today?
> FOCAILIN: None.
> CLOWN: Yesterday?
> FOCAILIN: None. Leave me clown. (*Gets up suddenly.*)[67]

Death is determined by committees and away from public scrutiny. Orders are given, but only so that they can be denied.

> F: You know what has to be done?
> O: Kill him.
> F: I didn't say that.
> O: I said it and you agreed with me.
> F: I said nothing. (*Turns to the door.*)
> C: What's the price of a revolver?
> F (*without turning*): I don't sell revolvers for a job like this.
> C: For a job like this, they're free.
> O: I said nothing.
> F: Then we understand each other.

Operator's belief system is premised on obedience. He is concerned with neither causes nor consequences: 'You've got to do as you're told' and 'Tell me what to do' are his mantras. 'Orders open doors and close minds', while questions, says Clown, 'open minds and close doors'. The questioners must be killed and the dissidents silenced. Fr Wilson was himself a target for Loyalist assassins, such as the Red Hand Commandos.[68] Since the end of the war the real extent of the collusion between British Intelligence and loyalist paramilitary groups has come to light. In Wilson's eyes, responsibility did not lie with the frightened Operator, but with the state and its agencies, and with a repressive state apparatus which included the hierarchy of the Roman Catholic Church. For example, when the Roman Catholic mentor of the British Army, Bishop Tickle, was challenged about the morality of

Figure 3. Focailin by Des Wilson, Belfast People's Theatre and Belfast Community Theatre, Conway Mill, Belfast, 1986.

soldiers obeying an illegal order to shoot unarmed civilians on Bloody Sunday, he remarked: 'If every soldier questioned himself before carrying out an order, where would we be?' When it was pointed out to him that the Nuremburg trial had refused to accept 'obeying orders' as a defence against unlawful killing, he replied that he 'Knew nothing about that'.[69] Fr Wilson's apothegm against violence makes clear his view of the culpability of such powerful elites in the manipulation of the historical situation of Unionism, a culpability since exposed by a number of reports into sectarian killings:[70]

> When you hear them talking about the sanctity of human life and that no political cause is worth shedding an ounce of blood for you don't believe them. And therefore you have to be very skeptical about the government's power to create peace. You know that it can create war.[71]

This analysis is embodied at a critical point in the play when Focalin encourages Operator to shoot Clown 'for asking questions'. The dramatic focus is the battle for Operator's lethal allegiance:

F   (*to Operator*):   Kill him! Kill him! (*O rises slowly with revolver in hand, aims at* C)

C   (*still turned towards* F):   Who am I Operator? What do I sell? Whom do I kill? Operator?

O   (*quietly*):   One voice at a time. One voice at a time. I can only hear one voice at a time.

F: Mine. What are you Operator? A coward?

O: I am a policeman, and a priest, a bailiff and a public servant. I sell duty done, orders obeyed. I kill the ones I'm told to.

C: Why?

F: Why not?

War corrupts all values: 'An institution that persuades good people to do cruel things is one of the most frightening monsters on earth'.[72] At the play's end nothing is resolved. The last line is spoken by Clown: 'I'll stay here and wait till you both come back [*Operator goes, fearful*]. And then we'll start all over again.' Despite its surface bleakness, *Focailín* is a hopeful play. The Clown is patient, an embodiment of Paulo Freire's conception of radical hope:

Hopelessness is a form of silence, of denying the world and fleeing from it. The dehumanization resulting from an unjust order is not a cause for despair but for hope, leading to the incessant pursuit of the humanity which is denied by injustice. Hope, however, does not consist in folding one's arms and waiting. As long as I fight, I am moved by hope: and if I fight with hope I can wait.[73]

This contemporary parable, with its emblematic characters and careful choreography, is a celebration of rational scepticism in the face of authority. If Fr Wilson's work has a unifying theme, then it is the call for the displacement of a disabling obedience, theological and political, by a radical hope. He would later write that if there was one thing he wished they had done more to achieve it was the eradication of fear.

We should have been tougher and worked harder to dismantle the fear that makes people hide inside their own minds ... our first conference was about fear because we believed that fear was the most pervasive and damaging characteristic of our society. Take it away and real change will follow.[74]

Conclusion

In 1996 Fr Wilson sent me a copy of a collection of his scripts for the People's Theatre, which had been collated by Springhill House. In an accompanying note he wrote, 'As you can see, the stuff I turn out (after many nights of agonizing) is more formal than one might wish. But it's the only way I can do it.'[75] There were no 'well-made' plays in this oeuvre, but no badly made ones either. Instead the People's Theatre work constitutes a bricolage of satirical skits and parable-like pieces, defined by a forensic intelligence and a playful and incisive wit. There is an exuberance about the use of stage space and the possibilities offered by a necessarily limited technical apparatus. The unique quality of Fr Wilson's writing lies in the blending of the rhetorical devices of the sermon with popular theatre forms.

The rehearsal process was conventional, with actors given their scripts and expected to follow them and take direction. The extant copies show some revision marks, the most common being 'Final version', indicating that there had been minor redrafts, sometimes, for example, the reordering of the verses of a song. And, while there was some improvisation in performance, these are not collectively determined texts. Nonetheless, it is possible to identify in this work something of the ethos of late medieval theatre, reflected in the radical expropriation of the Bible and liturgy, the irreverent attitude to state and Episcopal authority, and the use of emblematic figures, such as Woman/Soldier/Bishop/Child/Capitalist to explore the social experience of the community. It was, again like its medieval antecedent, a *meitheal* theatre, whose 'performers' came from and returned to an 'audience' which was at once spectator and actor, communicant and activist, teacher and learner, priest and laity. It was an affirmatory theatre, which used the stage to entertain, celebrate, educate, console, provoke, question, and, above all, to validate and affirm the dignity and rights of a people under occupation. It is notable that there are no radical clerics on this stage, and no suggestion that hope lay in priests like Fr Wilson. I do not think this was modesty (though he is an intensely modest man) but simply that he believed that salvation could not be achieved through the intervention of an intercessionary elite, but had to be realized on earth through the collective, practical and spiritual labour of a whole people to overcome injustice and oppression. What exercised the Roman Catholic Church authorities was not that this priest celebrated mass in the front room of a council house, or acted on a public stage, but that his life's work was premised upon a radical questioning of the legitimacy of the Roman Catholic state. For the Vatican, then, the suppression of armed Republicanism carried with it the added benefit of the necessary disciplining of a politicized and rebellious laity.

In a letter he wrote to the author in 1996, Fr Wilson said of his dramatic writings: 'Most of the futile, too gentle fury of the enclosed is directed against the Church establishment ... but by laughing at them we laugh at the whole corrupt boiling of them.'[76] 'Gentle fury' is an arresting phrase, which holds in powerful tension intellectual anger and spiritual humility. It was this 'gentle fury', directed against power in all its forms, and expressed in dramatic form over twenty years, which made the People's Theatre such a unique and important intervention into the war.

'At the Heart of the Struggle'

The plays of
Belfast Community Theatre

If you remove the English army tomorrow, and hoist the green flag over Dublin, unless you set about the organization of the socialist republic, your efforts would be in vain ... England would still rule you to your ruin, even while your lips offered hypocritical homage at the shrine for that freedom whose cause you betrayed.[1]

James Connolly

Republicanism is a broad church, and in the period of the Troubles it included in its ample ideological folds Marxists and humanists, social democrats and Trotskyites, practising Roman Catholics and committed atheists. It was possible, as we have seen, to be both Catholic and Marxist, believer and radical activist, secular politician and private votary. The ideological mix gave rise to tensions, but also to fruitful dialogues, and it underpinned the political and cultural energy which produced theatres such as Belfast Community Theatre. One of its founding members was community activist and educationalist Joe Reid, who was an important figure within the Springhill Education network, and had long argued the necessity for cultural activism, and of theatre in particular:

From 1969 in my case, some of us had been trying to wed theatre to the political struggle but events were such that we could never seem to break through with the importance of theatre. That changed largely through the involvement that many of us had at community level ... we were able to use our positions in local groups, Tenants' Associations, to highlight the value of theatre as a social commentator.[2]

Reid believed that a popular grass-roots theatre could foreground the community's experience of the war, and help to counter the state's ideological apparatus by offering alternative constructions of Republicanism:

We felt the need to try and provide a counter-information activity which could not only increase the self image of our community, but show the way in which the propaganda game works. Hence our involvement in writers workshops, production of pamphlets of people's poetry, prose etc. We wanted to speak about life in the occupied counties from the perspective of our experience, to offer a vision of hope for the future, and to play our part in the struggle for human dignity, freedom and justice.[3]

Reid is a socialist, who shares Connolly's vision of Irish unity as a transitional step on the way to a socialist Irish republic, and at the time we were introduced he was a mature student at Jordanstown University, reading for a BA in English and Drama. It was there that he had met lecturer Michael Klein. Klein had been raised in New York, and had worked for Luther King's organization. He was able to bring to his teaching a history of anti-racist action and activism in the anti-Vietnam and Black Rights' campaigns. Klein introduced Reid to the work of Piscator and Brecht, and to European and American underground films and writings. What Reid found in the American was an empathy with the working-class community that was absent from the rest of the academy. Klein encouraged Reid to write,

Figure 4. Oh Gilbert, by Jim McGlade, Belfast Community Theatre, Conway Mill, Belfast, 1984.

and became involved in the theatre process as it evolved in the period to 1987. The result was a rich formal synthesis, which brought to bear on a politicized working-class theatre the influence of a cosmopolitan radicalism. There is little doubt that Reid's experiences at Jordanstown University were to broaden both the historical scope of Belfast Community Theatre's work, and the formal experimentation which underpinned it.[4]

Reid was born and brought up on the Ballymurphy estate. Bounded by the Whiterock Road on one side and by the Loyalist Spring Martin estate on two more, and protected at its base by the Falls Road, Ballymurphy was the epicentre of militant Republicanism in Belfast. It was the birthplace of Gerry Adams, future President of Sinn Féin, and of Andy Tyrie, who was to lead the UDA for fifteen years, and co-author one of the few Loyalist play texts. Ballymurphy was an estate which, long before the Troubles, had a reputation for social disorder and entrenched poverty. In his autobiography Gerry Adams remembers the 'Murph' as being 'badly built, badly planned, and lacking in facilities'.[5] Although Ballymurphy was a mixed community in the 1950s, by 1969 most Protestant families had moved to the nearby Springvale estate. Springfield Road, which separates the two estates, would become one of the most violent and notorious flash-points of the 'Peace Line'. Until 1994 the Ballymurphy estate was, like many other working-class estates in the north, a war zone, and, together with the sprawling Andersontown estate which abutted it, would provide the majority of the group's members over the decade.

The company included Jim McGlade, a decorator and playwright, Pat McGlade his wife, a Springhill education worker, and Tony Flynn, also a volunteer at Springhill, and later a professional actor, whose credits include appearances at Abbey Theatre, Dublin. Joe Reid and Marie McKnight, another Springhill employee, and a fine actress, made up the group. In my first meeting with them in 1985, the group insisted that their theatre had not arisen fully formed, complete with methodological armoury and a political manifesto. Form, content and process evolved empirically in the unstable conditions of conflict, as also did their view of the theatre's political role. Belfast Community Theatre would include Republicans, Nationalists, Marxists, apolitical members, and others for whom the theatre was primarily a source of friendship and support. It was a combination which generated intense debate: 'That isn't to say that there aren't tensions. There are. There's a lot of disagreements. Because it's so important to us. We all feel very strongly about this.'[6] The group's first production had nothing directly to do with the war, but was a satire dealing with social responses to disability:

Belfast Community Theatre as such came into existence through a play originally written by Jim, a play called 'Oh, Gilbert!' And it was pretty straight forward ... it was like a comic farce ... and basically what had brought the group together was that there was a guy who had written a play and wanted it performed ... and coming from the political culture that we came from the answer was 'why not?' It was out of that came the nucleus, came the group as such.

The production was mounted at Conway Mill on the Falls Road, and was highly successful. One immediate effect was that it brought in Tony Flynn and Gerard McLaughlin to form a core of six performer/writers. Other community members would join later for specific projects. Marie McKnight: 'People come into the theatre through working together in other community groups. It's very much a community-based group that tries to deal with the issues. Each recognized a need within their communities for things to be said on social issues, on community issues.' The group's members were also teachers, carers, parents, tenants' leaders, community activists, and unemployed volunteers. Theatre was one element of a wider praxis. The Philippines Educational Theatre Association (PETA) has developed a term for such activists, calling them ATORs (Actors-Teachers-Organizers-Researchers).[7] It is a term which captures very well the complex role that group members played, and the critical relationship between these roles. This relationship produced a critical-creative dialogue between the community and the theatre which was central to its value. The group did not set out to create an ideologically and formally pure 'political theatre', but a rough, responsive and popular model. Reid insisted that

> Theatre must stand at the heart of struggle, and the tensions performed on the stage cannot be allowed to be abstracted from the reality of the audience's experience. Our community is our stage ... our theatre is not about abstract issues or arguments about this or that theory; theatre in this context is about life and death.

While the theatre group would welcome any and all who wished to take part, there was a permanent core of five or six who sustained the work.

> At the core stood people who were very, very committed and politically motivated, and who had, if you like, a particular vision of people's entitlement, people's rights. And although in the scheme of things people may argue the right to write a play is not a big right, to us it was a fundamental right because it stood at the very core of the struggle that was going on in this country. And that was the right to be heard, and the right to speak your truth, speak your experience.

Asked about the group's relationship to Sinn Féin, Reid, who was never a member (others were) responded:

You see, people talk about Sinn Féin as a political party, but what you've got to remember is ... the political aspirations were communal ... I would have found it pretty hard to produce a play that didn't deal instinctively with the issues *Sign on the Dotted Line* dealt with ... but always aware that theatre ... that expression ... needs to be free of any shackles ... Because we weren't spokespeople for Sinn Féin ... there were parallels, sure. But no way would my politics have been dictated to.[8]

These communal aspirations were most powerfully focused during the 1981 hunger strikes. Reid traced his growing commitment to cultural activism to this period and its aftermath, a period, he notes, of 'tremendous cultural and community trauma'.

The Hunger Strikes and the Birth of Constitutional Republicanism

On Sunday 1 March 1981, Bobby Sands, acting commander of the Irish Republican Army in the Maze Prison, Belfast, refused to take food, an action which signalled the beginning of a new wave of hunger strikes following the unsuccessful campaign of 1980. The hunger strike was the end game of the 'Dirty Protest' and marked the fifth anniversary of the British government's decision, taken in 1976, to end special category status for Republican prisoners.[9] The IRA saw themselves as prisoners of war, captured by an occupying army, and demanded to be treated as such. The issue came to dominate debate within the Movement, and the early eighties would witness the first signs of a significant shift in Republican thinking about mainstream politics. While the armed struggle remained the centre of its strategy, there were increasing signs of a willingness to accommodate civil campaigns and broad-front politics where they reflected the strategic priorities of the IRA Army Council. The most significant of these united fronts developed from the prisoners' Relatives Action Committee, which in 1979 brought together delegates from Sinn Féin, The Irish Republican Socialist Party, People's Democracy, the Trade Union Campaign Against Oppression, and Women Against Imperialism for a meeting at the Green Briar Hotel in Andersontown, West Belfast. The outcome was the founding of the National H-Block/Armagh Committee, whose sole aim was to secure political status for Republican prisoners. *An Phoblacht/Republican News* called for a 'mass single issue campaign aimed at drawing in whatever support possible – whether it be on a purely humanitarian basis ... or whether it be full blooded support for the IRA's armed struggle'.[10] Inside the gaols the prisoners were also mobilizing:

A few prisoners had begun to talk among themselves and with the Republican leadership on the outside about possibly resorting to a hunger strike in order to press their demands. Just prior to the Green Briar conference, Bobby Sands, the officer-commanding in the Blocks had written to his friend Gerry Adams, saying, 'I know you are strategically opposed to a hunger strike, but you are not morally opposed to it'. The Sinn Féin vice president replied, 'Bobby, we are tactically, strategically, physically and morally opposed to a hunger strike'.[11]

Hunger strikes were an unpredictable tactic, which had rarely achieved their goals. It is testimony to the power and status of the prisoners that they were able to overrule the external leadership, and, in process, bring about the most profound realignment in Republican politics since 1916. The new strategy evolved empirically. On 5 March Frank Maguire, the SDLP MP for Fermanagh/South Tyrone died, precipitating a by-election. After intense internal debate, it was decided to put Bobby Sands forward for election as the H-Blocks' candidate, and on 9 April he was duly elected as a Westminster MP. The election attracted considerable global media attention for the hunger strikers' cause. When Sands died on 5 May after sixty-six days without food, his death was headline news around the world. Nine more prisoners were to die before relatives ended the protest in October.

The hunger strike had three important effects. First, it is not too much to say that it saved the IRA by acting as a powerful recruiting agent for new volunteers. There was intense anguish and anger within the community, and, whatever local people's reservations about day-to-day tactics, the 'People's Army' would never again enjoy the same level of grass-roots support. Second, the community's response to the deaths led to an intensification of violence on the streets, and to sustained mass rioting across the six counties. Outside the prisons another 62 people were to lose their lives that year, while crown forces would fire 29,601 plastic bullets, more than in the previous eight years taken together.[12] Third, Sands' election to the British parliament marked the beginning of Republicanism's dual political and military strategy.[13] The scale of electoral support for the IRA man had surpassed all Republican expectations, and Sinn Féin had proven itself to be what it remains today: the most formidable political machine in Ireland. The idea was planted, and it drove the Sinn Féin's strategy from that moment on, that one day demographics would deliver what the armed struggle had not; though it would take another twelve years for the movement as a whole to accept this. Sinn Féin's new political strategy also led to a growth in community-based politics and cultural activism, as the movement sought to exploit and build upon the impact of Sands' election. Belfast Community Theatre developed from this complex interplay between the political, military and cultural wings of nationalism.

Early Work, 1984–86

The fact that members of the theatre group were active in communal and political networks was a great strength; but it also placed important limitations on the scale and form of the work, and the amount of time which could be committed to it. As Paula, a member in this period, noted: 'We're also equally committed to other aspects, such as community work. Some of us are ... well ... mothers! We have families and we have part time jobs, and the theatre must fit in there.'[14] These competing pressures gave rise in the early period to a flexible, popular entertainment model which the group termed 'Mixed Bags'. These were cultural events, sometimes spanning whole days, and staged at the theatre in Conway Mill. Theatre would be offered alongside poetry readings, music and dance, and reflected an eclectic and rich patrimony says Marie McKnight:

> Lady Gregory's plays had been written in the 1920s. We adapted them and changed the language a bit, to make them a bit more modern. But they were as relevant today as they were in the 20s. And they actually dealt with the supergrass issue, which is by no means a new thing, you know. We did a Brecht *On Education*, and pieces on George Jackson, Thomas Jefferson, James Connolly, Winnie Mandela.[15]

These latter were called *Oxygen Plays*, and were meant, says McKnight, to 'bring the air of truth, of understanding to the community'.[16] The adaptations of Lady Gregory's work included versions of *The Gaol Gate* and *Rising of the Moon*. The Brecht piece which McKnight mentions was a considerable reworking of *The Mother*, Brecht's own adaptation of the Gorky novel. Renamed *On Education*, the play celebrated the radical education system being developed through Springhill. These shorter pieces shared an emphasis on class, and class struggle as the lever of change. The focus on class politics would be the most important theoretical and ideological contribution Belfast Community Theatre made to Nationalist discourse.

REID: If there is a basic overall philosophy, and in our case it's a working-class philosophy, about the development of socialism ...

McKNIGHT: We didn't sit down and work it out first! (*Laughter*)

REID: We didn't sit down and consciously say 'Now listen to me, Karl, you write a *Capital* for theatre, and I'll write a series of workshop talks based on Leninism, and then you do one on comedy!' It was there because it is our experience. It's inherent in us. What we are interested in is our relationship with our audience, and with what we are saying.[17]

Theatre was a means to reach across the sectarian divide, and to help rebuild the political relationship between the working-class communities. The group has an important relationship with young cultural activists from the Loyalist Rathcoole estate, though the conflict meant that collaborations were heavily circumscribed. Reid:

> The issues we are tackling are as relevant to the Protestant working class as they are to ours. Unfortunately we haven't yet developed to the extent that we are performing on a regular basis within the protestant community. But I don't think they'd have any problem identifying with the issues we are raising.[18]

Drawing consciously on the example of the Worker Theatres of the twenties and thirties, and the more recent example of Joan Littlewood and Ewan MacColl's Theatre Workshop, the group created 'Living Newspaper' pieces, in which events on the streets were contextualized in montages which included material on popular struggles in South Africa, Chile, Nicaragua, India, and Britain. Material could be devised and performed on the same day, at Conway Mill and Springhill House, or in the Republican clubs, with audiences organised with great speed through the community's activist networks. Ghettoized by the war, confined by military occupation, the sketches placed the experiences of the community in the context of a global movement for civil rights and self-determination. It is of little moment here whether we agree that this was a liberation struggle; it was how the group perceived their work:

> The idea was there that this was a part of a national liberation statement, if you want, that echoed across the world. It was not something that belonged solely to Ireland. It wasn't Irish. This was a human experience that happened to be happening in Ireland. And so the link was made.[19]

Following the success of these plays, and with a desire to broaden both the scope and context for their work, the group decided to use theatre as a means to carry their people's experiences onto the mainstream stage.

'Corrupting the Enemy's Language' – *Eh Joe* and the Supergrass System

If the early 1980s represented a seismic moment in the history of the Republican movement, and the beginning of its slow, historic shift towards constitutional politics, it also marked the advent of a new tactic in the British state's war against insurgency – the Supergrass. The IRA and the loyalist paramilitaries had always been vulnerable to informers, and the period after

1981 was to see, in the words of one of the more famous of them, Sean O'Callaghan, informing turned into a 'full blown system, and one of the main weapons in the state's armoury against the terrorist organizations'.[20] The use of torture had become politically counter-productive by this time, with the British Government once more in the dock at the European Court of Human Rights. Yet the Supergrass system proved a double-edged sword for the state. The unreliability of witnesses and the tendency for many to recant at the last minute, citing brutality as the reason for making their confessions, was to render it unworkable. Nonetheless it created (and this was a key counter-insurgency aim) a climate of profound suspicion and 'blind panic' within Republicanism.[21] Betrayal went to the heart of the resistance culture, and it was the issue which shaped Belfast Community Theatre's next production. The catalyst was Reid's continuing and fruitful collaboration with Klein. Between them they decided that the group should get themselves onto the official Belfast Festival fringe programme for 1985. The Festival, based at Queen's University, was offered to the world as evidence that, despite a neo-colonial war in which significant proportions of the city's (working-class) population had been killed, mutilated, traumatized or imprisoned, 'Culture' survived. State support for mainstream cultural activity was an important element of the policy of 'Ulsterisation' instigated in 1976. The British state's aim was to de-historicize the conflict, and turn it into an issue of internal law enforcement. IRA volunteers were no longer to be seen as soldiers but apolitical gangsters whose motives were simply pecuniary and anarchic. Against this violent and causeless anarchy (understood as an issue of racial disposition) would be projected a constructed normality, which included the arts. Indeed it was because of Ulsterisation that political status was denied to Republican prisoners from 1976, a decision which had led to the hunger strikes. The concept of cultural struggle assumed greater importance in the post-hunger strike period, and Eoghan MacCormaic called in an essay for a kind of counter-colonisation of the oppressor's culture, and for actions which focused on 'corrupting the enemy's language, not just English, but the terminology and the built in assumptions on racism, sexism or class superiority'.[22] This neo-Gramscian analysis found resonance with Belfast Community Theatre, whose work was a de facto critique of the mainstream theatre. The group set out in 1985 to expose the use of the arts as a tool of counter-insurgency, and the consequent suppression of representations of the Nationalist experience. The vehicle chosen for this act of 'entrism' into the mainstream was an adaptation of Samuel Beckett's *Eh Joe*. Reid:

> *Eh Joe* was a play about betrayal. We were in the Supergrass period.
> There was a lot of betrayal. I use that in very guarded terms. But it
> was an issue. And I thought that the echoes in *Eh Joe*, the language
> in *Eh Joe*, we could tinker a bit with that. I liked it. You see I think

Beckett had some very good things to say. But working-class people had been deprived of what Beckett had had to say because it had been brought into this high art, and they had no access to the theatre. And people talked about Beckett in hushed tones. And I said, wait a wee minute, you know.[23]

The Republican enclaves were surrounded by forts and listening posts, and helicopters hovering over them twenty-four hours a day, taking photographs and recording conversations. The British intelligence service, MI5, ran agents and *agents provocateurs* who proved able to penetrate to the highest levels within the IRA's command structure. Many low grade agents operated at community level, gathering information and seeking to disturb or undermine community organizations such as Springhill House. In such a context, Beckett's intensely private, internal hell of betrayal became for Belfast Community Theatre a possible metaphor for a generalized condition: that of the community as undifferentiated suspect. Confident that the community would feel these resonances, the group decided to go a step, or rather two steps further. What Reid's innocent sounding phrase 'tinker a bit with that' amounted to in reality was the total redefinition of the piece for the stage. In place of the strictly set motions of the camera in the original, a spotlight marked the interstices in the text. This absolute rupture of the play's structure was extended to the text. In section 6, Beckett's words are excised, and in their place Belfast Community Theatre inserted the following:

> One phone call … that's all it took. Two meetings. Simple arrangements. What is her name, Joe … Where does her brother live? Tell us, Joe … A story about a bomb … Some rifles … The details don't matter … We'll fill them in … Information please … We'll fix you up with a new identity … Supply you with heroin … We'll take care of you … Across the water … University … Money … Nobody will know … One phone call … That's all it took, Joe … But what about me? What about our people, Joe?

The protagonist in this adaptation is a Supergrass. Reid explained the rationale for the work:

> The female character in it was calling Joe to account. That was what we were trying to say to people. You are responsible for your actions. You cannot Pontius Pilate yourself. You may escape, but your escape is always going to be one of exile. If not physical exile, it's certainly going to be emotional exile because you've put a gap between you and your community which will never heal. And in the darkness of the night you hear 'Eh, Joe!' You hear the accusing voice.[24]

The reaction of the Festival audiences to *Eh Joe* was, according to Reid and McKnight, one of outrage at the violation of one of Ireland's canonical texts. The violation of the rights of a significant proportion of their people by counter insurgent excesses was, it seems, less important. *Eh Joe* was an interesting act of cultural entrism, and was to mark the end of the group's experimentation with existing texts. For the next three years they would concentrate on new works based directly on the Nationalist experience. Important material for this work was to come from the prisons, including scripts, or sections of scripts, which were smuggled out of the prisons. Written on toilet paper or cigarette papers, these scripts were carefully reconstituted outside and offered to the group. To hold one of these texts, a paper trail of minute and laboriously pencilled dialogue and stage directions, is to be brought once more against experiences which challenge orthodox conceptions of the relation between theatre and politics. One prison script, performed as part of a Mixed Bag at Conway Mill, was Eoghan MacCormaic's *Night Before Clontarf*. Written in 1984, it offers an important example of how the prisoners' plays sought to intervene in the political processes outside.

Night Before Clontarf

The play's actions are set in 1843, on the eve of a rally called by Daniel O'Connell's Repeal Association and the militant Young Irelanders. The success of O'Connell's campaign, framed in the Emancipation Act of 1829, had been bought at the cost of the disenfranchisement of the poorest Catholics, and the banning of his own association.[25] The Young Irelanders, the precursors of the IRA, were a response to this accommodation, arguing against O'Connell's pacifism, and urging armed struggle against the British. Warned by the British authorities that the rally was deemed subversive and illegal, and would be crushed, O'Connell called it off. This 'caving in' to Westminster only served to sharpen the growing division in the movement between constitutional gradualism and physical-force Republicanism: a division which defined the internal politics of Irish Nationalism until 2005. It was this division that the play took as its content; although it is not so much a play as a series of dialogues. Five Nationalists, who are on their way to Clontarf, meet at a tavern. Two are from O'Connell's movement and three are from the Young Irelanders. Over drinks, the five contest the legitimacy of their opposed positions. While the Republican voice in the play, Cahir, is prepared to concede the commitment of the reformists, he counsels against taking small concessions for victories:

> Cahir: I cannot agree that the disappointments come from military defeats. There is always some comfort in the knowledge that at least you tried. The real disappointment comes when you think you have

won, and then suddenly discover that you have won nothing more than a moral victory. That is the danger of relying too much on moral force. Sometimes it takes real force to win real victories.[26]

The fear expressed here, of the absorption of revolutionary energies by constitutional processes, was real enough to the IRA. Militants would point to the cease-fire of 1975 as a moment where accommodation had almost led to the destruction of the movement. The play also spoke to the heart of the debate taking place in 1986 within the Republican movement. For it was at their 1986 Ard Fheiseanna (annual conference) that Sinn Féin voted to end seventy years of abstentionism from the Republic's parliament, the Dail Eireann, a decision that signalled the beginning of the political shift within the movement towards the Adams/McGuinness axis. The Good Friday Agreement of 10 April 1998 was the outcome of their slow struggle to convince the movement that Irish unity could now be achieved through demography, and the increasingly explicit indication of the British state's desire to disengage.[27] *Night Before Clontarf* was therefore deeply relevant. Reid's concern, as his hand-written notes on the back of the script show, was whether it would work on the stage. He notes: 'Dialogue too rhetorical, sounds like one long political speech: would not hold audience'. Below these comment, he lists a range of suggestions for making the text more theatrical. One idea was to set it in a contemporary bar with the characters 'as ghost figures', so pointing up the historical continuities.[28] Another note muses about the potential for creating new characters. In the end, his musings counsel strongly against theatrical considerations being allowed to 'lose the political content'. The play was performed as written, but with ballads added to break the static quality of the set-piece dialogues. Reid's notes also show that *Night at Clontarf* was a central text in a day-long cultural event for the West Belfast Festival.[29] In a further note Reid writes:

> Hold this play for August 9. Include it with 'Rising of the Moon', 'Jail Gate'. Reading from 'Why Me?': excerpt from Sands and 'Eh Joe'. Plus traditional music. Finish with poem by Donald Sutherland. Starting 6pm to midnight. Try to focus on Centre. 'Wicked Witch' for during the day. Kid's disco. Under 10s plus parents.

However, it was not *Clontarf*, but a script fragment from the H-Blocks dealing with interrogation and strip-searching which was to have the greatest impact on the group's work. From this fragment, smuggled out in cling film, came their best-known and most powerful play, *Sign on the Dotted Line*.

The Political Context for *Sign on the Dotted Line*

In the post-hunger strike period the Nationalist community was, in Reid's words, going through a 'tremendous cultural and community trauma'.[30] In Maghaberry Women's gaol strip-searching, an examination of mouth, vagina and anus, had been introduced for all prisoners whenever they moved anywhere within or without the prison. The Roman Catholic Chaplain at Maghaberry, Father Raymond Murray, wrote to the Under-Secretary of State, Nicholas Scott, to protest. Pointing out that strip-searching had been intensified at the very moment that the Roman Catholic hierarchy and local politicians had thought they had established a dialogue with the government over prisoners' rights, he continues:

> We took it [strip-searching] as the customary slap in the face to our community from our colonial masters. Since there is no internal searching of the women, as the Northern Ireland Office has often pointed out, what is the logic of stripping them completely naked, even during their periods, and visually examining the genitals and anus? Can you blame people for logically concluding that the purpose is to degrade and cruelly punish them?[31]

Nationalist lawyers petitioned the European Court of Human rights over the issue and the Anti-Strip Searching campaign was founded, based on an alliance between the H-Blocks Committees, Sinn Féin and the Women's Centres. *Sign on the Dotted Line* was Belfast Community Theatre's contribution to the campaign, and a performance of the play at Conway Mill on 18 March 1987 was my and John Goodchild's practical introduction to the group's work. Following the Adult Education visit we had kept in contact with Reid and McKnight, and had returned to see the production. It was our point of entry into the group's history. I want to use the performance as the basis for a more detailed exploration of the group's methods and as a means to demonstrate the decisive interplay between the political and creative processes. As always with these theatres, context was the dominant determinant of form, and of the theatre's radical effect.

The production was staged at the Conway Mill theatre and Father Des Wilson drove Goodchild and me from Springhill House down to the Falls Road. First, however, he checked the underside of his car for a bomb. Wilson was a constant target for Loyalist assassination, and had recently had a wrought iron gate fitted at the bottom of his bedroom stairs. On the way to the Mill we encountered two army road blocks, and a couple of burning buses. Security at the gates of the Mill complex was tight, and cameras checked us while we waited for Des Wilson to be recognized. There was a dull whirr, and the gates gave way to our touch. In the foyer we were checked again. The cumulative effect of these processes is emotional, and I associate theatre going in Belfast with fear: for myself, certainly, but mostly for those I was with. Conway Mill was where the majority of rehearsals for the group's work took place: a space where these ATORs' multiple roles intersected.

Once at the Education floor we bought a cup of tea at the bar, where our money was waved away. We made our way into the theatre. I noted the number of children among this working-class audience. Goodchild and I took seats at the back. Joe Reid was concerned because a singer they had booked had not turned up, and approached us. *Sign on the Dotted Line* was too short to fill an evening, and they now needed another act. Would we, he asked, be prepared to perform? It is important to stress that we had met only once before, during the visit I described in the introduction. Neither group had seen the other's work. This was also an audience of prisoners' families, made up of children whose mothers or fathers had been jailed by the British state. Our intention had been to watch the performance and go, and now we were being asked to take centre stage. After hasty deliberations, we borrowed a large cardboard box, an over-sized jacket, a scarf and a tie, and performed a simple agit prop style sketch on housing issues taken from our activist theatre work in Sheffield. Transposed from the Sheffield Galsworthy estate to the Falls Road, it still generated laughter as politics transcended the improvised nature of the performance. The Belfast Community Theatre group thanked us warmly and we returned to our seats, no longer invisible, but no longer, either, entirely strangers. There was a short break, and then the performance of *Sign* began. In the account that follows, I have drawn on both the unpublished text, and on memory, for the images made an intense impression. All quotations are from the unpublished script. By writing in the present tense I want to approximate something of the immediacy that defines all performance.

A Good Night Out on the Falls Road: *Sign on the Dotted Line* in Performance

The theatre doors are closed. From hidden speakers the mute bass of the Congolese Missa Luba rises and then dies away. The house lights dim. A single spot stage-left lights a solitary figure who is seated upon the floor. His legs are crossed, and he leans forward, one hand holding an ankle. The light catches his red hair like a rough halo. The image is held as he begins to sing. The song is Behan's 'The Auld Triangle'. His voice is beautiful, clear and youthful, the innocence contrasting with the harsh reality of the song's account, its rising notes set against the confined pose. From the rear of the hall another voice joins in, deeper and more powerful. The duet encloses the audience, as past and present meet; the continuity of struggle, and of art's response to it, is implicit. In the image of the confined prisoner, Ireland finds its most potent metaphor.

Scene One

As the song ends, the lights dim to blackout. When they come up again, they create a corridor of half light along the front of the stage. Just behind, on a raised dais, you can barely make out a table and three empty chairs. At each corner, down-stage right and left, a figure is crouched. Further back, near the table, is the Narrator. As the play progresses it becomes apparent that she is there to act as the audience's guide, the players' friend and prompt, alter ego and spare performer. In a mixture of Boal's 'Joker' system and Brechtian aesthetic, she is ubiquitous, detached, and omnipresent. It is as if she calls the play's stylistic shifts into existence, demanding new forms to meet the needs of the material, or of a shift in perception. For now we see her hover nervously as the two figures begin to whisper across the space dividing them. One of them is busy ruling lines onto a small piece of toilet roll. The other prisoner, for that is what they are, calls to him:

> KEVIN: Hurry up. Be careful. Are you ready?
> DONAL: Just a minute.[32]

A voice shouts in from stage left: 'Be quiet in there!' We assume it is a guard. The Narrator gestures to them. The two prisoners now whisper in Gaelic. Again the voice calls from off stage: 'You pair shut up, or I'll have you both on report. And give up talking in that foreign babble.' This is enough to tell us that they are Republicans, and we experience the incongruity of the Irish language being referred to as 'foreign' in Ireland, and the pejorative use of the word 'babble'. It is the word of colonialists for 'native' tongues and it carries deliberate overtones of the subhuman, of infantilism. Language and the land are indivisible: the one is called for through the other. Repressing the use of one is an attempt to suppress the struggle for the other. We hear retreating footsteps. The prisoners pause, and then they begin again. Why, Kevin asks, are two prisoners accused of insurrection writing a play on toilet paper? What is the meaning of that response? And why do this under such difficult conditions, risking beatings and solitary confinement? What is the purpose of this theatre? Donal's answer is for Kevin, it is for the group, and it is for the audience whose sufferings the play contains:

> DONAL: Listen, Kevin, I know how you feel ... but ... what's
>   important is that we are writing the play, and that when we
>   do get out, people will remember.
> KEVIN: Will people really go to hear what we have to say?
> DONAL: Of course they will.

The 'we' in 'we are writing' is the most important word in the scene. 'We' are writing, not outsiders, or middle class radical playwrights who will try to imitate our lives: the theatre is ours through and through. It is permeated by our struggle, our experiences and our language. There is again this Brechtian nod towards the artifice of theatre: we are hearing Kevin ask if anyone will hear. As the two turn to setting down the script painstakingly on the tiny piece of paper, Kevin pauses. He has forgotten, he tells Donal, what comes next. Donal's answer is for Kevin and for the audience, for the moment and for history.

DONAL: I haven't forgotten. We don't forget anything.

There is a blackout.

Scene Two

As the lights rise, the Narrator comes forward. The tone now is urgent and business-like:

NARRATOR: The scene is Ballymurphy. The time is the present. Tony Murphy's house was raided on a cold, damp morning at 5am. Tony was swiftly arrested under the infamous section 11 of the Emergency Provisions Act. He was then placed in a land rover and taken to Castlereagh interrogation centre. Once in Castlereagh he was handed over to the Special Branch for interrogation. The Special Branch file on Tony Murphy included reports about him mixing with 'subversive types', including well known Ballymurphy Republicans Patsy Mulligan and Toni Tinnsley. This is Murphy's first time in Castlereagh. But there have been others there before him.

The flat tone, the matter of fact directness, which prepares the audience for Murphy's interrogation, is suddenly undercut. The lights change to a single spot. The Narrator moves into it. The physical shift indicates a rupture. A tin whistle is heard. She begins to read a Bobby Sands poem. The switch is in fact foreshadowed in the last line of the narration. Once again Republican history reaches out and claims all individual experiences for its own.

NARRATOR:
   I scratched my name but not for fame, upon the whitened wall,
   Bobby Sands was here I wrote with fear, in awful shaky scrawl,
   I wrote it low where eyes don't go, it was just to testify
   That I am sane and not to blame should I come here to die.

The poem, simple and halting, is crucial to the unfolding of the drama. Not only in its evocation of the hunger strike, but through the values it presents. The Republican hero is revealed as vulnerable, fearful, and modest. Yet, he starved himself to death, privileging Irish freedom before his own life. As the last lines are spoken, a guard brings in Tony Murphy. He is placed on a chair on the raised rostra, and left alone. The interrogation is about to begin.

Scene Three

The zonal lighting, which is central to the play's aesthetic, now plays upon the rostra. Behind Tony there is blackness. He is restless, fearful, breathing heavily. He wrings his hands, turns this way and that, licks dry lips and moans gently. The light intensifies his isolation. We hear voices, and two Special Branch officers enter. One is telling the other a string of bad jokes. They ignore Tony and sit down. One of them, Haddock, places a file on the table. He studies it, looks at Tony, and studies the file again. The question when it comes is chatty, like a bank manager checking on your overdraft needs:

Figure 5. *Sign on the Dotted Line*, by Belfast Community Theatre, Monteney Community Centre, Sheffield, England, 1987.

HADDOCK: O.K., let's see ... hmmm ... hmm ... right ... when did you
           join the Provos?
TONY: I'm not in the Provos.

Haddock slams down the file, turns to McMullan.

HADDOCK: Talk to him!

The interrogation has been prefigured. They claim to have evidence that
Tony has been knocking around with known IRA men and women. They
press him. Did he know they were in the Provos? No, he didn't. They
probably aren't. It is a game of mirrors. If Tony wants his freedom he'll
have to implicate others. Either he goes down, or others do. They raise the
stakes. They tell him that his house is being raided. His elderly mother won't
like that. If he co-operates she can be told where he is. He again protests
his innocence. Haddock leaves to check on the progress of the house raid.
McMullan stands staring at Tony. He smiles. He asks Tony to tell him a
joke. It's a kind of grotesque reversal of bar room chit-chat. Tony tries and
falters. He excuses himself. McMullan brushes the apology aside, and asks
casually:

McMULLAN: Tell me Tony, do you know anyone called Mulligan. Patsy
           Mulligan?
TONY: No, I can't say I do.
McMULLAN: Are you sure?
TONY: Yes, why?
McMULLAN: Oh, just wondering.

The pressure is drip-drip, the accusations, the house raid, and his mother.
The powerlessness is absolute. Interrogation works because it goes to the
heart of our value system. What matters to us? For Tony it is love for his
mother. In the space between this love, and his fear of what might be done
to her, the interrogators do their work. Haddock rushes back in. They have
found bullets in his house. Who put them there? If Tony didn't, it can only
mean one thing, his mother did. He denies this. They pressure him. They
bang the table, shout, plead, accuse. Tony's head jerks from one to the other,
seeking an anchor in this bewildering farce. The scenario is banal, B-movie
stuff. Finally, Haddock pretends to lose his temper and tears off his jacket.
He walks behind Tony, grabs his hair and yanks his head sharply back. He
raises his fist. Tony cries out. McMullan pretends to shield his eyes as if he
can't bear to see violence. They are acting a script, and Tony, they intimate,
is a bad actor. He knows enough of the plot, but he won't take his cue.
They offer now to leave him to think things over, to 'get his act together'.
As they go Haddock offers him the final twist in the narrative they are all
creating together:

HADDOCK: I'll tell you what, sonny, we're going to go for a cup of tea
now. You have a good think to yourself while we're away,
all right? We'll continue this when we get back. Mind you,
it was a pity that your mother took that wee turn when
our boys were searching the house. They had to call for the
doctor. I hope you start co-operating because I wouldn't like
to be held responsible for the consequences of interrogating a
sick old woman.

They go, leaving Tony alone. He stares into blackness, shaking. From offstage we hear snatches of the 'Old Triangle'. In the interrogation cell you
are never alone. History and its myths crowd in. Names that have been
scratched on walls call to you. McMullan re-enters. He's got a deal to offer
Tony. They're prepared to forget his non-existent Provo activities if he'll
play a part for them. Tony can go free, and his mother will be left alone, if
he informs against his community. McMullan freezes. Tony sits staring out
into the audience. From behind the audience a voice cries from the back of
the hall. It is the Narrator. She sets out Tony's options. Heads they win,
tails you lose:

NARRATOR: Don't do it Tony ... Think of your self-respect, your dignity.
If you turn informer you'll always be found out, you'll have
nowhere to go and nobody to turn to. When they've finished
with you you'll be like a stray dog! But you can't let your
mother take the rap, she's an old woman with a bad heart,
she couldn't stand up to the interrogation. There isn't any
choice. There's no way out.

Tony must choose between his mother and the community, between his self-
respect and her life. The Narrator's speech acknowledges this. There is no
condemnation, just the calculation of damage. The interrogators now close
in, physically and metaphorically. They lay a piece of paper on the table:

McMULLAN: Well, Tony, Mr Haddock and I have already prepared a
statement. All you have to do is sign on the dotted line.

There is a long pause. McMullan holds a pen out to Tony, who turns and
looks at it. They freeze. The lights blackout. We do not know what he
chose, anymore than we can know what choice anyone makes in the terrible
loneliness of the interrogation cell. The play does not condemn those who
sign, nor does it fete those who do not. The theatre does not invite judgment,
but a complex and historically aware solidarity. It does not ask, 'What do
you think of what he or she did?', but rather, 'In their place, what would you
have done?' It asks knowing that, in truth, we do not know the answer.

Scene Four

A single spotlight down stage left. A young girl walks into the light. The spot lights only her face, so that it looks as if it were suspended above the earth:

> GIRL: My name is Maria and I was fourteen the day they stopped me growing to be fifteen … They told my mummy and my daddy I had been throwing stones at them, that I was a threat to their armoured cars … I was only going to the shop.

So begins a monologue which stands as a memorial for the sixteen children aged under sixteen who have been shot and killed by plastic bullets in the north of Ireland. Children such as Carol Anne Kelly, aged 12, killed on 12 May 1981, or Julie Livingstone, aged 14, whose face was removed by a plastic bullet on 22 May 1981. The monologue's combination of innocence and bewilderment, of forgiveness and childish musings is devastating. The speech closes:

> GIRL: I can't forgive the papers or the men who came on TV and said how regrettable it was that I had to die, such a waste of life they said … but did I have to die? What harm could I have done to them? No, I can't forgive all the silent people who watched a girl of fourteen not being allowed to grow to fifteen.
>
> *The light fades.*

Scene Five

The Narrator moves forward. We are about to witness the second interrogation, that of Patsy Mulligan. Her name is familiar from Murphy's cross-examination. Haddock and McMullan enter. They debate whether to swap 'roles', but Haddock knows Patsy, and they decide against it. It would disturb the 'plot'. McMullan goes and reappears dragging a woman by the arm. She resists and he is forced to push her into the centre chair. They take a seat either side of her. Once more, they begin their mockery of human intercourse.

McMULLAN: Well Patricia, or is it Pat?

> *She says nothing, staring straight ahead, impassive and mute.*

McMULLAN: Well, I'm Detective Sergeant McMullan and this is Detective Constable Haddock.

HADDOCK: Oh, Patsy and I go back a long way. Isn't that right Pat?

McMULLAN: Well now, Patsy, what would you like us three to talk about?

Again, there is this grotesque inversion, as if Patsy had called them in for therapy. She says nothing. Indeed, the motive power of this scene, its dramatic locus, is her silence, her refusal to acknowledge the game, to give them a foothold into the routine. She is being held on a seven day under the PTA.[33] It happens regularly. They get up, circle her, probing, stroking her hair, touching her breasts and thigh. She flinches, goes to push the hand away, but stops herself. She stares ahead. The innuendo is aggressive, sexual:

HADDOCK: There'll be no fucking about with your Provo boyfriends this weekend. Mind you, from what we hear, you'll be missing it a hell of a lot more than they will.

They lean towards her. Freeze. Black out.

Scene Six

The lights rise down stage right. The white light is replaced by reds and greens. Music is playing. The Narrator is busily arranging chairs around a table. We are in a club. Yet, we have not left the interrogation room. Always at the back of the stage, as at the back of the community's mind, sit the confined ones. Several women enter, chatting. They sit down; they remove coats, laugh and point. A waitress (the Narrator) brings drinks. Between the gaps in the war, the scene suggests, life carries on, but it is life qualified always by what is absent: peace, a comrade, a lover. The scene is played naturalistically. It is a Friday night outing. In front of the dais, three women discuss a forthcoming marriage. As we watch, we feel the deliberate aesthetic choice being made in this counterpoising of an assumed normality with the still image of the oppressed woman, who is both of and apart from the community. Just as normality is constantly ruptured by uncommon violence and suffering, so the naturalistic scene at the stage's front is denied its stylistic integrity. The scene is about Patsy, not them. As they talk it becomes clear that Patsy has been arrested for her fight against strip-searching. They admire her. Her struggle is theirs, it is symptomatic, historical, and the community owns it. It is also, and this is now becoming apparent, a struggle about the double oppression of women. And because violence breaks into the everyday without warning, so the scene is suddenly undercut in mid-sentence as the Narrator turns towards the stage and the light comes up once more on the trinity of players on the dais.

Scene Seven

Haddock jumps to his feet, screaming into Patsy's face, banging the table:

HADDOCK: I'm biased? Sure didn't Murphy tell us earlier that Tinsley and this bitch here were going out to shoot policemen? Yes, you! Answer me! I'm talking to you!

He pulls at her blouse, which rips. She grabs at it. McMullan moves across, pretends to restrain him. The double act is in full play now. We also note the reference to Tony Murphy. Did he sign? We don't know and nor does Patsy. What we can see is the ripped blouse, the violent gestures, two men alone with one woman. Patsy stays immobile, silent. Haddock hits her, tears at her hair, screams abuse, and then storms out. We do not feel this time that it is pretence. He hates her. A long silence. Patsy is still, McMullan stares at her from stage right. He sits down next to her. His voice is full of concern. If she goes to gaol how will her little child or her ageing mother cope? He leans forward, parent to parent, he offers understanding:

McMULLAN: What age would she be now? Two? Three? That's the age my own wee one is. You know she nearly screams the place down every time my wife leaves her; she can hardly go to the toilet without the child crying after her. For Christ's sake Patsy, wake up! If you're not worried about yourself, think of your child!

He gets up. Patsy hasn't moved. Her eyes stare ahead; her face is closed against him. He walks around slowly, talking, coaxing and threatening by turn.

McMULLAN: You know that unless we make some kind of deal here that you're going to Maghaberry. Maghaberry, Patsy! It's no bloody holiday camp. Come on, you've been around, your mate Joan Maguire only got out a few weeks ago: she's bound to have told you what it's like … All you have to do is sign, and I'll see you're all right. Hmm?

He goes, leaving Patsy alone. The lights dim. She stays sitting. The Narrator steps forward. She is caught in the back light. As Patsy responds with her face, the Narrator acts as her alter ego, voicing the thoughts Patsy would not speak out loud. We are now allowed to know the inner turmoil that her stoical exterior hides:

ALTER EGO: Christ, I hate those bastards! Scum, who do they think I am? That I would sign other people into this hell hole? … God, what about wee Sinead … her granny'll be putting her to bed around now, and she'll probably forget to give her that old blue jumper … it's full of holes but she can't sleep without it. She's so shy. If they put her in one of those homes she'll be so distracted.

Now Patsy calls on the two forces which shape her life, Catholicism and

Republicanism, God and a United Ireland, in whose name the present must surrender to the future.

ALTER EGO: Oh God, help me do the right thing ... Hail Mary full of grace ... she'll be growing up and I'm going to miss it all ... But I can't sign anything. I can't. Oh Jesus, I can't! What about wee Sinead ... what about all those other wee children ... but no ... no ... think ... what kind of world will they grow up in if we don't do what's right!

She is totally distraught, her face an agony of repressed tears, her body tensed and contorted, the hands grasping at the sides of the chair, holding herself on. Haddock comes back in. He screams into her face. She is facing conspiracy to murder. Patsy is going to Maghaberry for life. They freeze. There is a black out.

Scene Eight

From off stage comes a verse of the Missa Luba Sanctus. The stage is in total darkness, except for a low light on the Narrator who is stage right centre. She is once again the alter ego for Patsy. A loud voice is heard:

VOICE: Right, strip!
ALTER EGO: Silent young woman
Alone, so forlorn
Awaits in subjection
No clothes adorn.
VOICE: Come on, get them off! We haven't got all day you know!
ALTER EGO: Maiden there standing
No pity knows
Waiting just waiting
Her nakedness shows.
VOICE: Right, you bitch, let's have the sanitary towel!

So the scene unfolds, with this counterpoising of the simple haunting beauty of the poetry, and the crude banalities and cruelties of the voices. It is an evocation of ritual defilement which speaks of martyrdom and holy solitariness: Christ among his tormentors: Connolly strapped to his chair in the cold light of dawn: Sands defiant in his cell. There is raucous laughter. The light slowly fades.

Scene Nine

After the noise and brutality of the interrogation, and the still, painful dignity of the last scene, Patsy's entrance into Maghaberry is almost domestic in its ease and warmth. After the corruption of closeness and touch, it is also a

Figure 6. Sign on the Dotted Line, by Belfast Community Theatre, Monteney Community Centre, Sheffield, England, 1987.

celebration of love, of caring, of women in solidarity. Once again, there is the deliberate interplay of styles. The scene opens with three women sitting in a semicircle front stage centre, talking amusingly about their education courses. They had been denied access to books with 'political ideas' in them because they constituted a 'security risk'. Patsy enters but stands unnoticed. It is the Narrator who interrupts the talking, and speaks to her, offering comfort. The women make room for her, and ask solicitously about her experience. They allow her for the first time to acknowledge the horror of what she has been through. The need is palpable. She clings to the women, they rock together. Patsy breaks down. In between her sobs they soothe her, but make clear the consequences of her choice. Strip-searching, humiliation, abuse – these will be the condition of their lives together. The scene ends in affirmation:

> ROSA: You're all right now, love. You can trust us. We're all in the
>   same boat. They may be able to frame us ... to humiliate us
>   ...
> PATSY: But by God, and by Christ, they will never, never break us!

She is on her feet now, defiant. The light focuses upon her, her clenched fist raised in a salute to the audience. The lights cut out.

Scene Ten

Darkness. The Kyrie from Missa Luba begins. It stays throughout the scene. Two lights come up stage left and right. Tony and Patsy, the two prisoners, step into them. They begin a paean to the Irish struggle, and to all freedom struggles. From within the audience other voices join in:

VOICE: Let freedom ring from the mountains of Kerry to the hills of Antrim, from Soweto to Greenham Common!

PATSY: Irish men and Irish women, in the name of god and the dead generations ...

TONY: We declare the right of the people of Ireland to the ownership of Ireland. We declare the right of the peoples of the world to live free from poverty, tyranny and fear ...

PATSY: And freedom from imprisonment and degradation ...

TONY: As Connolly ...

PATSY: And Countess Markeiwicz were imprisoned before us.

VOICE: Our day will come!

ALL: Venceramos! Our day will come! Our day will come!

The music rises now to a crescendo as the Kyrie comes to its conclusion. The lights are held to the final note, and then they snap out. There is silence. As the applause rings out the players come forward to bow, and then melt into an audience from which they came, and to which they belong. It was at that point that I realized why there were so many children with only one parent in this most family-orientated of cultures. These were the Sineads, come to see why mammy or daddy was in prison.

The Making of *Sign on the Dotted Line*

Sign was the product of a deeply political and communal reflex. To place this in a more concrete context, here is how group member Paula accounted for the play's genesis:

> The beginning of the play was written by two men in the H-Blocks of Long Kesh. It was smuggled out of the gaol on small cigarette papers and tissue papers, and it was passed onto the community theatre. We built our play around that. We felt that there were a lot of issues that needed to be raised, such as strip searching, such as plastic bullets and so on. So four women members of the group got together for maybe a week in each other's houses. We sat around and we talked to women. We invited along ex-prisoners. Women who'd been through strip-searching, who'd been through interrogation, who could relive, if you like, what they'd been through. Then we talked about what they'd said. We talked out a script into a tape recorder,

and then picked out the best parts. That's how the whole second section dealing with Patsy was written. The women members of the group felt it was really important to bring out the strip-searching issue through women. The play grew around that. There was the section on plastic bullets written by Joe. The introduction and ending was written separately.[34]

Contained within this account, if it were minutely dissected, each of its relationships and actions given their proper scrutiny, is not only the history of a theatre that is political through and through, but of the political history of Ireland, of which a forty-five minute piece of theatre is only the visible, public and partial expression. Even in this short statement we get the sense of the piecemeal accumulation of material. The theatre is created in a cell, a kitchen, a community space, a theatre and in one man's head: it arrives through the agency of cigarette papers smuggled in mouths from a prison, a tape recorder, paper and pen, debate and argument. It is begun by men, and taken forward with a deeper agenda by women. It is part reportage, part text, and part improvisation. A particular issue, interrogation, becomes a prism through which other experiences are refracted. However, while the script exists, and can be reinterpreted, what cannot be reproduced is this process, the collective 'method' by which the play came to be made. It was a method conjured out of the interaction of people with an unstable reality, and negotiated amid politically created limitations on access, resources, space and time. Belfast Community Theatre demonstrated a politics of improvisation that moves us beyond notions of devising, to embrace both the sequence of human activities which produced the script, and the means by which Nationalists survived an unpredictable and hostile reality.

When rehearsals began there was no plot or narrative focus. It was through the practical testing out of script fragments and the counterpoising of images that the group arrived at the plot and narrative. Marie McKnight: 'It grows from a conglomeration of ideas. People chip in and say "Look, I think this would work, or that would work". And we would try them out. It grows, basically, by consensus.'[35] It was a consensus that was achieved through passionate and tense debate. The level of Republican commitment in the group ranged from passive support to those who, like Paula and Mairead, were extremely active. A key advisor in ensuring the play reflected the reality of interrogation and strip searching was Mairead Farrell, later to be shot dead by members of the SAS in Gibraltar in 1988.[36]

Influenced by Brecht's theories, Reid and Klein insisted that each image or script offered by the group should be constructed into a scene or scenario that would be rehearsed as a stand-alone. 'If it worked on its own, it worked,' Reid notes. Only when the different elements were in place did the issue of structure arise, of finding a device to cohere what Reid calls a 'stylistic mish-mash'. The Narrator, a figure who was conceived as an historical interlocutor, was the formal device that they used. Reid comments: 'We weren't concerned with *form*: what we were concerned with was getting the message across. What medium suited the message?'[37] The play was in itself a statement about this process, about the right to mobilize all forms or styles in service of the ideas and feelings being presented. The choice of the alter-ego to voice Patsy's feelings during her interrogation was not made for aesthetic effect, argues Paula, but because it met a concrete need:

> Patsy is a strong character, because she doesn't actually say anything through the whole interrogation. But she's human. Those feelings are what's going on her head. Even though she's physically upset, with her crying you can't hear what she's saying. So we thought we'd bring someone else in to speak her thoughts. She's human after all.[38]

As noted, some sections of the text arrived in developed form. The Plastic Bullet scene, which Reid wrote, was one example. Sections of the interrogation scene with Patsy were also well advanced before rehearsals. The rehearsal was a means to test and refine these texts. Direction was shared, and members would step into scenes they had directed in order to let other players out to watch, comment and advise. Local people coming into the Mill for classes or a drink would also be invited to watch rehearsals and to offer their responses. Not only did this help enrich the process, but it also helped to spread the word about the production. This continuous interplay between reception and production was a key aspect of the creative activity. At other moments specific groups would be brought in to help develop the play's authenticity and to refine its politics. As well as Mairead Farrell, a local women's group challenged what they saw as patronizing and inauthentic elements, and their analysis was fed into discussions at the next rehearsal. As the work progressed and was bedded down, Reid's job was to take material home each night and write it down ready for reworking. It was a process of refinement using improvisation within very defined parameters. A point would come when the scene was felt to be right, and it could be set. *Sign* was always conceived as work-in-progress, one which remained open to the world it described. One of the group's objectives in writing the play was to help break a barrier which existed within their own community, between those who had been through interrogation, and those who had not. For after the terrible isolation of the cells, many prisoners felt unable to convey, even to loved ones, what they had been through. Paula, who had herself been interrogated at Castlereagh on several occasions, told me:

> No-one can ever understand what you personally go through. It's like a woman being raped. No-one can understand what she really experienced. So a lot of people who have been through interrogation,

who have been through strip searching ... even after the event is over ... after they are out of prison ... they still feel isolated.[39]

The analogy with rape underlines the fact that *Sign on the Dotted Line* is also a play about patriarchy, and about the double oppression of women within the Nationalist community. When the show was seen by the women whose experiences it was based upon, the impact was even more striking. Paula again:

> The first time we performed this play we performed it for the women we had spoken to earlier. And they were just shattered by the whole thing. By the very fact that you could see what was happening on stage. If you like, they were outside looking in.[40]

The women's response goes to the heart of Brecht's concept of *Verfremdungseffekt*. For it registers absolutely the idea of 'making strange' what has become naturalized, of revealing as abnormal what has come to seem normal. Reid has talked about how the group had wept when they recognized what they had created in *Sign*. The *Verfremdungseffekt* is not limited to public performance. Performance and reception constitute a continuum that is present throughout the production of this theatre. The first people to be alienated are not the audience, but the players, who in rehearsal are both performer and audience. The political effects of theatre are dispersed throughout its processes, and theatre changes first those who create it. The production helped to open up a debate on these experiences, providing both therapeutic support for the women, and supporting mobilization against the practices it excoriated. For, as Brecht notes, 'true A effects are of a combative character': epic theatre was not supposed to stimulate theoretical discussions, but praxis.[41] The relationship between stage and audience in a situation of insurgency is dynamic. Uptal Dutt, the charismatic impresario of Bengal's Marxist theatre movement, said of the audience's relationship to such performances:

> They bring their actual life experiences to bear upon the stage. They react to plays from the standpoint of their own personal sufferings and have the strength to alter the values enshrined in performance. The audience is the link between life and theatre.[42]

This sense of an organic relationship, and of theatre as part of a wider nexus of socio-political life, in which culture is embraced as part of a universal and progressive human project, permeated Belfast Community Theatre's work.

The Tour of Belfast Community Theatre to South Yorkshire, November 1987

Both Goodchild and I were deeply impressed by the power and quality of *Sign on the Dotted Line*, and determined to organize a tour of the group to South Yorkshire. For help in achieving this we were able to draw on a support group comprising Adult Education workers, Troops Out activists, youth workers and local tenants' association representatives. We decided to make it a community-based tour, and performances were arranged at venues in the city's council estates, including the Frecheville Open Door Centre, Manor Community Centre, Sheffield and District Afro-Caribbean Community Association, and Monteney Community Workshop. Performances were also held at the Sheffield Centre Against Unemployment, and Rotherham Arts Centre. Manor Campaign Theatre, Lower Manor Tenants' Association, and the Manor Community Shop contributed to the financial costs of the tour, and local residents paid for, and hosted, a community meal at a local public house for the visitors.[43] These were all venues at which Goodchild and I had performed, or held theatre workshops, or which were, as in the case of the Manor, the bases for local activist theatre companies.[44]

A great deal of effort went into developing an audience for the shows, which took place 23–29 November 1987. The group came over with Michael Klein. Joe Reid did not come. He had been advised, by which sources he would not say, that travelling to Britain would not be a good idea. The group asked whether one of us would take over Joe's role as Haddock, which is how John Goodchild came to be a temporary member of the Irish company. Michael Klein rehearsed him into the part during rehearsals at Monteney Community Workshop. Goodchild's English accent in some ways intensified the play's realism, for it pointed up the active relationship between British intelligence and the Northern Ireland Special Branch. At all times in the period we were acutely conscious of working against the dominant media images of Republicans and Nationalists. The war in Ireland had entered one of its most bitter phases, and the *Sheffield Star* newspaper reflected this in a series of articles in the period leading up to the visit. 'Belfast Hate-filled Kids Still Brick our Soldiers', was the headline on 28 September 1987, in an article by Philip Andrews. Chesterfield MP Tony Benn answered with a call for a United Ireland in a column on the 11 November. A joint City Council/ Troops Out delegation report, published in November, recommended that Sinn Féin councillors be invited to the city to help build a dialogue. Roy Mason, a Barnsley MP, and a former Northern Ireland Secretary, accused its authors of 'encouraging links with the IRA'. He warned local councillors of how terrorists and Republicans 'visit Britain in their various guises'.[45] Presumably this included visiting in the 'guise' of performers.

This level of attack and counter-attack was to persist during the tour, and made the local centres' decision to host Belfast Community Theatre an act of political courage. A combination of personal contact with local groups, and the efforts of local workers, trades unionists and activists, meant that the four shows were seen by over three hundred local people. The reception was favourable, and the tour was deemed a success by both parties, creating the basis for a relationship that was to span the next decade. In addition to the performances, joint workshops were held with local groups Manor Campaign Theatre and Castle Theatre Workshop at the latter's base above a local library. And while Belfast Community Theatre was only to come to England once, Goodchild and I crossed the Irish sea on a regular basis over the following years, performing and running workshops.

The instability of the situation and the lack of funding meant that these visits were limited to one- or two-week stays over the period. Nonetheless, we were to perform in West Belfast in 1987, 1988, 1989, 1990, 1992 and 1994. While all visits included a show at Conway Mill and Springhill House, 1989 saw a more organised tour of Republican Clubs. Although we had developed pieces on issues such as the Birmingham 6 case in 1988, the main focus of performances was sketches on working-class issues from Britain, such as the Poll Tax and the then Conservative government's attacks on the trades' union movement.[46] The sketch-based style and satire were the elements Reid and Wilson most liked. Alongside the performances was a series of workshops in 1987, 1989, 1992 and 1994. Confined initially to work with Belfast Community Theatre or with local people at the West Belfast Community Festival, the 1992 programme was organized more formally through the Belfast Institute of Further Education, where Joe Reid was then a lecturer. Advertised as a series of 'Community Drama Workshops', the sessions took place daily through 9–13 March, and spanned the political and religious divide, from the Falls Road Library to the Loyalist Glenand Workshop, from St Agnes's Catholic Centre to the multi-faith Shalom meeting rooms. The workshops became for us a new way to engage with the contending narratives of the war and its causes.

Two images from the workshops stand out. The first was a Network Image created by the Shalom Interdenominational Christian Peace Group, who represented themselves as intermediaries between the warring factions. In the image these factions were shown being manipulated by both criminal and political interests. In the centre of the tableau, positioned between Republicanism and Loyalism, was a figure with arms outstretched, the crucified Christ. The Troubles, the image said, could be ended through an appeal to a common value system based on a Christian heritage. Earlier that week, at the Whiterock Centre on the Westrock Road we had played 'Rock the Boat' with Belfast Community Theatre. The exercise involves a group of stage players moving in space, 'rocking the boat', while a group of audience players watch. At a given signal the stage players must 'balance the boat' by creating a unified image. The process is repeated until the audience players see an image they can work with. The relative value of each image is determined by the theme the group is investigating. Here it was the war. At one point the group had frozen in another arbitrary image. We saw a man held while two others leant towards him, one with his hand near the man's knee. A few yards away two women held a third woman close. The held woman had her face hidden. The interpretation offered by two group members was this: the man is being knee-capped by the IRA for antisocial behaviour. The woman is his wife. Those holding her are comforting her ('she is not involved') and helping her to accept that while personally traumatic the action is objectively necessary. The sharp contrast between the brutal act and the loving act, connected by the inexorable political logic of Republicanism, and the IRA's de facto status as a community police force, was painful to apprehend and accept. Later, Joe remarked that the work had raised a powerful issue for them all, but that, with due respect to us, they were not about to have that debate while we were present. The demarcation was not personal but political.

1988 'The Rights of Man' and *Ecce Homo*

In the period following *Sign on the Dotted Line* Reid continued to work on material for an epic drama based on the hunger strikes. The group meanwhile turned its attention to an issue, which, on the surface, could not have been more alien to its community's belief system, or more apparently marginal to the overall Nationalist struggle – Gay Liberation. The resulting play, *Ecce Homo*, was to be the group's last, and was never performed. Several of the pieces which we performed on our visits focused on gay issues, and Goodchild's uncompromising political activism around gay and lesbian rights had helped to bring about, in 1987–88, an important development within the Springhill community when, supported by him, several young men had 'come out'. This inevitably fed into the Belfast group's politics, as Reid acknowledged:

> We started to look at issues that people wanted to explore within the group ... and the gay issue came up ... people in the group wanted to highlight the gay issue ... and out of that came *Ecce Homo*. *Ecce Homo* was never produced and never will be. And maybe that doesn't matter.[47]

The text began as a series of improvisations, which were taken and written up by Reid. In the same interview, he traced the elements which had led to the script:

> We are in a heavily politicized situation, and it's about rights. How do we treat people inside this politicized situation? Within this family?

I have a right within the family to ask those questions. So, how can we on the one hand have the Rights of Man, and yet not seriously consider how we demand those rights? And out of that came *Ecce Homo*. It was also an attempt to highlight what I still regard as the oppressive nature, the insensitive nature, of organised religion.[48]

Ecce Homo is both a provocation (to the Roman Catholic Church and the community's conservative members) and a celebration (of sexual diversity). Oppression, the prologue tells its audience, is socially constructed, and it relies upon the assent of the oppressed:

> The theft of the mind
> Is the theft of the spirit
> Those who would oppress you
> Those who would exploit you
> Need your assent.[49]

The play tells the story of Emanuel, a young working-class Catholic who is planning to move into a flat with a young woman, Veronica, and another friend, Simon. Emanuel works on a building site as a labourer. His plans worry his parents. Is Veronica pregnant? Will they be living in sin? As the mother rushes to the priest for advice, and the father reflects that at least his son isn't a 'fruit', Emanuel decides to come out. It is this decision which precipitates the play's actions, as he confronts in turn his mother, his friends, his father, his work mates, and finally, an army patrol which stops him as he is coming out of a gay bar. Only his mother reacts with a confused but unconditional love. For his lover, Simon, the action is not worth the pain. Recognizing that he is confined, geographically, ideologically, militarily, Simon wants to fence off his sexuality: to make it a private space in which he can be free. Emanuel's response to this is as unrealistic as it is dangerous:

SIMON:We live in a straight world. We can't change that.
EMANUEL:Aye, straight and narrow. And maybe we can't change it, but we
        don't have to accept it!

And so the precipitate rush to confront the world begins. The play's last scene takes place on the building site. Emanuel has come out to his work mates, an action triggered by hearing them leer over the photograph of a topless model in a tabloid newspaper. As they abuse him, he grabs the newspaper:

EMANUEL: (*As he speaks he drops crumpled sheets of the newspaper
           to the floor around him*) Man (*reads*) Queer! (*Balls sheet
           and throws it down*) Poof! (*Balls sheet and throws it down*)

Pervert! (*Balls sheet and throws it down*) Faggot! (*Screws up rest of sheets one by one and throws them down, stops, pauses*) Faggot. They call me a faggot. I'd like to explain what a faggot is. In the Middle Ages, when they persecuted and burned witches, the majority of whom were lesbians, they used to collect all the gay men in the village, tie them together, place them at the bottom of the bonfire, and burn them first. That's why they call us faggots. (*Takes a box of matches from his pocket and steps on to the pile of newspaper*) Well, I'm gay. I'm a faggot. (*Holds out matches towards audience*) Who wants to burn me?

The image was taken directly from Theatreworks. It had been created by Goodchild many years earlier, and had been part of our repertoire of sketches. The play also borrows, without acknowledgement, from the writings of Bertolt Brecht, and the speeches of Nelson Mandela. Reid is forthright about his 'quotation' from Theatreworks:

That seemed perfectly logical to me. You don't reinvent the wheel. Here's a man ... here's two men who have been through a particular experience ... have done theatre ... and it works and it has something to say to us. If I like what you say – and that's what I want to say – use it.[50]

Such 'quotations' insist on the existence of a movement, of a community of endeavour, that reaches both back and across history. For Reid, as for Badal Sircar in India, Augusto Boal in Brazil, or Ngugi wa Thiong'o in Kenya, the history of liberation theatre is rendered contemporary through engagement, through its practical use and re-use. In one of the play's most poetic sections the narrator talks of a 'Freedom Line' which weaves through the world, connecting the sites of suffering and liberation, connecting individuals and collectives, groups and societies, and drawing them into a network:

Where the Freedom Line began or will end, no one knows. It was seen the day that a tired black woman refused to give up her seat to a white oppressor ... it was seen and heard on the streets of Derry, Yorkshire and Alabama.

This ideological continuity is to be found in part in the play's constant and striking attacks on the authoritarian Church. One scene shows Emanuel's mother being consoled by a priest, who asks her to pray for God's help in turning her son against his 'evil ways'. Emanuel appears stage centre, and as the action freezes, speaks over the priest's head:

> I saw the crucified Christ three days ago.
> He did not hang by the cross,
> But lay instead on a Belfast street.
> There were no nails in His limbs,
> No crown of thorns, no open wounds.
> The Queer bashers had left nothing
> But a gaping gash upon His head.
> And he did not cry: 'Forgive them lord!'
> But only lay there, gazing at the rain filled sky.

This is not the Gay Christ, but the Inclusive Christ. He is also, and this is telling, an unforgiving Christ. The quotation is deliberately cut off before the biblical coda, 'For they understand not what they do'. Yes, says Reid, they do. The Faggot Sketch deliberately echoes and interrogates this image. For the Christ Risen, in terms of gay liberation, is the activist in the Faggot Sketch. He also offers his body, not as a transcendent sacrifice, but as an act of radical, material transgression. And, in this new context (a working-class Catholic community) the image takes on a fresh and many nuanced potency, conjuring as it must not only with concepts of human rights, and liberation, but with its audience's most profound belief systems. The proffered immolation echoes in an iconography infused with the fires of hell, the *auto da fe* of the Inquisition, and the irrational barbarities of witch burning.

The play was never staged. As I have noted earlier in relation to internal criticism of the IRA, the community operated its own censorship. Jim McGlade wrote a piece entitled *Belfast in Hell* which was a critique of the IRA's treatment of informers. It was never performed. Internal censorship by the community existed in a symbiotic tension with the censorship of the state apparatus. This was not a matter of proscription in any settled way, but of constant internal negotiation, and was related to the prosecution of the military struggle. While Reid and the group were committed to a liberation strategy, and wanted to move the analysis beyond a pan-Nationalist agenda, it was work effected from the ground of a critical but unconditional solidarity. Reid:

> This community is not perfect, but I want to be part of the solution to its problems. I'm not going to be, or lend, ammunition to any outside bourgeois, imperialist forces … I'm using clichés I know … but you know what I'm saying … to help those people hammer us. We'd had enough of being hammered. The boot was on our neck. And you had to get people standing up first and starting to push that boot off. And maybe *Ecce Homo* didn't have the same priority. And I hold my hands up, mea culpa. But I reckon it was probably one of the best things we've ever put together.[51]

Figure 7. Joe Reid in Father Des
Wilson' *The Soldier's Synge*, Belfast
People's Theatre, Conway Mill, Belfast,
1999.

Criticism of Nationalists for not foregrounding gay issues during an irredentist war is similar to that aimed at the South African Black Consciousness movement for their perceived failure to take on the class dimensions of apartheid.[52] It is a complex matter: fractions within the community did, like Belfast Community Theatre, push identity agendas, and take risks with them. Dan Baron Cohen of Derry Frontline shared Reid's reading of the dilemma facing the community: 'Inevitably, there are so many contradictions within the most progressive cultures of opposition or resistance, each contradiction reflecting an unevenness of development determined by vulnerability and survival'.[53]

'It was a Moment', 1990 and the end of Belfast Community Theatre

By 1990 the group had ceased to operate in the same regular way. Events on the streets, the development of different imperatives as nationalism moved towards the historic accommodation represented by the Good Friday Agreement of 1998, and the need for members to earn a living – all these impacted on the group's longevity. There was instead a greater focus on workshops within the community. Belfast Community Theatre did not utilize any specific methodology in this work. Reid has never to my knowledge read Boal's *Theatre of the Oppressed*, and would no doubt agree with the member of Derry Frontline who reputedly replied, when asked why he did not use Boal's 'Cop in the Head' techniques, 'What do I need a cop *in* the head for, when I've got one *on* me head?' In reality, the workshops were always a sporadic element in a practice circumscribed not by a lack of will, but by a geo-pathology that rendered work outside the area dangerous. For Reid, McKnight and the others theatre had never, in any case, been a profession: it was an intervention, one action among others in the broader struggle. What such theatre offered, besides political commitment, was what Reid called 'the authenticity of the voice'. Form was derived from the desire to give the suppressed Nationalist experience shape, a concrete form that, as in *Sign on the Dotted Line*, could nourish hope and strengthen resistance.

> Within the struggle for socialism, the arts, and theatre in particular are usually relegated to some sort of aesthetic void, removed from the mainstream of political activity. I believe this to be a fundamental mistake. Theatre, like all the arts, must be part of the overall political consciousness building which has to develop side by side with the political struggle.[54]

Rooted in Irish culture, Belfast Community Theatre's range – the use and reworking of Beckett, the performance of texts by Lady Gregory, Yeats and Brecht, the writing of new plays, the 'Living Newspaper' forms, and so on – demonstrated a breadth of dramatic interest which places it outside the British political theatres of the 1960s and 1970s. To find a comparable concentration of elements, of a coherent, geographical, class-based experiment that was, in every sense, catholic, one would have to turn to Littlewood and MacColl's Theatre Workshop, or, more appositely, the Workers' Theatre groups of the 1920s. Belfast Community Theatre belongs to this lineage, a lineage defined by a double project: to educate its community not only through theatre, but also about theatre. They searched theatre history for inspirational examples, finding in Lady Gregory's plays, or the pedagogic theatre models of Bertolt Brecht, forms and contents that could help illuminate and articulate the immediate experience. For Reid and Belfast Community Theatre, theatre was a social practice and an inherently political art form of great power and beauty:

> I could reach into it tomorrow, pick it up again. Hopefully I will do in the near future. It's not the be all and end all. But to me it comes close to being the be all and end all as a means to expression, as a means of empowerment. And there was a philosophy at work there … we met people … yourself, people from England, Scotland from all over the world … so it wasn't a theatre hammered out of insularity. It was a theatre hammered out of an awareness that the plastic bullet that was fired here today could be fired in Sheffield in the morning.

Could be fired in Scotland next year. That the judicial tactics that they used here could be used in Sheffield in the morning ... And so Belfast Community Theatre was a moment ... was an experience. It's still alive because it's alive in everybody who was involved in creating it.[55]

'The University of Freedom'

Theatre in the H-Blocks

> I always keep thinking of James Connolly, and the great calm and
> dignity that he showed right to his very end, his courage and resolve
> ... there have been thousands like him, but Connolly has always been
> the man that I looked up to ... I may die, but the Republic of 1916 will
> never die. Onward to the Republic and the liberation of our people.
>
> (Bobby Sands)[1]

As I have noted, the 1981 hunger strike and the election of Bobby Sands
to the British Parliament marked the beginning of Republicanism's dual
political and military strategy.[2] The other critical, though less visible, impact
of the hunger strikes was manifested within the prisons. The No-Wash
protests and the deaths of the ten men led to a reassessment of political
and social organization within the Republican prisoner community, one
effect of which was to foreground the role of culture in the 'Long War'. As
a consequence, the sixteen years which elapsed between Sands' death and
the second IRA cease-fire in 1997 would see a radical rethinking of the
concept of cultural struggle, including debates about the forms, method
and role of a revolutionary people's theatre. One prison in particular, Long
Kesh, became the *locus* of this paradigmatic shift in Republican attitudes
to cultural action. Situated outside Lisburn in County Antrim, Long Kesh
prison was rebuilt and re-branded in 1976 as HM Maze Prison, though both
Republicans and Loyalists continued to call the prison by its original name.
The new prison had a unique cellular layout which earned it the alternative
sobriquet of the 'H-Blocks'. It was as the H-Blocks that it would, through
the agency of the hunger strikes, become a global symbol of neo-colonial
oppression and revolutionary resistance. To those who viewed the IRA as
freedom fighters, the H-Blocks were Ireland's Robben Island, a fact given
eloquent force by Bernadette Devlin McAliskey who, in a series of powerful
speeches throughout the eighties, repeatedly called on the British state to
'give me back my Mandelas'. The H-Blocks' cells became the IRA's school, its
university, and the 'empty space' in which the practice and theorization of an

indigenous cultural movement evolved. An *An Phoblacht/Republican News* leader column in October 2006 remembered Long Kesh as a 'University of Freedom' in which prisoners educated themselves to Ph.D. level, and created the 'Jailtacht' Irish language centre.[3] 'We were not just prisoners', writes former IRA volunteer Dr Laurence McKeown, who survived seventy days on hunger strike, and is now a social researcher, author, playwright and journalist, 'but political activists and theorists whose intellectual influence could expand beyond the confines of the prison camp'.[4] Central to this influence was the revitalization of the Irish language, for it is not too much to say that it was the Republican prisoners of war (POWs) who were primarily responsible for the late twentieth-century renaissance in Irish language in the north. As Kiberd notes, 'the struggle for self definition is conducted within language', and language had always been at the core of conceptions of Irish identity. Young Irelander Thomas Davies, a Protestant, had caught this precisely when he wrote that 'a people without a language is only half a nation'.[5] The English poet Edmund Spenser had encapsulated a principle which would define the colonization process over successive centuries when he asserted in his 1596 *A View of the Present State of Ireland* that, 'The speech being Irish, the heart must needs be Irish'; a view which was to have fatal consequences for native speakers. Spenser thought the extirpation of the Irish language and the terrorization of its people the soundest basis for colonial policy, though he did reserve a grudging professional respect for Gaelic poetry.[6] It was not in the cosmopolitan centres, however, but in the rural hinterlands that the language survived into the twentieth century. As the rural poor were increasingly dispossessed, and pushed actually and metaphorically to the margins of both land and social order, so the Irish language became synonymous with poverty and backwardness, and both with incipient irredentism. When the Northern Ireland government outlawed the Irish language and the flying of the Republican tricolour in 1954, it was enacting into law Spenser's fear of a fit between language and rebellion. Moreover, just as this legislation helped to produce what it sought to repress, so it was that the response of the British state to the No-Wash protest created the conditions for cultural renewal.

Locked in tiny cells, naked, and denied books, TV, radio, writing materials, and social association, Republican POWs were obliged to find ways to develop both themselves and their understanding of their struggle. The Irish language offered obvious tactical advantages, as it rendered prisoners' communications unintelligible to guards, and helped to facilitate the planning of escapes. However, there was also a more fundamental political and cultural impulse at work behind the revival, a process of conscious linguistic decolonization. From their cells POWs improvised a remarkable Irish language education programme taught 'out the doors'. This involved prisoners standing at their grille and shouting out phrases which other 'students' repeated and memorized, and, when feasible, wrote down.

Slowly and incrementally, knowledge of, and facility in, the Irish language spread among men who had, for the most part, been 'failures' at school. This method applied to other areas of knowledge. McKeown:

> The teaching of the Irish language is one example of how the prisoners developed an informal system of education during the years of the Blanket Protest in which the 'pupil' became the 'teacher' once he had arrived at a particular level of competence ... The same applied to other knowledge that people acquired, be it about economics, socialism or history, but it was in the teaching of the Irish language that the principle was most apparent.[7]

From an actual poverty of resources, and in the context of a protest that brought repeated beatings and punishments, the POWs improvised a school whose books were the embodied knowledge each brought to these empty spaces. When Jacky McMullan, who had taken part in the No-Wash protest and survived 49 days on hunger strike, received a copy of Paulo Freire's *Pedagogy of the Oppressed* in early 1982, it spoke directly to his experience:

> The pedagogical theories of Paulo Freire impacted greatly upon me. Freire argues that education in its true sense should be a revolutionary force and through what he calls a process of conscientisation learners are treated as subjects, active agents, and not as objects, passive recipients. They engage in discussion of their lives and community and together examine the forces, economic, political, social and cultural which impact on their lives and through discussion develop strategies to deal with these forces. I felt exhilarated on first reading Freire.[8]

McKeown shared this response. He also recognized that Freire's democratic method would pose a challenge to the hierarchical military organization of the camps. Inspired by the Brazilian's ideas, McMullan, McKeown and like-minded POWs initiated an intensive discussion within the cell blocks. Debating in pairs or small groups to encourage participation, POWs were asked to reflect on 'the Republican structures, what criticism they had of those structures, and how they saw their role within the camp.'[9] From these debates there evolved, incrementally, radically new approaches to life in the H-Blocks. Says McKeown, 'Freire came to act as a guide to the practice, processes and structures through which we organised our lives.' Many of those drawn into the struggle had been labelled failures by the school system, and the debates laid the ground for a 'radical political education programme designed to cater for the individual'. Imbued with the spirit of the Blanket protest it was 'a collective and communal process not an individualistic or competitive one'.[10] Classes (in Irish *rangs*) were organized, for example, in Republican History, Political Theory, Historical Analysis, the Role of the Cadre, and Women's Studies. While there was fierce ideological debate about these matters, McKeown writes that 'the dominant ideology among Republican prisoners in the H-Blocks in the 1980s was that of a revolutionary, left-wing, socialist, Marxist orientation'.[11] Some POWs took Open University degrees in Third World Studies, and produced the 'Freelimo documents', a series of discussion papers on the future of political education in the camps, which they were able to circulate and debate in the guise of 'coursework'. Such developments marked a distinctive break with the conservative leadership of the pre-hunger strike IRA, whose commanders had tried to banish Marxist literature from the Long Kesh cages. Freirean methods opened up the 'culture of silence' which had defined Republican irredentism and the new educational programmes constituted a radical break with convention.

One of the most important outcomes was the establishment of poetry workshops. The workshops were viewed sceptically at first, and then with increasing enthusiasm. Poetry was produced in workshops whose ground rules reflected the new spirit of an open, communal but critical pedagogy. Brian Campbell, the moving spirit behind the workshops, and later a playwright, recalled that 'you had to write, and criticism was expected, and you had to take it'.[12] Gerry Kelly, whose escapes and exploits rendered him a mythical figure in Republicanism, noted that Sands had helped to make poetry acceptable, and not the 'effeminate thing' of traditional IRA culture.[13] There was a sense that an ancient and historical tie between Irish armies and their bards was being recovered in the cell blocks. McKeown felt that writing poetry gave POWs the confidence to articulate emotions, and that this emotional literacy and openness was a critical element of Freirean pedagogy, of the needed integration of 'personal and political consciousness'. The poetry workshops were thus integral to a conception of struggle, to the production of what Fanon had termed a 'literature of combat'. 'Every revolution has its revolutionary culture, including its revolutionary literature. Ours in no exception and it is another step in our political development to become part of that culture. These poems are linked into that process of awareness.'[14]

In 1988 Campbell put together the first edition of *Scairt Amach/Shout Out*, a 'small typewritten A5 booklet of collected works from the poetry workshops'.[15] *Scairt Amach* was the prototype for what was to be an extremely ambitious cultural development – the establishment of a prisoner's magazine with high production values, which could be distributed across the pan-Nationalist community, including the USA. It would embrace political analysis, social commentary, poetry, short stories, satire, cartoons and art works, and would be a celebration of the cultural work of the POWs. The result, *An Glor Gafa/The Captive Voice*, was launched in autumn 1989.

Figure 8. Laurence McKeown next to hunger strike commemorative gable end, Belfast.

The cover image on the first volume is a line drawing which shows a hand holding a pen and haloed by barbed wire. This first edition contained short stories, poems and cartoons as well as essays on cultural imperialism, the struggle for women's rights, and the political implications of the break up of the Soviet Union. Over the following ten years *An Glor Gafa* would be produced three times a year to the same impressive production standards. While every edition contained poetry and short fiction, original art works and cartoons, each also focused on a specific theme, for example ecology, feminism, gay rights, liberation theology, education, and theatre. The influence of Gramsci's concept of hegemony is manifested in the first editorial:

> The state is not sustained by force alone … The media, the education system, the churchmen and politicians all play their part in guarding against the dissemination of revolutionary ideas. Thus, the gaols have been the arena for a different struggle, the struggle through education. Time and a common purpose have enabled us to study the nature of the world in which we live and to educate ourselves to become better able to bring about change in the Ireland of today. We hope our *Captive Voice* will be heard by all those who share our vision of freedom in a socialist republic.[16]

Republican irredentism was carried out not by mercenaries, but by volunteers. The People's Army represented a cross section of the Republican community, and the overall effect of counter-insurgency tactics was to sweep into the gaols, interrogation centres and torture rooms of the north a radicalized generation of intellectuals, poets, writers, musicians, artists and social commentators. *An Glor Gafa* was one expression of this reality. The other came through theatre.

The Pageant Dramas

On 24 January 1972, six days before Bloody Sunday, Father Edward Daly, curate of St John's parish in Derry's Bogside, received a letter from the Ministry of Home Affairs in response to his request to mount a concert party at Long Kesh prison. In part the letter read: 'You may be aware that a number of concerts were staged at Long Kesh at the end of last year. However, it was never intended that this arrangement would extend beyond the Christmas season and I regret that it is not now possible to allow "live" shows to be staged at the Internment Centre.' Daly notes that, although disappointed, he was 'not surprised'.[17] The concert parties were simply a continuation on the battlefield of a cleric-led amateur dramatic patrimony that had defined pre-Arts Council Irish theatre. However, while the state managed to keep the curate out, concert parties and their equivalent continued to take place within the jails and remand centres. IRA POW Paddy Devenny has talked about the 'skits' which were a traditional part of prison culture, written by POWs and which were 'invariably slapstick, comedy sketches' that alleviated the 'bleakness of life on remand'.[18] Sketches, songs and parodies were also used to mark and celebrate rites of passage: entry into prison, marriage, release, birthdays, and the like. Alongside these lighter dramatic forms were the annual acts of commemoration which defined Republican culture, and which reflected the continued dominance of the hierarchical militaristic model of organization of the pre-hunger strike IRA. Eoghan MacCormaic's list of such commemorations reflects this focus: they included, he writes, 'Easter Commemoration, Military Drill, Roll of Honour, Proclamation', and so on.[19]

MacCormaic, a POW, playwright, cultural theorist and now academic, was a prominent critic of the failure of these enactments to recognize the changing nature of contemporary Republican experience. There was a need, he writes, to 'deritualise Easter', and to create new forms which could engage prisoners and which would both 'capture their imagination (i.e. entertain) and make a statement (educate)'.[20] MacCormaic felt that the basis for such a performance was already available within the oral traditions of the Irish 'seanachai' or story-tellers. The outcome was the development of an open, communal and epic model of theatre which, drawing consciously or otherwise on medieval models of *meitheal* drama, turned the Easter commemoration into a 'Pageant of Irish history'. The first of these pageants was produced in 1984, with original pageant scripts being circulated within the blocks over the following years, sometimes being recreated two or three years later by a different group in communal areas. The creative energies generated by the pageants found expression over time in more ambitious dramas on social or historical subjects. MacCormaic again: 'We had plays on Daniel O'Connell, on Strip Searching, on the relevance of Connolly and Pearse 70 years on, or mixed marriages, and even a "radio debate" between a number of patriots and radicals from the past 200 years.'[21] Echoing Brecht, MacCormaic stresses that the role of the H-Block theatre was to educate through entertainment. The dramas were structured as 'open' scripts, subject to modification through performance and debate. A short piece, for example on the 'Show Trials' or 'the Paid Perjurer System', would be prepared by a company from one wing. During rehearsals topical material relevant to the audience in another wing community would be incorporated into the performance. Once the drama had been performed, the audience was encouraged to debate the issues raised, and, critically, invited to propose amendments to the script. As the plays were passed around from wing to wing, they were consequently amended and developed in response to their audience's view of the issues.

The pageant dramas would seem to have served five interlinked functions: they were a critical element in the political education system being developed by Republican POWs, and prepared the intellectual and ideological ground for the reception of Freirean pedagogics; they provided a means to construct a coherent cultural patrimony through the pageants and related dramas; they provided a safe space for the mediation of contentious issues around IRA organization and military and political strategy; they offered a celebratory entertainment to mark rites of passage through the prison system; and, finally, through the circulation of scripts between wings they reinforced a collectivist culture. The commemorations had the advantage of requiring the maintenance of a repertoire of pageant material, and of treatments of socio-historical issues. Some of the scripts were smuggled out of the prison, or taken out by released prisoners, and were performed by community theatre groups in Belfast. The Belfast Community Theatre was one of the groups who would use the prisoners' scripts as the basis for productions outside the prison walls, including a version of MacCormaic's *Night Before Clontarf*.[22] Over the following decade, as *An Glor Gafa* flourished, theatre would become one strand of an expanding cultural front that transcended physical barriers. The history of Republican resistance culture is, in part, the history of the POWs' determination to maintain within the prison walls its political and military organization. However, this was not, as we have seen, a reductive or instrumental urge; on the contrary, culture was seen increasingly as central to the self-conception and values of the Republican movement. The concrete walls, barbed wire and watch towers that separated jail and community were shown to be a porous membrane through which writings and ideas would pass. Nor was this a one-way process, whether through the influx of liberation writings sent into the cells, or though the influence of the teachers and artists who periodically came to the prison to work with the POWs. Republican prison drama would reach its apotheosis through one such encounter, which saw the production in August 1996 of *The Crime of Castlereagh*.

The Crime of Castlereagh: Beginnings

Tom Magill is one of Ireland's foremost community theatre and applied theatre facilitators. Co-director of the Educational Shakespeare Company, which he founded in 1999 with Andrew Stokes, Magill's work with ESC has earned the company an international reputation for its innovative programmes, including *Mickey B* an award-winning version of *Macbeth*, created in 2007 with inmates of the north's Maghaberry prison. The company has also won praise for its work with young people from Loyalist and Republican areas as part of the project 'Exploring Conflict Resolution through the Performing Arts'.

In 1994 Magill was working in Belfast as a freelance director and writer when he received a telephone call from the Arts Council of Northern Ireland. The welfare section of the Northern Ireland Probation Services was looking for new ways to engage inmates in educational and artistic activities within the prisons, and it had been suggested to them that they consider using theatre. Their response had been positive, and the Arts Council had consequently made funding available for twelve drama sessions. There was no detailed brief for the work, and Magill was left to negotiate any process directly with the prison authorities and the prisoners. His first task was to meet with inmates from the Republican IRA and INLA, and the Loyalist UDA, UVF and the LVF, in order to assess their interest.

Magill was an excellent choice for this work, having returned to his native Belfast in 1990, following twenty years in England. This exile was rooted in an upbringing that was a microcosm of the Troubles. Born and raised in the Lower Shankill, the heartland of Loyalism, Magill's family had left for England in September 1969, the month that the first crude 'peace line' was erected to separate the two communities.

> The reason for our hasty exit was only made clear to me many years later, when I found out my mother's family were Catholic, and my grandmother, who was from Dublin, had changed their names to live in Brown Square, lower Shankill, where they first settled when they moved to Belfast.[23]

His grandmother had been a Republican sympathizer, and an uncle had been responsible for maintaining the Republican Milltown cemetery on the Falls Road. Yet Magill had been raised as a Loyalist, and he felt a powerful allegiance to a heritage inimical to his grandmother's tradition. The revelation of a Republican patrimony had left him deeply conflicted. His return to Ireland was a means, he writes, 'to face the problem of cultural identity' posed by his heritage.[24] He brought with him to his country of birth an approach to theatre that had been shaped by two critical encounters.

The first took place in 1987 in the Chapeltown district of Leeds, where he came into contact with the African theatre company Gbakanda (Stubborn Resistance), led by the charismatic Yulisa Amadu Maddy, a playwright, poet, actor and dancer. Born in Sierra Leone in 1936, Maddy was also a resident artist at Leeds University Theatre Workshop, and in 1987 the company mounted a production of Athol Fugard's *The Island* in the Workshop's theatre. Magill had reservations about the production, and he asked to meet Maddy so that he could talk about his response. Maddy listened carefully to him, but said little during their meeting. However, a few days later he made contact with Magill, and invited him to join the company, where he would spend three years as the only non-African performer. When Maddy was challenged about employing a white actor, he would say that Magill was 'black' in spirit, and that this was all that mattered. Magill believes that he was chosen for a far more prosaic reason; namely, to play the role of a white butler in Maddy's play *Big Berrin*. Whatever Maddy's motives were, Magill was offered an invaluable and formative education in the company's aesthetic. It was an ethos defined by what Magill says was an African disregard for the western theatre's tendency to see acting, directing, writing, and dancing and so on, as discrete creative roles or professions. Instead, Maddy believed in 'the breaking down of the barriers between all artistic roles', and the assertion in its place of a holistic conception of 'the performer'.[25] Magill's commitment to a dynamic physical theatre that integrated dance and song, movement and music, would be further deepened by his experience as the assistant director for Michael Bogdanov's production of the Seamus Heaney translation of *Beowulf*, which was staged at Trinity College, Dublin in 1994.

The second decisive influence was the work of the Brazilian theatre director, Augusto Boal. Magill met and trained with Boal in 1989, while studying for an MA in Cultural Studies at Leeds University. Boal's 'poetics of the oppressed' would become a principal methodology, a way for Magill to integrate a story-telling theatre with socio-political goals. What Maddy and Boal shared was a belief in theatre's agency as a tool to counter oppression, and to celebrate and manifest the stories of ordinary people. Magill's work in the H-Blocks would reflect these influences, and the outcome would be a process founded on a unique interplay between Boal's Image Theatre methods on the one hand, and the holistic aesthetics and exuberant physicality of Maddy's narrative dramas on the other.

Approaches

Although the theatre workshops were offered to all groups within the prison, it was the Republican POWs who expressed the strongest interest, and a meeting was arranged between Magill and a group of the IRA POWs. Having been told by the prison staff that H-Block 5 where he would be working was a 'zoo', the home to 'two hundred animals', Magill approached the prison for the first time, he told me, in a state of 'fear and apprehension', and with a profound sense of 'facing my nemesis':

> I remember the first day I arrived at the prison. Razor wire around the steel fences, the wall in front of me grey granite – all I could think of was a border post somewhere in the old GDR or the Soviet Union. I was taken in and photographed, then briefed as to what I had to avoid in conversation – the 'Troubles' and my personal life. Meeting the prisoners for the first time, I was struck by the quality of stillness, silence and control common to all of them. I drew out some of the ideas I have about theatre and was not surprised to hear what they expected: they wanted a community project, contemporary and relevant and popular and about Belfast.[26]

IRA prisoner Dan Kelly recalls that Magill had brought along a copy of Oscar Wilde's *Ballad of Reading Gaol*, which he offered to them as a potential starting point for an exploration of their experiences. The POWs agreed to consider it. In debates over the following week the idea arose of adapting Bobby Sands' epic trilogy comprising the three long poems, *The Crime of Castlereagh*, *Diplock Court*, and *Torture Mill – H-Block*. Sands' work had been inspired by Wilde's poem, and he had sought to reproduce the taut metre of the original in a sequence that took as its subject the Republican prison experience. The debate within the cells as to which source should be used was intense, says Devenny, and 'both suggestions were given a lot of hard thought and consideration'.[27] In the end, and perhaps inevitably, Sands' poems were chosen. The POWs felt that this was literature which spoke for them and of them, and that this proximity would help overcome any technical deficiencies, and would allow them 'to contribute more in terms of ideas, images, emotions'. Sands' poetry was, writes Kelly, 'rich in language and imagery', and work on it would fulfil the twin tasks of cultural work, which were the tasks of 'developing ourselves' and of 'articulating the experience of our community'. At the next rehearsal they put forward their idea. Magill's experience with the Bogdanov adaptation of *Beowulf* was, he says, fresh in his mind, and he was consequently excited by the way that you 'could take a text off the page with an ensemble'; but he was also intensely aware of the challenges the group faced. Bringing the *Castlereagh* trilogy to the stage would mean transposing over 200 verses into stage images, a demanding process of selection, empirical experimentation, and compression. Dan Kelly remembers that 'Tom warned us of the magnitude of the task we were about to embark upon'. Nevertheless, embark upon it they did, and in conditions determined not by choice, but by the exigencies of the battlefield. The resulting production would later be described by IRA POW Paddy O'Dowd as 'the most thought provoking, emotionally charged and energetic play ever performed in the H-Blocks'.[28]

Rehearsals

The workshops would take place each Monday in a sixteen-foot square, grey-painted classroom in the H-Blocks' educational and recreational centre. Sometimes the space had to be shared with other education classes, including a basic French course. Workshops were interrupted by periodic head counts, and prison officers watched all rehearsals through a spy-hole in the classroom door. The theatre group was composed of men who were considered among the most dangerous in the western democracies, and their theatre would be made within a prison whose perimeters were guarded by elite units of the British Army. The first task facing Magill was to create an ensemble which had a shared theatre language and a shared conception of the aesthetic that would be needed to translate Sands' poem to the stage. Drawing on Boal's Image Theatre techniques and Maddy's physical theatre methods, Magill worked with the group to evolve an effective rehearsal method. This task was greatly facilitated by the poem's innate theatricality and exuberance, and its evocative, raw and compelling language. Because the poem defied naturalistic treatment, it became common to talk about the emerging form as both 'minimalist and surreal'. This 'surreal minimalism' was felt to be a new aesthetic, which had been born out of a fruitful clash between performance space and text, between a material poverty of circumstance on the one hand, and a non-naturalistic source on the other.

For the POWs, none of whom had had any drama training, the workshops were a revelation, an introduction to a totally different conception of theatre, and to ideas about 'style, movement and expression'.[29] At the core of Magill's approach was Boal's conception of the interplay between image and reality, or more precisely, between 'the reality of the image and the image of reality'. Judges were not, after all, pigs in a literal sense, nor do our inner demons and anxieties have an external existence as 'real' bats or snakes. However, to embody the poem, the actors would need to concretize these metaphors as a physical score. As Micheal MacGiolla Ghunna noted, demonstrating a clear understanding of Boal's method: 'We created our own world with its own rules and deeper truth rather than conforming to naturalistic conventions ... which image is the true one: the Diplock judge as a distinguished man in a red cloak, or as a pig, snorting contemptuously

Figure 9. Brian Campbell (third left, front row) and Pam Brighton (first right, second row), with members of the DubbelJoint theatre company, Belfast.

at justice?'[30] When a group member dropped out, or was released, his replacement was first initiated into what one company member described later as the 'alien acting style' demanded by the piece.

Asked by the group to define what an 'actor' was, Magill told them that an actor needed three virtues: to be active, to be committed, and to be a volunteer who gave freely to the creative process. This, he told me, caused a great deal of laughter. 'No problem there,' one of them said, 'all of us in here are active and committed Volunteers!'[31] It was their willingness to translate that commitment to the theatre which ensured its success even when the exigencies of life in a high-security prison presented obstacles to the work. Kelly records that there were many times when members could not attend rehearsals because of 'visits, education classes, and the myriad daily activities of the wing'. As the planned twelve-week programme stretched into nine months, greater strains were inevitably placed upon individuals' commitment to the theatre. The rehearsals also created emotional crises with some POWs finding the intensity of engagement with the poem's content too 'emotionally draining' to be sustained. Rehearsals were described as being 'hard and exhausting' and 'intense and tiring', although they often left members feeling, paradoxically, exhilarated.[32] What prevented the process collapsing was that the theatre was viewed as a political task, part of a broader cultural struggle, and it was consequently sustained by the *meitheal* solidarity, and democratic education and communal praxis, which defined the H-Blocks in the period.

Over the weeks a working method emerged. Dan Kelly has written evocatively of a process that appeared to be driven by 'a spontaneous combination of ideas and images', although he had a clear-eyed sense of the reality of theatre making:

> Like all art, it was as much about perspiration as inspiration. The months of routine rehearsals and exploration of the text were a long hard slog, requiring stamina and single-mindedness as well as creativity. Often we were tired ... however, when the mish-mash of disjointed actions and images came together and we found we had a scene completed, we gained a powerful sense of purpose which carried us through to complete the rest of the play.

It was this sense of purpose which allowed them to sustain the work when Magill's first period of employment ended. He would return two months before the first performance on the insistence of the POWs, but for long periods the group assumed total responsibility for the production. It was a period of personal and communal creative learning, says Kelly: 'We were constantly learning new skills and creating new images; we were organizing our own exercises, directing each other's performances.' During the early rehearsals the 'surreal minimalist' style brought with it disabling doubts about the value of what they were producing, and even of their right to be doing it in the first place. There was a feeling that their theatre was elitist, its aesthetic alien to their community, its message mediated by a physical language which their community would not understand. In order to reassure them, Magill arranged for several respected POWs to come and watch the work-in-progress. Did they understand the play? Was it accessible? Did it feel real to them? Their answer to all these questions was affirmative. In Magill's words, 'they got the semiotics right: they got what the work signified'.[33] It was, he told me, a major breakthrough. Later, when the first section was completed, Chrissie Poulter, a drama lecturer at Trinity College, and Imelda Foley, the drama officer for the Arts Council of Northern Ireland were also invited in to the prison to see what by then had developed into a half-hour piece. They were impressed by what they saw, and they encouraged the group to carry on with its work.

The most significant crisis, however, came six weeks before the planned performance and after Magill had returned to the prison. The group arrived at the rehearsal space and told him that they would not be doing the show. When he asked why, he was told that, as none of them had been on hunger strike or lived through the Blanket protest, they had no moral or political right to re-enact those experiences, or to decide how they should be represented. There were POWs in the H-Blocks who had been through these experiences, and it was they who should be doing the drama. It was an extremely difficult moment. In one sense, Magill told me, they were questioning the validity of their own experience as POWs, who had also been through interrogation, the courts and now incarceration. He reassured them that as committed Republicans they had every right to dramatize these critical episodes from a shared history. The issues being raised in that moment about acting and authenticity, and about the politics of representation, are fundamental to our understanding of these theatres, and I return to them in part four's summative analysis. The production survived these challenges, which were dictated not by aesthetics, but by the historical and political context of performance.

On Sunday 6 August 1996 in the canteen of H-Block 5, Long Kesh, *The Crime of Castlereagh* received its first performance. Over the coming months, the play would be performed in all the H-Blocks, and, through an ingenious manipulation of the parole system, at the Féile an Phobail (West Belfast Festival) on 14 September 1996. The prisoners who brought the show to an improvised stage were – Paddy Devenny, Paddy Fox, Eddie Higgins, Steve Jamison, Dan Kelly, Micheal MacGiolla Ghunna, Mairtin Og Meehan, Marty Morris, Jonathan McCann and Frankie Quinn. In a programme produced for the Féile an Phobail each reflected on the devising process and performance experience. It is an invaluable and rare record of theatre made by and for an insurgent army and its community.[34]

The Crime of Castlereagh at Long Kesh

On that August Sunday, then, the eighty POWs of H-Block 5 gathered for one of the more remarkable world premieres of an original drama, and in one of the more unusual theatres. It was, notes Kelly with wry humour, 'a captive audience'. What the group did not know was if it would also be a captivated one. They were, understandably, as nervous as any amateur dramatic group. Marty Morris: 'We took a decision to put the play on in our block, whether it was perfect or not. In the end there was a bit of mayhem with final preparations, nerves jangled as the time approached, props and staging were checked, double checked and triple checked.'[35]

Although no video recording exists of the first performance, a film of the West Belfast Festival production was made. I have seen selected footage from this video, and there are also photographs available which were taken by the Republican press, and also, for reasons I return to, by the ultra-conservative Unionist *Newsletter*. These fragments, taken together with Sands' poem, and the comments of audience and cast members, provide a kind of performance *bricolage*, from which it is possible, necessary I feel, to attempt to recreate something of the ethos of the performance, and of its place within Republican culture. It was a *meitheal* theatre, created on the battlefield, its conditions of production defined by the war. It belongs in the history of political prison theatres, the improvised theatres of insurgents, irredentists and 'terrorists'. This history includes, most famously, a performance on Robben Island, when Nelson Mandela and other ANC POWs produced a version of Sophocles's *Antigone*, a production which included Mandela as Creon. Athol Fugard, John Kani and Winston Ntshona would later recreate the production in their play *The Island*.[36] What the Republican prisoners did, says Dan Kelly, and these actions were prefigured in the South African context, was to create from the given conditions the resources and space of a theatre: 'A small number of props and costumes had to be made from the limited materials we had on the wing – scythe from a brush pole, a wig from a mop head, a judge's cloak from a red mattress cover, a mask from a football cut in half and painted.'

For Paddy Devenny the restrictions had a beneficial effect: 'the minimalist approach in relation to scenery appealed to me because there was more imagination and less actual prop-making required'.[37] A stairway, used as an image of the mechanistic processing of Republicans through what Sands had called a judicial 'breaker's yard', was constructed from upturned prison lockers. Magill also used the staircase as an image of hope and resistance, expressed most strongly when Frankie Quinn, who played POW1, defiantly hauled himself up the makeshift structure step by painful step following a torture session. The 'empty space' also had to be defined:

> A stage had to be designed and layout agreed. The wing canteen had to be transformed into a mini theatre. Everything a drama group outside would take for granted we had to improvise. All this had to be organised while we were in a period of intense rehearsal and jangling nerves.[38]

The sound effects for the play were conjured from a bodhran, a tin whistle, and assorted kitchen utensils and other objects scavenged from within the prison. The challenge was 'to choose the right music and sound effects for the images the lads had created. This took a lot of consideration and trial and error before PD and myself came up with what we thought would be the right sound or song to set the appropriate atmosphere for each image.' These improvisations mirrored the poem's production. What is striking about Sands' work, and his longer poems above all, is that any stylistic unity is achieved at all, or any narrative sustained. Here, after all, were poems written on bits of toilet paper or cigarette paper, inscribed with a biro end, which was wrapped in cling film and secreted, to avoid confiscation, in his anus. The repetitive rhyme was perhaps the key to its thematic unity: its iterative beat has an internal impetus, which impels the poem forward, and gathers up its discursivity and repetitions into a whole. It is poetry which has to be read aloud, a point acknowledged by Brian Campbell, who reviewed the Féile an Phobail production. Admitting that he 'was never a great fan of

Bobby's poetry, maybe because its use of rhyming couplets seemed to give it a forced quality in my eyes', Campbell acknowledges that it is precisely this quality which gave the poetry its dramatic force.[39]

The company had not attempted to render the poem as stage dialogue. Rather the 90-minute drama was an extended mime, a physical score which embodied Sands' verse in physical actions and soundscapes. An important aesthetic choice was to have the narrator offstage, and so invisible to the audience. This alienating effect was intensified in the festival performance by the use of a microphone and sound system. Pam Brighton, director of DubbelJoint, thought that the vocalization by Micheal MacGiolla Ghunna was 'outstanding', but would have liked to have him present on stage.[40] But for Paddy O'Dowd, who watched the first show in the Maze, and who wrote a detailed review for *An Glor Gafa*, the invisibility worked powerfully as a potent and political symbolism: 'the walls themselves seemed to speak the words. And what better narrator of this trilogy than the walls of a H-Block.'[41]

The Sands trilogy comprises three interlinked poems: *The Crime of Castlereagh*, *Diplock Courts* and *The Torture Mill – H-Blocks*. The opening lines proclaim its dominant themes of individual suffering, resistance, and community:

> I scratched my name and not for fame
> Upon the whitened walls;
> 'Bobby Sands was here,' I wrote with fear
> In awful shaky scrawl.
> I wrote it low where eyes don't go
> 'Twas but to testify.
> That I was sane and not to blame
> Should I come here to die.[42]

In the video recording the camera focuses on a bed, which is centre-stage. A lone figure enters, the broken tempo of his movements denoting the effects of the beatings; the iterated image here is of a paradoxical loneliness under surveillance, of an induced paranoia: 'I heard the clink of metal link/The Watcher was abroad/He squeaked and creaked, tip toed and sneaked/On shoes that were not shod.' [107] Left alone, removed from the immediate community, the prisoner is always in limbo, a liminal state of recuperation between the last beating or interrogation and the next. The sounds of metal on metal are set against the prisoner's groans. The experience of interrogation and physical beatings brings disorientation, and a profound mental disequilibrium caused by shock, however anticipated: 'Depression, friend, it did extend/In waves through every cell/Crept up behind and bit the mind/Like shock from bursting shell.' [107] However, the dominant image is not of darkness, but of searing light and exposure:

> White Walls! White walls! Tortured sprawls,
> With ne'er a window space
> And so confined a quaking mind
> Goes mad in such a place.
> The monotony so torturously
> Cuts deep into the mind.
> That men lose hope and just elope
> With charge of any kind. [108]

Two figures enter. They are dressed in black but wear white masks. The masks are elongated, ghoulish. The insistent couplets issue from MacGiolla Ghunna's deep and evocative bass voice, which is amplified, slightly distorted, and driven by the pulse of the bodrhain and a syncopation of pans, whistles and utensils. The figures dance and weave around the tormented prisoner, who crawls, cowers, and seeks escape. They carry white towels which will become instruments of pain, and of false succour. The movements have an intense energy. It is a *Ballet Guignol* of torture and derangement as the prisoner struggles with his inner demons, represented here by the masked ghouls. The movement in and out of images is precise. At one point the ghouls smoothly divest themselves of mask and cloak, and become prison guards, as the imagined pain becomes real, and the imagined oppressors are actualized. The protagonist is pinned to the floor, trodden on, and then, with precision, inverted, his feet looped over a horizontal broom held by two of the guards. He is face upwards. His legs are spread wide, his face, chest and genitals vulnerable to the blows which now rain down:

> Like withered leaf or side of beef
> They hang you by the heels,
> The kidney crunch with heavy punch
> To torture jiggling squeals.
> Bones are bruised 'cause boots are used
> To loosen up your tongue.
> So men admit a little bit
> When nothing they have done. [118]

Another sequence on the video showed the *Diplock Court* sequence. The Volunteer was sentenced on the basis of information supplied by those who have broken under interrogation, or on the evidence of perjurers and Supergrasses. No corroborative evidence was required. The language here has a muscular and compelling, if melodramatic, theatricality:

> A prosecuting hawk stood up
> I sat as sparrow prey,
> His shrivelled beak unleashed a shriek

That pinned me in my stay.
And ne'er I dared to even speak
For this was judgment day.
And one by one they came slithering forth
And one by one to lie,
Those writhing snakes and dirty fakes
Called 'witnesses' and why?
Because they witness what they wish
From closed or opened eye. [130]

The stage actions replicate the poetic imagery. The perversion of centuries
of jurisprudence and rights is rendered as a grotesque mime.

They walked me through the door of doom
Like pig to slaughter pen.
But pigs are treated better
Than prisoners are, my friend.
And I in lonely fetters
Of captured Irishmen. [133]

Paddy O'Dowd's review for *An Glor Gafa* captured graphically the
sequencing of images in the *Diplock Court* section: 'This was unsurpassable:
the re-enactment of torture, the slithering of snakes of witnesses, swooping
prosecution hawk, pig-in-wig judge, the circle of lies – all done effortlessly
and still with the ability to induce an emotional response from the
audience.'[43] The poem is also a justification of IRA armed resistance. To
Sands, the Diplock system, built upon torture until it was banned, and
later on interrogation and other forms of physical and psychological abuse,
created the necessity for physical-force Republicanism. It is not Republicans
who are on trial, but the colonial power:

And men asked why men rise to fight
To violence do resort,
And why the days are filled with death
And struggle's black report.
But see they not, these blinded fools,
Lord Diplock's dirty court. [133]

The defining ethos of the third act, the *Torture Mill*, is of a cycle of
resistance. We see the POWs smearing excreta on the walls of their cells,
being dragged away and beaten while the cells are cleaned, and then being
returned, and beginning again. We see men standing in the filthy cells, and
joined in song, in a transcendent solidarity. The dominant image is of the
'torture machine', which was created using upturned prison lockers in the

original H-Block production. In the Féile an Phobail performance a more complex stage prop was used. In a 'still' from the performance, we see one of the young prisoners suffering a breakdown caused by the pressure of the Blanket protest. He sits, his face contorted, his eyes closed. He leans away from two others who are standing and who lean forward to touch him. One has a hand on the side of the boy's head, the other supports the back of the head with his right hand, while his left holds the young man's hand against his chest. They are draped in blankets: it is an image of tenderness. In the Festival production, a smoke machine combined with orange and green lighting to impart a biblical feel to these sequences, as blanketed figures move in and out of the hazy light. At moments, as the images are held, the figures also appear like exiled Roman senators, possessing a still if deadly dignity. The dominant motif is not of pain, but of calm and stoical resistance. The final image shows three Blanket men standing facing out towards their audience; at their feet a prisoner lies stretched out in a rictus of pain. A judge and a guard crouch menacingly over him.

The acting in the filmed performance has a focus and intensity born of a political and communal ethos. There are none of those languors, the indeterminate moments in amateur theatre when 'I' am not speaking, but am simply waiting/not acting/in the space but not *present*. Its precision and purpose is inseparable from the larger political and military purposes of Republicanism. The encounter between actor and text, and actor and body had entailed risk, an opening up which the POWs found extremely hard (thus the constant reference to 'emotional exhaustion' during rehearsals). The labour on the text had required the prisoners to confront not only their technical limitations, but their deepest and most painful experiences, and had called for an emotional expressiveness which was not common within Republican culture. There is also present the spirit of what Grotowski called the *via negativa*, and which Sands' poetry taken as a whole focuses: why do we choose these actions and with these painful consequences? The answer for Republican activists as for the actors of the Poor Theatre is the same: in the *via negativa* the choice we make is not to not do it.

Reception

The response to the first performance in the prison canteen was, for Magill, 'one of my most profound experiences in theatre … there was silence at the end that seemed to last for an eternity, and then an explosion of appreciation. We knew we had given birth to a significant and historical piece of political theatre.'[44] The POWs agreed, and Paddy O'Dowd summed up their reaction; *The Crime of Castlereagh* was, he said: 'the most thought provoking, emotionally charged and energetic play ever performed in the H-Blocks'.[45] The actors talked of 'a great feeling of pride and achievement', of 'a truly rewarding experience', and of an experience that had been 'very emotional and unlike anything I had done up to then'. What is manifested here, and in all these reflections, is a deep appreciation for the arts of theatre and for the artistry conjured out of a (material) poverty of resources. O'Dowd's observation that there was 'no room for idle props' ('idle' is a telling word), echoes Grotowski's statement that when the actor enters the space of theatre, everything they need is already there.[46] But what for Grotowski was an aesthetic injunction, a deliberate stripping away of what was *available*, here frugality was imposed. Nonetheless, the effect was the same, we can argue, for it was clear that this enforced poverty brought a revelation of the power of the imagination, of the power of *their* imaginations, and a delight, an important emotion in theatre, in its exercise.

Commenting on the inventive use of the prison towels, O'Dowd describes how they became 'a noose, creating a mock gallows from the bedstead, and staging a mock hanging', but were also re-imagined as shackles, batons, a headdress, and, at times, even a towel. If objects can be transformed through a change in function and our imaginative assent, then so too can actors. The necessity for doubling became another source of delight in technique: 'a casual costume change on stage (subtle but effective) transformed the ghouls into two interrogators'.[47] What everyone present in the prison canteen agreed on was that this was the most important and complex piece to come out of the Blocks, and that it had built upon and developed the earlier experiments. For Brian Campbell it was genuinely 'revolutionary' because its aesthetic had brought something 'radically new' into Republican culture.

The production also broke new ground in another way. In the weeks leading up to Christmas, members of the H-Block group applied for individual parole for the holiday period, which was granted. Once outside, the group came together to perform the play to their community. *The Crime of Castlereagh* was performed at St Agnes's Parish Hall on December 27, 28 and 29, 1996. Gerry Adams and the Republican leadership were present at the first night, as well as the recently released Brian Campbell and Laurence McKeown, and 38 members of the hunger strikers' families. Magill again:

> Dan Kelly took Magill to meet Bobby Sands' sister, Marcella, at the end of the production. Kelly asked Marcella, 'Did we do Bobby's poem justice?' To which Marcella replied, 'That play is the only justice our Bobby ever got.'[48]

The production was revived again in June 1996 as part of that year's West Belfast Festival.

A Revolutionary People's Theatre

The success of *The Crime of Castlereagh* was evidence, wrote Brian Campbell, that 'the idea of culture and education being an arena of liberation continues to be taken to new heights in the jails'.[49] In an important article Micheal Mac Giolla Ghunna, who had narrated the drama, contextualized the production in the field of global liberation theatre. While the performance was rooted in the Irish experience, it was not, he argues

> A narrow, localized account of the experiences of a political prisoner. The story could easily be set in any part of the world, for it contains universal themes and experiences of imprisonment – fear, isolation, loss, of family, physical pain as well as principled resistance, comradeship and courage.[50]

Acknowledging that there are other narratives which have yet to be told, including those of the prison officers and state officials, MacGiolla Ghunna sees *Crime* as an important and specific contribution to an 'historical understanding of this phase of the conflict in Ireland, and in particular the experience of imprisonment'. *The Crime of Castlereagh* had been made possible by the decade of cultural work which had preceded it. Freirean pedagogy had been the inspiration for 'the educational and cultural basis of our prison community. Thus the cultural struggle in the H-Blocks has come full circle – the pedagogy of the oppressed has prepared the ground for the theatre of the oppressed.' Addressing himself to the Republican Movement, Mac Giolla Ghunna argues the case for seeing cultural production as 'central to political change' and to the task of 'raising the political awareness of the mass of the population'. The theatre was part of a counter-hegemonic project which necessitated 'the creation of alternative social meanings and values which challenge the dominant ideology of the ruling class'.[51]

In December 1988, in a prescient article published in the internal Sinn Féin discussion document *Iris Bheag*, Eoghan MacCormaic had called for the establishment of a Revolutionary People's Theatre, to be funded by Sinn Féin. The model and material for such theatres existed in the H-Block plays, he argued, to which could be added other pieces on topics such as 'the effect of the war on one Nationalist family, or on wider questions like liberation theology, fascism etc.'[52] The concern of such a theatre, he wrote, would be with the widest possible conception of culture as 'a summary of our way of life'. Theatre as an 'art form and cultural expression' could be promoted directly through the Sinn Féin Cultural Department, which 'should take on the responsibility for establishing one or more groups, recruiting a core of actors and organizing a programme for the coming year'. What MacCormaic envisaged was a pan-Nationalist theatre which would create dialogue between the working class of the Republic and the north. Mirroring the Active Service Units (ASUs) which were the basis of IRA military organization, actors would be cultural cadres, the vanguard of a programme of political-cultural radicalization and renewal:

> The drama group I have in mind need not be very large, no more than three or four regular members all based in one area, but prepared to tour with the drama and capable of acting various parts. (The best will and eagerness to 'act' is not enough, the core group would actually need that bit of ability to put words into life.) This core of actors would recruit others, local Republicans, to fill any additional minor parts while on tour, giving time to put into rehearsals and pass on drama skills in the process, and their expenses for travel, equipment etc could eventually become self-financing from door money in local halls and functions.

The Revolutionary People's Theatre would eschew large venues and the panoply of the mainstream, and would set up in 'the corners of pub or lounge, in a small village or on a street corner if need be, to deliver its message to the public'. The model of theatre proposed in the article can be found replicated in more or less diluted forms within the history of radical theatre within social democracies as well as within anti-colonial and anti-imperial struggles.[53] What is revolutionary in the suggestion, therefore, is not the proposed forms, methods, contents or performance contexts, but that the actors would be combatants in an armed movement seeking to overthrow the existing state. It would be a revolutionary theatre, the article argues, because it would be a theatre made by revolutionaries. In the summation, which locates Irish irredentism in the broader frame of anti-imperial struggles, MacCormaic calls for the 'culturalisation of the struggle' to bring it into line with movements in the South:

> Isn't it about time Republicans began creating a revolutionary literature to replace the apologist shoneen and contra-literature (in book, verse, drama and song) which has been used regularly to attack and belittle our struggle by the establishment 'Arts World'? Surely we can find an Ernesto Cardenal, an Amilcar Cabral, or Steve Biko or a Benjamin Mobise in our ranks to write and reflect, to evoke and depict the social causes we espouse, the struggle we engage in, the contradictions of the state we oppose, and the beauty of the social order we propose.

An Glor Gafa and the H-Block dramas, of which *The Crime of Castlereagh* was the summation, were manifestations of the Movement's response to this challenge.

Conclusion

Tom Magill's achievements, both within the H-Blocks and in the Shankill community, constitute one of the key narratives of this history.[54] His interventions have produced a unique and historically significant body of theatre work. In their reflections in the Féile an Phobail programme notes, Frankie Quinn and other IRA POWs would pay fulsome praise to Magill's theatre skills and to the considerable personal courage he showed in seeing through a project which had immediate and negative consequences for his employment by the Northern Ireland prison authorities. Nor did they underestimate the risk involved in a 'son of the Shankill' involving himself in a play which celebrated so powerfully the experiences and political aims of the IRA and the Republican movement. In an article Magill compared the H-Block production with the Shankill Community Play which he had worked on a few months previously, seeing in both a necessary affirmation of each community's cultural identity.[55] Had he been allowed to work again in the Maze, he would have pushed, he says, for a more self-critical and reflexive analysis of the Republican Movement and their role in the war. Nonetheless, *The Crime of Castlereagh* remains for Magill 'the most effective piece of physical ensemble theatre that I have ever been involved with'.[56]

By July 2000 the Maze was empty of its political prisoners, and in December it closed, the closure another step in the slow finale to one of the twentieth century's longest neo-colonial wars. Ireland's most famous prison would count among its former inmates a number of Doctors of Philosophy, including Dr Patrick Magee, who had tried to kill the entire Conservative cabinet in Brighton in 1984, and who is the author of the definitive work on representations of Republicanism in contemporary fiction.[57] Another alumnus, Dr Laurence McKeown, has written the first auto-ethnographic account of the social construction of Republican prisoners. He and Brian Campbell, the inspiration behind *An Glor Gafa*, would become the Republican playwrights of the Peace Process, where art became the continuation of struggle by other means. 'We are not', wrote Mac Giolla Ghunna, 'shifting our attention from the political struggle to the arts – rather we are making the arts part of that political struggle'.[58]

Derry Frontline and the template for liberation

Introduction

Fr Des Wilson was not the only priest in the north of Ireland who had a keen interest in theatre. Edward Daly, curate of St Johns' in Derry's Bogside was also an enthusiast, although his taste in theatre, and his view of its role, could not have been more different from those of the Ballymurphy activist. In the weeks leading up to what became known as Bloody Sunday, Daly had been spending his spare time directing Frank Carney's melodrama *The Righteous Are Bold* for local amateur theatre group the '71 Players. The group had been rehearsing since mid-January, and, as the day of the January 31 civil rights march approached, Daly noted his apprehension that it might lead to more rioting: 'My main concern was to have a good rehearsal of the play with my cast late on Sunday evening when, hopefully, all would be over.'[1] The rehearsal was never held. Instead, Father Daly would become a central figure in one of the most iconic images of the Troubles, as, holding a white handkerchief aloft as a sign of his peaceful intentions, he led the group carrying the dead body of seventeen-year-old John Jack Duddy from the Rossville Flats. Duddy was one of fourteen people, eight of whom were under the age of twenty, who were shot by British Paratroopers on that day. For many Nationalists Bloody Sunday marked a point of no return in the conflict with the Unionist state. John Hume, later leader of the moderate SDLP, was present at the march, and told RTE Television in an interview, 'Down there [the Bogside] people now feel it is a united Ireland or nothing'. An editorial in the Dublin *Irish Press* agreed, warning that: 'If there was an able bodied man within the Derry area who was not in the IRA before yesterday's butchery, there will be none tonight.'[2] Faced with the killing of fourteen of his parishioners by the British army, and the consequent intensification of the insurgency, Edward Daly also made a judgment on the morality of armed resistance, but his was a very different response from Des Wilson's. Speaking as a witness to the killings, he concluded

There may be some circumstances where and when armed conflict is necessary and constitutes the only possible way forward. In such situations, it may be morally justified. It is my conviction that such circumstances did not exist in our situation.[3]

While he would intervene to save the lives of the 1981 hunger strikers, Daly's view on the immorality of the IRA insurgency did not waver. In August 1986 he joined with Cahal Daly, Roman Catholic Primate of Ireland, in demanding that Republicans renounce Sinn Féin and the IRA, or leave the Catholic Church. Sinn Féin's Martin McGuinness responded by enquiring if the Roman Catholic Church only accepted SDLP members, and demanded that Daly pronounce also on the morality of Partition and state terror. Daly did not respond. Instead the moderate and anti-Republican Nationalist press defended his position, with a leader column in the *Irish News* describing Sinn Féin's stance, somewhat histrionically perhaps, as 'a blasphemous challenge to Christ Himself'.[4] But it was not as blasphemous, presumably, as the actions of Fr Patrick Ryan, a former quarter-master of the IRA, who was arrested in Brussels in the same month on suspicion of gun-running.

Daly's condemnation would be dramatized in the play *Inside Out*, the first production by Derry Frontline, which opened in July 1988 at the Pilot's Row Community Centre in the Bogside, Derry. In the play's prologue, a local priest reads out a pastoral letter from the diocesan bishop. The staccato-like verse serves to emphasize the sermon's simplistic theological binaries:

> We know it is a sin
> To join organizations committed to violence
> Or to remain in them
> We sympathize with the police forces ...
> We call on our people
> To co-operate with the police ...
> It is a choice between good and evil
> Our task as Catholics
> Is to join the forces of law and order
> In the prevention
> Of terror and murder.[5]

Like Fr Wilson, Derry Frontline would also engage with the twin oppressions of state occupation and the institutional Catholic Church, but they would do so through a form of engagement which could not have been more different in its philosophy, modes of production, performance forms and contexts from the 'gentle fury' of the priest's satirical revues. One critical difference was that Derry Frontline, despite the presence of Republican activists and artists in its membership, had its roots outside the Bogside and Creggan estates; indeed outside the island of Ireland itself.

Biography of a Method

Derry Frontline's founding member, writer, director and theorist, Dan Baron Cohen, hailed from the leafier environs of London's Hampstead, and came to cultural activism via Oxford University, where he studied English Literature, and Manchester University's Division of Continuing Education, where he was a tutor. Derry Frontline was part of a personal journey which antedated it, and which continues to the present, defined by the use of 'cultural and educational work' in the development of 'a community based anti-imperialist culture of collective action'.[6] This approach, he writes, evolved

> Through an adaptation of Paulo Freire's pedagogy of the oppressed literacy methods and Augusto Boal's theatre of the oppressed techniques developed within and beyond Brazil; the linkage between culture, education and community participation embodied in the Kamiirithu anti-imperialist rural theatre project coordinated by Ngugi Wa Thiong'o in Kenya (1976–77); and the narrative techniques and rehearsal methods of the rational theatre developed by socialist English playwright Edward Bond.[7]

The practical laboratory for these adaptations was the work of two companies – Quantum Theatre Company Manchester (1984–86) and Frontline: Culture and Education (1986–90).

Founded in 1984, the Quantum Players evolved from an adult education class being led by Baron Cohen at Manchester University's Division of Continuing Education. The company's first production, in March 1985, was Edward Bond's *The Woman*, to be followed in June by the same author's *Human Cannon*. Both productions were performed at local community centres, and at benefits for the local miners' strike fund. In 1986 the company metamorphosed into Manchester Frontline: Culture and Education, hereafter known as Frontline. One of those to stay with the new company was Derry sculptor Locky Morris, who was studying at Manchester University. Other members included Donna Sullivan and Jan Robinson, who, together with musicians Derek Suffling and Harold Hammond, formed the core of Frontline until 1990, when they were joined by Jim Keys and Carol Deehan from Derry.

The new company focused its work in Manchester and Salford's inner-city working-class communities, where the cumulative effect of rising unemployment manifested itself in intra-communal aggression, racist violence, drug abuse, ill health, crime and social alienation. Frontline's aim was to use theatre as a vehicle of social and political change through a comprehensive programme of radical education and cultural training with young people, particularly the young unemployed. The company's founding charter declared that it would offer those it worked with 'education and the cultivation of cultural skills' through cultural innovation in the fields of 'new drama, new music, videos and exhibitions'. The cultural work, it continued, would address 'the critical points of conflict and need in our society', and would support struggles for self-determination, in particular in Ireland, where the solution to the war lay in the 'political, military and economic' disengagement of the British state.[8] Frontline's first major project was *Struggle for Freedom*, based on the life of black boxer and Communist Len Johnson.

Struggle for Freedom

On Tuesday 30 June 1987 *The Guardian* newspaper ran a feature in its Education supplement entitled 'In the Frontline'. Written by Maureen O'Connor, it was the earliest national response to the company's work, and focused on *Struggle for Freedom*, the first project to manifest Frontline's cultural programme. Her opening paragraph graphically describes the context:

> Take a hundred teenagers from three inner-city schools in Manchester: two groups, of mainly Asian and Afro Caribbean origin, come from traditionally antagonistic boys' schools, the rest from a mixed Catholic comprehensive where 80 percent of the pupils are of Irish background. Add the heightened tension which followed the murder of an Asian boy at one of the schools last year ... plus an inquiry into race relations in the area, and it would be not unduly pessimistic to predict some sort of trouble.

Instead, what emerged, O'Connor writes, was an 'impressive production', whose themes of 'discrimination, cultural conflict and the role and rights of women' resonated in 1980s inner-city Manchester.[9] Epic in structure and scope, and utilizing Living Newspaper techniques, *Struggle for Freedom* used Johnson's life as a point of entry into the great themes of twentieth-century political history. Born in 1902 to an African father and Irish mother, Len Johnson grew up in inner-city Manchester. In 1926, and against bitter local opposition, he married nineteen-year-old Annie Forshaw, herself the daughter of Irish immigrants. Johnson earned his living through the fairground booths which toured the region, and was recognized as 'the greatest middleweight boxer of his generation'.[10] When eyesight damage forced him to retire from the ring, he became a political activist, joining the communist party in 1944. In 1946 he was instrumental in the formation of the Pan African Congress

(PAC) in Manchester, and later the New International Society, which was based at the New International Club on Ducie Street in Manchester's Moss Side. When Paul Robeson came to Manchester in 1949 to sing at a protest against the racist trials of young blacks such as Alfred Beard in Alabama, USA, the PAC members refused to be part of a mixed-race audience. Robeson solved the dilemma by singing in the street. Interleaved with this narrative, *Struggle for Freedom* is Annie's struggles against the opposition of her own Irish community as she organizes local campaigns around housing conditions and poverty. The Great Strike of 1926, the Spanish Civil War, the rise of Mosley's Blackshirts, the Second World War and the new anti-colonial struggles in Algeria and Africa are brought into dramatic focus through the couple's joint and separate struggles.

In *Struggle* Frontline achieved the first full-scale manifestation of what was to become a model of cultural activism. The mix of local history, democratic workshops, skills teaching and anti-imperialist practice would become a hallmark, as also would the use of Edward Bond's work and philosophy. The scene 'Learning' from his play *Red, Black and Ignorant* was a key text in the development of the rehearsal strategies for *Struggle for Freedom*, helping, says Baron Cohen, to 'pinpoint the origins of dogma and authoritarian, vindictive and reactionary models of behaviour'.[11] *Struggle for Freedom* was also to provide the company's entrée into Ireland.

The 1987 Irish Tour

According to Derry-born builder Jim Keys, his involvement with Frontline began with a chance remark. His friend, the sculptor Locky Morris, had returned from Manchester in June 1987. Morris had joined Frontline at its inception, and took part in the early *Struggle for Freedom* workshops. He was returning to his native city to fulfill an arts commission from Derry City Council. While there, he set about organizing an Irish tour for the *Struggle for Freedom* production. When Baron Cohen arrived in Derry to check on the preparations for the tour, Jim Keys was invited to join in the discussions. He declined:

> I said I didn't know anything about politics because I wasn't taught history at school. I remember standing in the hall of the house, they were going into the front room to have the meeting. He asked me 'Have you ever asked yourself why you weren't taught history?' It was like a corridor of doors opened up. After that wee epiphany I joined them in the meeting and by the end of it had decided I would go with Locky and the play on the two week tour. By the end of the tour or maybe even by the end of that first meeting I had decided to finish up my work as a building contractor and go to Manchester to work for Frontline.[12]

Keys would stay with Frontline, playing a pivotal role as an actor, facilitator, designer and production manager in both Manchester and Derry, until the company folded in 1994.

The Irish tour was sponsored by Glór na nGael, the Irish Language Association. In an article in the *Andersontown News* on the first day of the tour, a Glór na nGael spokesperson called for a warm welcome to be extended to the company, noting that 'We must develop links between the Irish in Britain and Irish people here. We share a common concern about the defence of our identity.'[13] Opening in the West Belfast Andersontown Social Club on 3 October and ending on 13 October at Queen's University, the tour also took in shows and workshops in Derry, Dublin, Navan, Cork and Newry. The reception was passionate, with new dates at the Whiterock Centre and Mac Airt Centre in the Short Strand, Belfast quickly added to the original itinerary. Reviewing the production for *An Phoblacht/Republican News*, Jane Plunkett wrote that 'this was not simplistic agit prop where the workers are good and the bosses are bad'. She commended the company for asking its audience to face 'uncomfortable issues', and, in particular, the racism of the Irish community in 1920s Britain.[14] When Annie reveals that she has married Len, her father banishes her from the family home, his racism embrocated with the fear of a projected sexual potency: 'They steal our daughters and seduce our wives! Never thought it would happen to my family! Run off with a black man!' 'My daughter is dead!' is his final, cruel statement.[15]

Plunkett felt that the play's greatest strength was that it took on the difficult contradictions that inhabit all revolutionary struggles: 'The aim isn't to send us out into the night feeling right-on-revolutionary pleased with ourselves.' Another laudatory response to the production came in a letter written to the author by Joe Reid. He wrote:

> An English based group, 'Frontline' has just finished a tour of community venues here with their play '*Struggle for Freedom*'. I don't know whether you have heard of them or seen them. The play itself is excellent and deals with the life of the black boxer Len Johnson, his experiences of racism and work for the Communist Party. They performed at the Mill and got a great reception. The form was very similar to the Unity Theatre's Living Newspaper production 'Busmen'. They were really worth seeing, and I was very impressed – it's so refreshing to see material that is directly relevant.[16]

While Republican activists were enthusiastic about the Frontline play, Dan Baron Cohen was critical of Republican and Nationalist cultural activity. In an article about the tour written for the journal *Red Letters*, he later described how the company's workshops had demonstrated to a group of 'shy' Republican activists at Conway Mill the 'importance of producing a forward-looking culture'. For, up until that moment, he writes, Republicans had been exposed 'only to the musical celebration and lament' of Irish song, with the consequence that 'the revolutionary potential of culture remained unrecognized and untapped'.[17] On the contrary, as we have seen, Republicans had already absorbed Freire and Boal into a radical and indigenous political and cultural project, including theatre, both within the H-Blocks and across Springhill and its networks. The Mill Theatre where Frontline held the workshops was the home of the People's Theatre and Belfast Community Theatre, as well as of writers, poets, artists and craftspeople. In August 1987, before the Frontline tour began, the Mill had witnessed the inauguration of the annual West Belfast festival or Féile an Phobail, which continues to showcase the cultural production of the Nationalist people. Baron Cohen's misreading of the situation was the misreading of an outsider who had little first hand knowledge of the complexities of the war. His belief that Republicans lacked a sophisticated understanding of liberation theory and culture, and that it was this understanding which he could offer to their struggle, would not be modified by his experience in Derry in the following four years. This is not to take away from the tour's success, which laid the ground for the establishment of Derry Frontline and an Irish base.

On Methods

In his introduction to the company's collected plays, Baron Cohen writes that Derry Frontline's work was grounded in three interrelated concepts. The first, derived from the work of Augusto Boal, was the idea that 'the stage is a unique, simultaneously empathetic and analytical cultural space', offering the possibility for communities and societies to 'question and define itself'. Second, that the transformation of individuals, communities and societies which cultural activism proposes, is achieved 'through *dialogue* (with others and within ourselves) centred in our knowledges, our needs, our questions, our critical imagination'. Third, that 'resistance is knowledge' but, and this is the critical axis of Baron Cohen's analysis of Republicanism, that 'the barricades we use to protect ourselves can transform themselves into resistance to liberation, the key focus for cultural action for freedom'.[18] The central task of cultural action in the 'struggle for democracy' is the 'decolonization of the mindful body'. He would elaborate on this concept, which was derived from the ideas of the Kenyan writer, academic and liberation theorist Ngugi wa Thiong'o, in a series of articles and chapters in the following decade.[19] These three concepts would be elaborated in a creative programme consisting of four interrelated phases:

- Story-telling: in which the experiences of participants was shared, and the generative themes for the project were identified, and democratic and consensual working methods agreed.

- Experimentation and critical questioning: here 'key dilemmas' were identified from the story telling sessions, and then placed within 'limit situations'. This is Freire's term for those situations in which the contradictions and tensions within a given socio-political reality are most symptomatically expressed. The insurgency provided illimitable 'limit situations'.
- Narrative construction: this phase involved the creation of a 'collective narrative' based on exploratory improvisations. At this stage the project's aims might be modified and the balance of the 'key dilemmas' identified in phase two altered. The final workshops were taped, and then developed into a final script by Baron Cohen. Later Baron Cohen would publish the scripts under his own name, an action which effectively appropriated the authorship of what were evidently collectively determined texts.
- Production – or the process of realizing the script as performance: this was the most complex phase, embracing as it did casting, rehearsal schedule, production roles, administration, publicity and the achievement of a finished production.

One of the features of Frontline's praxis was the clear articulation of a set of themes and cultural/aesthetic objectives for each production. For example, a key aim of *Inside Out* was 'to demonstrate the potential of cultural action to the Republican Movement specifically through drama, sculpture, poetry and music'. As I have indicated, this was perhaps a presumptuous goal for an outsider to set. Another aim was to 'pass on skills of cultural action to engaged youth, their families and their communities'. One of the play's 'thematic concerns' was teenage sexuality, and a 'woman's right to choose abortion as essential elements of a progressive cultural politics of self-determination'.[20]

Taken together, these four steps constituted the 'collective participatory workshop methods' which defined Derry Frontline and which would be adapted to meet the contingencies of each collaboration. What is striking about the company's dramatic achievement is that plays which are comparatively conservative in their structure, and restrained in their dramatic action and formal techniques, emerged from such a complex and highly structured cultural praxis. In Derry these cultural methods were brought to bear within a working-class Republican community during the last phase of the Troubles, 1988–94. Derry Frontline's work is defined by three plays, *Inside Out*, *Time Will Tell* and *Threshold*, and by the 20/20 Vision Festival in 1989.

The Early Derry Frontline Productions

Inside Out was premiered at the Corn Beef Community Centre in Derry on 27 July 1988 and subsequently performed at Conway Mill in Belfast on 30 July as part of a short tour of Republican venues in the north. The production grew out of a series of cultural workshops which brought together performers, musicians and the Bogside Sculptors, of whom Locky Morris was a key member. The play's three central themes – struggle, abortion and social change – were reflected in a sculptured triptych, which was placed prominently on the stage area. The sculptors were Anne Deehan and Cathy Friel, who also acted in the play. The production notes summarized the plot as follows:

> The accidental and unwanted pregnancy of a fifteen-year-old girl triggers a series of arguments which question the relation between the State, the Church and the home in present day Derry. Within the context of imprisonment and the past twenty years of conflict, two young people are forced to examine why women are locked inside the home, and how people are trapped within an economic and political stalemate.[21]

The production was intended, says Baron Cohen to 'contribute to the moral and political reflection and debate within the Republican movement', and to help it 'hear its own censored voice and understand the contradictions within its own culture'. One of these 'contradictions' was the Catholic/Republican attitude towards abortion. Abortion is used as a prism to focus the wider oppression of women, their subjugation within the home and church, and to open up for debate 'two complex social and moral questions – the right to choose armed struggle and women's right to choose abortion'.[22] The play was the first to introduce what would become Derry Frontline's defining political and ideological concern, namely that the war was being prosecuted by militants whose radical challenge to the colonial power was contradicted by a reflexive conservatism when it came to the historical 'colonization' of women, gays, lesbians and all minorities by the repressive theologies of a corrupt and misogynistic Church. To interrogate the family, the play argues, is to be led ineluctably to a confrontation with a belief system in which the twin oppression of women, both by class and gender, remains unexamined. The challenge to the Republican community, argued Derry Frontline, was to move beyond resistance to a liberation culture in which the total way of life of the people is opened up for examination; in which national liberation facilitates rather than represses liberations of gender, sexuality, race and disability. Liberation was not a goal, but a process, a praxis, a method, a way of life. What kind of society, the play asks, is being defended? The question is a powerful one, and was being addressed elsewhere within the

Republican Movement, including in the pages of *Iris Bheag* and *An Glor Gafa* as well as in the plays of the People's Theatre and Belfast Community Theatre. Important as it was, Derry Frontline's intervention was only the latest in a series of important cultural interventions. In the next two productions these themes would be elaborated in different ways.

Time Will Tell

In January 1989, Derry Frontline members Jim Keys and Mary Gallagher travelled to Manchester to train with the English company, and to take part in a programme of exploratory workshops. One of the aims of the programme was to 'enable the Derry activists to return to develop the cultural movement of resistance and self-determination in Ireland'.[23] The rehearsal process would see the addition of a form of collective lyric writing to the arsenal of cultural methods. Besides Baron Cohen, the joint company also included Susan Strongitharm, Carol Deehan, Locky Morris, Jan Robinson and musicians Harold Hammond and Derek Suffling. The resulting show, *Time Will Tell*, was devised using the story-telling methods outlined earlier, taking the histories of participants as the basis of its content. The company's gloss on the play in its annual report for 1990 is worth quoting at some length, as it expresses clearly the complicating forces at work in the drama:

> A father burns his daughter's clothes and then sacks and evicts his son from the family home. With their two teenage children out of the home, this Anglo-Irish family are forced to examine both their own relationship and the cause of their father's violence ... there is an undisclosed past of unresolved pain and conflict within the father's past which is responsible for his volcanic temper [...] When his son returns home from a tour of duty as a soldier in Derry, and his daughter declares her own lesbian identity, the father is forced to confront his own past [...] As a Protestant who has fled the Troubles at their outset, he learns how those who do not learn from the past are bound to repeat it, repeat crimes against themselves and their own without understanding how they came to commit them.[24]

Time Will Tell received its first performance in Manchester on 13 March, before a tour of northern venues which would include Sheffield on 5 May. It would later be revived as Derry Frontline's contribution to the 20/20 Vision Festival. The idea for a Sheffield performance came from a meeting John Goodchild and I had held with Baron Cohen and Jim Keys in their Manchester base in November 1988, to debate our different approaches to cultural activism. The visit by the company to South Yorkshire on 5 May was sponsored by the Sheffield Troops Out Movement and the Anti-

Racist Alliance. The venue was the Sheffield and District Afro-Caribbean Community Association (SADACCA). Its large hall had staged productions by, among others, CAST, Red Ladder Theatre, Banner Theatre, and the Women's Theatre. Belfast Community Theatre had performed there in 1987, as would Theatreworks, with a version of Des Wilson's *Focailin* in 1990. The company included, besides Jim Keys, Susan Strongitharm, Katrina McHugh, Frances Simpson, Derek Suffling, Carol Deehan, Harold Hammond, Martin Hyams, Tony Ricard, Jan Robinson and Mark Shotter. Baron Cohen was not with the troupe, but had returned to Derry, leaving Jim Keys to manage the tour.

Performance

SADACCA's main hall was an important theatre space for radical theatre, but it was never an ideal one. It is a long narrow room. The stage, a small arrangement of rostra framed by two pillars, is on the left as you enter, and situated midway against one of the long walls. The wall opposite is made up of windows looking out over a busy thoroughfare. The door to the bar is directly across the room from the entrance. It is a meeting room and a transit room, and performing there meant accepting interruptions and a certain level of background noise. Seating in 1989 comprised loose plastic bucket chairs which were arranged according to choice in front of the stage area. There were some forty people present for the Frontline show on that May evening, most of them active in different ways in campaigns around the Irish war, or anti-racist work. The play was staged on the little rostra, with a space, stage left, where the band was placed. *Time Will Tell* is subtitled 'scenes and songs of resistance and hope', and the play's six scenes each closed with a song, with actors, where necessary, joining the musicians. This was a touring production, and the lighting was correspondingly minimal, enough to mark the scenes and the transition points within them. The set was likewise sparse and indicative.

As the play opens the wife, Susan Knott, is standing in the garden next to an open fire. The fire has been set by her husband, Jim Knott, who is burning his daughter Katrina's clothes. Katrina enters. We learn, as they talk, that Susan has been beaten again by her husband and that the burning of the clothes is an act of calculated cruelty, the symbolic immolation of a daughter whose self-image challenges him, though he cannot say why. Katrina decides to leave home, and goes to collect what remains of her possessions. Left momentarily alone, Susan's face is contorted by a silent scream. The goodbyes with her daughter are strangely muted, abrupt. The lights fade. The singers sing a song about the exploitation of a worker: 'bench and machine well tied/you netted for him for fifty years'.[25] When the lights rise again they show a living room: there is an old armchair where Susan sits, a rug, a table and a simple chair. Jim is at the table.

He is a builder, and is busy pricing up the next job. It becomes clear as he talks to his wife that they are in financial straits. His calculation is a precise one; he must sell himself cheap enough to get work, but not so cheaply that there is no profit:' I could push the estimate to three eight but it's taking a risk. We'll pay the car. The gas. Save five on the food. You can kiss the coat goodbye.' [94] This is the first mention of a coat, but no context is given. The line hangs in the air as their teenage son Shane enters, tired, dishevelled, and wearing a combat jacket which is spotted with blood. Has he been in a fight? He has no idea, as he has been drinking heavily, and the days are lost. Jim's reaction is delivered without any sense of irony: 'If I find out you were fighting, I'll put you through that wall so fast you won't know what day it is.' [95] As the conversation develops it becomes clear that Shane works for his father, and had left the work-site early the previous Friday, leaving a job unfinished. Jim's pride, as well as his business, is at stake: 'When we say we're going to do a job we get it done. On time! That's our bread and butter!' [97] Shane is paid by his father for his work, and then is supposed to pay rent and board back to his mother, but he has drunk that month's payment. He is in debt to them as a son, as a lodger, and as a worker, or so Jim asserts. The argument escalates. Jim wants all the owed money by the end of the week. Paying up will free Shane, because in Jim's worldview to be free means to pay your way, to be your own master, to earn your bread.

> Jim: When I left Ireland I vowed I'd never again work for another man's food. I'm not paying for mansions and colleges I'll never use. I'm not paying for those snobs to send their sons to schools where they learn to rob us. I'm working for my self to be free of all that. And I'm going to do something that I can take pride in. That's still my dream. That and to make you freer than I ever was ... I admit there's a price to be paid. You may have to leave your own people behind. But freedom costs. [99]

Shane begs for more time to repay the money but his father is implacable. When he tries to leave, Jim attacks him, wrestling him to the ground in order to take away his house keys. Shane is thrown out without clothes or money. The singers sing of the violence done to mother and children: 'When you hold me now do you not feel/The bruises his anger left behind?' [101] Violence defines Jim's relationships. It is the price paid by his wife and children for an historical inarticulacy. Challenged by Susan to say what drives him to lash out at his family he replies 'I don't know how to'. [113]

Indeed, it is the play's central point that Jim, like his children, had also run away. Born and raised a Protestant in Derry's Fountain area, he had fled from his native land in 1969, just as the Troubles ignited. He had run, but we do not know yet, in this moment as he seeks to reassure Susan, why he ran. Later, ineptly, he will offer Susan flowers for their anniversary and bring her a present. But when he finds out that Shane has returned, and broken into the house to collect his clothes, he decides to have his son arrested. The law is the law, he tells his wife, and another lesson must be learnt. He tries to coax Susan to come out with him. He has bought her an expensive fur coat. He is happier now that his children have gone; an economic and emotional burden has been lifted. 'We can live again' he tells her. [109] He is jocular and flirtatious in a suit and dark glasses. He offers her a new coat: 'Put it on before I kiss you. You don't have to wear it if you don't like it. Just put it on.' [111] Susan tries the coat on, and pretends to model it, but she is ill at ease. They are on a different trajectory. He wants her to come out but she cannot. She needs to know why he has driven their children away.

> Susan: You drove them away. I spent ten years holding on. In two nights you tore it all down. Look around you. What's here for me now? An empty kitchen. A ghost house. Your life's at that table. I feel dead. Empty. Used. [113]

She goes to the kitchen and returns with a bread knife. The scene is the play's thematic core and implicit in her actions are the history which drove her husband from Ireland and the unresolved emotional traumas which have damaged (or so the play argues) an essentially decent man. Susan is centre stage here. She faces backstage towards Jim and we hear, but cannot see clearly, as she stabs at the coat. What we do see, our gaze focused on him, is Jim's reactions as she iterates the litany of abuse:

> Susan: You made my daughter feel raped! (*Slit*) You made my son beg! (*Slit*) ... And you never listened (*Slit*) I can't plead anymore! (*Slit*) Now I can't bear you! (*Slit*) I can't bear your look (*Slit*) I can't bear you near me (*Slit*) I can't bear you in me! (*Slit*) I can't bear your voice (*Slit*) I loved you, Jim (*Pause. Exhausted*) Now I am numb. [114]

She leaves the room as Jim screams after her: 'Don't go!' [115] The lights fade. The singers sing of hope.

Meanwhile Katrina has found a lover, Sandra, and in the next scene we see them clearing out their books and any possessions that might reveal their relationship. Shane is coming to stay and the truth must be kept hidden. In a deliberate echo of the first scene, Katrina now burns her letters and diary – another loss, another painful divestment suffered to appease an angry man. Sandra challenges her submissiveness. Patriarchy and its violences have marginalized women, she says, pushed them to the edges of life, and for lesbians this invisibility is greater:

Sandra: Do you know how hard it is to find anything from our past? Wherever I turn I find the same lies. We're sick. Unnatural. We should be burned at the stake. Sometimes I find a fragment after months of searching. A letter some woman wrote in a cellar. Or a poem a woman wrote to herself on the back of a receipt in the middle of the night. Sometimes I find our secret locked away between the lines of a book a woman signed as a man. Or in the margin. For years you can search and find nothing ... save the diary Katrina. You don't know how useful your childhood thoughts might be to the future. [122–3]

But Katrina burns her memories, and pleads with her lover: 'Don't tell. Anyone about. This. Sandra! Promise ... I'm. Afraid. Sandra. I'm. Afraid.' [124] The song which follows iterates the play's theme that there are many battlefields, and they all deny safe space: 'Outside of our doors/You go marching/Round the rooms/Inside our homes.' [125] The scene now shifts back to the family home. It is eighteen months since Shane left. He has joined the British army, and now returns home from a tour of duty in Ireland. As mother and son falteringly re-engage we learn that he had been round to Katrina's but had not stayed, had felt uncomfortable. Susan is happier, has worked through the crises, stayed loyal to Jim, whose actions she tries to excuse. Shane is obsessed by his experiences in Ireland: 'Get the anger and frustration out in the open. Nice and legal. Take it out on an eight year old. Release it in a raid.' [130] The killing, the deaths of friends, the obligation to violate homes, all have unnerved him, and so he has decided to leave the army. But when Jim arrives and finds out that his son is a soldier he is pleased. How could he want to leave when he had everything he would need – a secure job, respect, money, a future. He is blindly provocative, and his provocation leads to the play's most theatrically compelling scene:

JIM: If you're not man enough for the job then get transferred!
SHANE: (*Stands suddenly*) Man enough? (*Susan stands as he kicks over the coffee table*) Yes, sergeant! No bomb under here, sergeant!
JIM: What are you doing?
SHANE: Pull up the floorboards? Yes, sergeant! Right away! (*Lifts chair and turns it over*) Just shift this chair! (*Kicks another chair over*) No guns under here sergeant! (*Brushes books off the desk and lifts it*) No bombs here neither!

Jim tries to restrain Shane

JIM: Get off that –
SHANE: Sit down old man! (*Throws Jim onto the couch*) Got something to hide? Want your sons locked away? Your

daughters stripsearched? Any detonators upstairs? Handguns in the oven?

As Shane's violence escalates, Jim makes a final plea:

> JIM: This is our house!
> SHANE: Shut it Fenian scum! You'll get compensation for the door!
> JIM: You have no right!
> SHANE: You invited us in!
> JIM: Tommy bastards!
> SUSAN: Stop! I beg you to stop!
>
> *Silence. All are standing. Furniture lies upturned across the room.* [134–5]

Play and reality, the theatre of war and the theatre about war, the violation of families and family violences, are skilfully conflated as the play pushes the war into the living-room, transforming what is safe and distal into the proximal and disturbing. Shane's is an act of literal and symbolic violation. He really does wreck his parents' room, and we are meant to understand that this intrusion of the war is also a way of returning the war to its source in England, to the colonial centre. The violence, at once real and simulated, brings Jim's *cri du coeur*. The moment of crisis intimated earlier had occurred at Burntollet Bridge, when Loyalists and off-duty B-Specials had attacked a civil rights march on 4 January 1969. This historic moment, which was to help ignite the Troubles, was also a moment of personal choice, and Jim, armed and ready to attack the young students, made his:

> JIM: You can't blame me. You can't hold me responsible. I never took sides! Why do you think I came over here? I saw that war was coming when I left my home! I left my home and my city so that no one could accuse me of those crimes! (*Stands*) Your self pity disgusts me! I was there on Burntollet Bridge when the march for democracy was destroyed! The police just stood by! Some were there in jeans and boots, but I knew who they were! They were leaning against their Union Jacks cheering in time to the lembeg drum, chanting: 'Up to our knees in Fenian blood! Up to our knees in Fenian blood!' You don't know what cruelty means! I saw farmers punching women down the slope to the river, heaving rocks the size of footballs at their faces ... I saw a girl lying face down in the river while men hit her with nailed clubs ... yet I gripped this club and did nothing. You think you've suffered? Pulled the wrong trigger? I never once raised my hand! Still they pointed! You lost your nerve! Sold out your people! With

> every look they branded me a traitor! With the whole world
> sneering I turned my back and walked away! I never took
> sides in my life! [136–7]

Shane leaves. Jim stands shaking and silent. A song now tells of the historical
wrong as the unemployed youths of one nation kill and are killed in turn
by the unemployed youths of another. A final, brief scene brings Katrina
and Susan together. Shane's actions have brought a kind of closure, Susan
tells her daughter, and she and Jim have a future. But what is central to the
scene is the power and warmth of the women's relationship. Susan accepts
her daughter's sexuality. They exit laughing, the one to organize a march
for Irish women prisoners, the other to her husband. They are both strong
women who occupy the hidden battlefields.

The performances were very good, especially Jim Keys as the father and
Susan Strongitharm as the mother. An anonymous reviewer in Manchester's
City Life agreed, writing that the 'performances are excellent, well beyond
the usual amateur fare of "community drama"'. If the production had a
fault, the report went on, it lay in 'the attempt to cover too much ground,
and make too many points in a six scene play'.[26] This was true, but it
seemed to me in that moment an important achievement, not least as a
dramatic intervention which brought the war, figuratively, into the living
rooms of England. That was its theatrical cleverness. The play explores
also the continuities or interplay between the body politic and the political
body. The play's aim, wrote Baron Cohen later, was to help its audiences
'understand the capacity of the oppressed to become the oppressor and the
relationship between patriarchy and colonialism, to construct a politicized,
empathetic bridge between the divided Protestant and Catholic working-
class communities of Manchester and the north of Ireland'.[27] Feminists
might balk at the idea that male violence against women can be explained
by reference to colonialism: violence against women transcends all racial,
cultural and class boundaries, and all histories. Male violence against
women predates western colonialism. The positive ending leaves Shane's
future unresolved, though presumably another woman, or women, may have
to pick up the pieces of that personal/historical crisis, and the accompanying
trauma. The play's subtext, and one of its most important achievements, is
to represent the trauma of war, the terrible damage done to people regardless
of ideology or affiliation. And, of course, the trauma of the hidden war, the
systemic abuse of women and of children, which became the central theme
of their last play, *Threshold*. Domestic violence was not a unique feature of
the Troubles, as researcher Valerie Morgan notes:

> Domestic violence is a major human rights issue and a key element
> in structural violence. During the 1980s there was also increasing
> awareness of the extent and impact of domestic violence. As in a

number of other societies experiencing political violence, including South Africa, the Middle East and parts of Latin America, the response to domestic violence in Northern Ireland was for a long period one of ambivalence or denial. As feminist writers such as Simona Sharoni, writing about women's experiences in the Arab/Israeli situation, have shown, in societies experiencing violent conflict at the community level, the direct relation to domestic violence is often affected by the overall situation ... In addition cultural attitudes sometimes accept and excuse male violence against women, especially by men involved in the paramilitary groups and the security forces, labeling it as a response to stress.[28]

By the late 1980s women's groups in the north had organised networks to support the victims of domestic violence, and were campaigning for increased legal and civic action to eradicate it. The situation was complex, for it was also the case that a significant number of women took up arms, or provided important logistical support to the IRA and INLA, and viewed the prosecution of the war as a greater priority than tackling internal community or gender based violences. Performances of *Time Will Tell* exposed these political contradictions within the community. When the production was revived for the 20/20 vision cultural festival in Derry in August 1989 it received, the company's annual report noted, a 'hugely emotional and analytical response' from the largely Republican and Catholic audience at Pilot's Row Community Centre. However, while the working-class community could relate to the mother and daughter's 'emotional torment' at the hands of a violent man, they were less ready to embrace an analysis of familial and political trauma expressed 'through the eyes and fears of a lesbian'.[29] It was another example to the company of that 'resistance to liberation' which Baron Cohen repeatedly analyzed as a defining feature of Republicanism. Derry Frontline's attempt to counter this projected resistance would reach its apogee in the August 1989 20/20 Vision Festival in Derry.

The 20/20 Vision Festival

1989 was the twentieth anniversary of the arrival of British troops on the streets of the north of Ireland, and was marked by political and cultural events across the Nationalist and Republican community. The 20/20 Vision festival was Derry Frontline's contribution to the commemorations. Six weeks in preparation, the festival included 'plays, concerts, discos, debates and workshops that would tackle health, sectarianism, sexism, censorship, alternative economic and political structures, armed struggle and abortion'.[30] These themes were also addressed in talks and participatory workshops, and included sessions on liberation theology (held, intriguingly, in Bishop Street), culture and liberation, and Irish political prisoner writings.

The plays presented during the festival included a revival of *Time Will Tell* and a Derry Frontline production of *The Visit* by Eoghan MacCormaic, which explored the emotional impact of war and poverty on a working-class community. Dublin based Line Tosaigh contributed a production of Edward Bond's *Black Mass*, the English playwright's take on the Sharpeville Massacre and the historical ubiquity of state terror.[31] Established in 1988 by Michael Rush and Liz Riches, Line Tosaigh had evolved a practice based on Frontline's original template for cultural action. *Black Mass* had been their first production, in November 1988, and they would go on to produce Bond's *Human Cannon* in 1989, as well as a devised piece with unemployed activists at the Larkin Unemployed Centre in Dublin in the same year. The relationship with Frontline would last until 1990. Art exhibitions included works by sculptor Locky Morris, the Bogside Sculptors, and Carol Deehan and Aine Murphy. A Children's Festival ran in parallel to the adult events.

In hindsight the 20/20 Vision Festival can be seen to mark the zenith of Frontline's achievements. It brought together the three branches of the company in a festival of culture which expressed the core conception of a radical people's culture as embracing the totality of its way of life. It also convinced Keys and Baron Cohen that only a permanent cultural centre, properly resourced, could guarantee the longevity and effectiveness of the company's work. In the following year they would expend much intellectual and practical energy to securing the resources, including space, to make this possible. In September Jim Keys, Carol Deehan and Baron Cohen returned to Manchester, and, although letters show that they were conflicted about being away from Ireland, they believed that the time had come to 'concentrate on internal development and lay foundations for the opening of a cultural centre within two years'.[32] The centre would never be achieved and 20/20 Vision remained as a model, a template of an integrated cultural praxis. In April 1990 Baron Cohen and Carol Deehan returned to Ireland in order to 'reopen Derry Frontline', and to initiate the *Threshold* project.

The *Threshold* Project

Originally planned as an eighteen week workshop programme, the *Threshold* programme would last for two years, and would incorporate, besides a full length naturalistic drama, the development of a People's Banner, sculptures, mural art, music workshops, and political and cultural education programmes, including a Women's Living History Circle. Initially conceived as a 'critical celebration' to mark the approaching tenth anniversary of the hunger strikes, the play developed into a more complex exploration of experiences of violation and violence. Colonialism, patriarchy, the cultural conservativism of the Roman Catholic Church and globalization were focused through the single and singular image of a 'freedomstriker' – a young Catholic woman who is raped on the streets of her own community.

In this sense *Threshold* developed and intensified themes present in the earlier plays. Baron Cohen:

> *Threshold* extends the idea of the hunger strike, a long standing method of Republican political protest in Ireland, into that of a 'freedomstrike'. In the play a woman decides not to eat as a protest against what she sees as the refusal by her community to acknowledge the parallels between its silencing of the issues of rape and abortion and the violence and censorship of the state.[33]

The rape is collectivized and historicized and the personal violation presented as the result of an historic collusion. The abused are the victims of the undeclared war, the collateral damage of a militarized and theocratic community:

> MARIE: You raped me Derry. Entered me without my consent. Your
>   darkness hid the rock that knocked me unconscious. Your
>   streets held me down while you tore me open and emptied
>   your lust into my womb. I will not give birth to that. This
>   child will speak for them who walk your streets in fear.
>   This child will cry out against your unborn crimes. Even
>   you planted a seed of pain inside this womb. I'll not carry
>   your suffering into the future. No child of mine will be a
>   monument to revenge. That is my choice. And none of your
>   laws or constitutions or flags of war will change my mind.[34]

Marie's action precipitates intense debate within the Church, the community, and the media. The freedomstrike draws in young Republican activists, including Protestants, who have set up an underground radio through which she communicates with the city's people. Some suspect a hoax, an elaborate ruse by the security services to destabilize the community by generating paranoia. Marie's action elicits a passionate response from women across the region. There are mass rallies. In what seems like a veiled criticism of the 1981 hunger strikers, Marie eventually calls off her strike, refusing martyrdom in favour of political activism:

> MARIE: Imagine if I died. If I wasn't assassinated by the tabloids
>   or smeared by the Church. I'd be turned into a martyr. A
>   portrait to be hung on the wall. They'd turn me into an ideal.
>   An ideal of sacrifice. Another Virgin Mary! The very last
>   thing we need! [293]

Marie's 'freedomstrike' intersects with the return of businessman Sam Doherty to his native Derry. Forced to emigrate, Doherty embodies in his substantial girth some of the most potent myths of the relationships between Irish and American history. Working-class, Catholic, son of Derry, and a successful business man, Doherty, in a deliberately ironic reconfiguration of Irish history, is the impoverished emigrant turned international inward investor. His is the counter-narrative to the gun-running of NORAID, and the romantic tin rattling of the east-coast Bostonian revolutionaries, who funded the IRA's war. Where they brought guns, he will bring dollars. Globalization has reduced conflicts between nations to the status of localized squabbles, and the age of transnational capital has rendered the nation state an anachronism, the deaths in pursuit of Irish unity a tragic irrelevance. At one point he scoops up a young boy, Sean, into his arms and addresses a local journalist:

> SAM: Andrew, this is Derry! Real salt of the earth Derry! This is
>   why I've returned! This wee boy and his mother! These are
>   my people! And these are the people I have fought for all my
>   life! We don't have to apologize anymore! We don't have to
>   beg for work in foreign countries! We don't have to hide who
>   we are or block out the world in some ghetto bar! ... Derry
>   people have no reason to beg, Sean! Not any more! And we
>   will not lower our eyes in shame, Sean! Never again! The
>   future is yours! You are a citizen of the world, Sean! [168]

It is a bravura performance, a piece of improvised but highly effective theatre, the prodigal son as inward investor. Economic regeneration is the new ecumenism. Political and religious differences are to be levelled out by Capital. A few moments later Sean is abducted, and is found in one of the shopping centre's new toilets, unconscious and covered in blood. His cries had not been heard above the noise of the shoppers, and the self-congratulatory media circus which surrounds Doherty. The voices of the powerless, literally, will not be heard. 'It's a miracle he escaped unharmed', a priest later tells Marie.

> MARIE: It happens round here all the time. And you know it. The
>   blood's washed away. The scapegoat's sedated and entered
>   into a file. And you catch up onto your sleep. What you don't
>   notice is the drugs wear off. And the wain out for revenge.
>   Til he knifes his girlfriend or jumps into the Foyle. Then you
>   write a sermon. And the file turns into a crime. [173]

One of the play's arguments is precisely that intra-communal and intra-familial violence was sanctioned by the need to maintain the coherence of resistance. In a further complication we find out that Doherty is Marie's uncle. She sees his dream of economic regeneration as yet another front in the war, and the myth of economic renewal a means to deny 'the slaughter that's meant to stay out of sight'. Later the priest will agree with her, telling a television chat show host: 'Do you know what inward investment really is? Mass rape. The calculated rape of a whole people.' [232] However, although the play projected this analysis, the company still chose to take part in the IMPACT 92 Festival. The acronym stood for International Meeting Place for the Appreciation of Culture and Tradition, and the festival was the cultural wing of Derry's inward investment economic programme. The decision to participate in IMPACT activities was to generate fierce internal debate. By performing at the Playhouse were the company allowing their radicalism to be absorbed and neutralized by the mainstream culture? Was the act of performance in fact an act of ideological submission, or were they, as Baron Cohen argued, refusing to be barricaded into the ghetto, their appearance a means both to foreground working-class Republican experience and to reach other constituencies? Given the company's commitment to class solidarity, the Playhouse seemed to offer a rare space for communication with the Loyalist community. It is clear from Baron Cohen's interview with Lionel Pilkington that the rehearsal process was defined by intense internal debate and disagreement. These were of two kinds, though connected: the first centred on the play's themes, the second on the implication for those themes of performing outside the community. Central to the debate was the play's ambiguous representation of 'martyrdom'. At one point in the play a young man, Eamonn, smashes a photograph of his brother, an IRA volunteer, who had died on active service. Eamonn has taken a position with Doherty's firm in order to secure a career and support his young family, but, in an impassioned speech, he is accused by his mother of soiling his brother's memory: 'I didn't bury a son and the sons of ten mothers before him so you could hand this struggle over on a plate.' Doherty, she says, is a cannibal: 'He consumes peoples and continents. In the name of freedom.' [201] There were, says Baron Cohen 'constant outbreaks of doubt that the smashing of the portrait of the volunteer, or Marie's refusal to be idealized into martyrdom, could be understood as condemnation of the armed struggle'; a condemnation that would be doubly powerful for coming from within the community.[35] Hunger striking was presented as a metaphor for the victim as endurer, for what Terence des Pres calls 'the allusion of grace.'[36] It is this grace which Marie refuses, and which the play confronts.

Impatient to stage a play which had gestated for nearly two years, Derry Frontline embarked on a production process which, Baron Cohen admits, created 'strained or tense relations and occasional flashpoints of anger'. This process included auditions, and an eight week rehearsal period which prevented the development of 'a collective understanding of the whole play'. While the rehearsal process utilized role-exchange and other collective methods to help the cast develop 'objective understanding' of their characters, these exercises were not enough, says Baron Cohen, to correct 'the experience of having been cast or the uneven depth of understanding of the script'.[37] These choices, which defined the *Threshold* production, gave rise to 'avoidable contradictions which seem to recur in community theatre's decision making, organization, and the relationship between its "skilled" and "unskilled" producers'.[38] The play's aesthetic reproduces these contradictions. The dominant impression is of a naturalistic aesthetic, though this is periodically ruptured by monologues or direct addresses to the audience. The precision and detail of stage directions is a notable feature: 'An upholstered Balmoral suite surrounds an oval Queen Anne coffee table which stands on a Chinese rug decorating a polished wooden floor. A well-thumbed catalogue lies open beneath a book of accounts beside a vase of satin flowers on the table.'[39] In total the play utilized seven sets, each as detailed. The aesthetic economy and epic dramaturgy which had characterized the earlier touring shows had been superseded. The *Threshold* set was less a response to the needs of the play, than to the possibilities offered by the Playhouse theatre.

The internal crises which threatened to destabilize the IMPACT intervention were rooted in long-standing tensions spread over the preceding two years, and were analyzed in the company's most striking internal document, produced in 1992, and entitled 'Everything You Always wanted to Know About Derry Frontline (but were afraid to ask)'. Written by Baron Cohen, the document is at once a potted biography of the company, a guide to its membership structure and aims, and a reflection on its internal problems. In a covering letter addressed to members, he offers the following summary of issues:

> At different times, people have asked for information about Derry Frontline, unsure about who are its members, who takes decisions, who has rights or responsibilities in decision making, who receives expenses and why, whether there is a planned training programme for becoming a co-coordinator, and how people can become involved in a full time role.[40]

The 20/20 Vision Festival and *Threshold* project had seen an expansion in both the scope of activity, and in the personnel involved in it. Boundaries between the different initiatives had not been clear, causing confusion about ownership and responsibility, and leaving local group members feeling disempowered by the lack of communication, and lack of debate about the theatre's overall role. An important initiative, the Women's Living History Circle, was twice set up and twice suspended due to 'lack of resources, personnel and inadequate organization'. The same reasons were given for the failure to revive 20/20 Vision and restage *Inside Out*. Arguments over money also played a role. In contexts of mass unemployment and endemic poverty, the economic ecology of a community can be easily upset, and indeed the letter began by hoping that Christmas had not left members 'crippled by debt'. Frontline had a system of full, associate and project membership, with the different forms of membership determining the individual member's ability to influence the company's strategic development. While all members received expenses, Full and Associate members received additional money. The challenge, says Baron Cohen, was how to maintain these differentials without 'threatening the trust between coordinators and the community'. It is clear that that challenge was not met, and that behind Baron Cohen's impressively articulate and seamless liberation rhetoric, lay a severe and practical democratic deficit, a failure of politics. Although the company did not fold until 1994, *Threshold* was the final product of its model of cultural activism. A video of the *Threshold* production was completed in 1993, and a collaboration on a mural project with Bogside children and artists from Managua in Nicaragua. More mural collaborations followed in 1994, this time with Chicano–American community artists, culminating in the mural/sculpture 'Decode' for the Texan–Austin Irish Studies conference 'Remapping the Borders'. April saw the company perform Ariel Dorfman's *Death of a Maiden*. It was be their last production. In May, and partly in response to a lack of funds, the group, says Baron Cohen 'temporarily closed its community drama and Parenting and Young People's workshop'. They remain closed. Once Baron Cohen had left Ireland, Derry Frontline was not revived by local cultural activists.

Conclusions

One of the most significant documents produced by the company, and the one which most powerfully reflected the company's analysis of Republican political culture, was the *20/20 Dialogues*, written by Jim Keys and Dan Baron Cohen in 1994, before the company folded. Based on papers which had been contributed to cultural debates at a 1991 internal Sinn Féin conference at Derry City's Guildhall, the *20/20 Dialogues* operate as a kind of valedictory address to the Republican movement. Conceived as 'an imaginary dialogue between a political activist, a cultural activist and a politically active young working class woman', the 20/20 papers are artfully constructed, including direct citations from earlier documents and writings. Under the general heading of 'The Role of Culture in the Liberation Struggle', the papers are organised around three headings, 'What is Culture?', 'From Survival to Resistance', and 'From Resistance to Liberation'. 'The Role of Young People in the Struggle' is dealt with in a further section. Defining culture as 'our social, political and economic relationship to the world. It is both how we understand who we are, and how we live out that understanding,' the *Dialogues* propose that 'art is one of the most advanced languages which allows us to shape and pass on culture.' Echoing Sean in *Inside Out* with his cry of 'They own our minds!', the Cultural Activist argues that a liberation culture must be a process of critical reflection on reality. Liberation culture is a culture of hope, and this is why the Republican Movement cannot be a liberation movement. Republican culture, according to the *Dialogues*, is 'purely oppositional, contradictory and offers no vision of the future'.[41] It is a movement which represses women, silences the young, and has 'no imagination or belief that we can win'. The price of speaking out is humiliation. The cause, says the Cultural Activist, is that the Movement simply reproduces colonial structures and repressions. Republicanism is a culture of domination. The solution is for it to learn from the liberation movements of Africa and Latin America, whose successes were based upon their understanding of the importance of cultural struggle. 'Self determination', it goes on, must become 'a method' rather than simply an objective. Sinn Féin's failure is the failure to harness the young people of its constituency: instead its political relations are 'directive', based upon 'monologue rather than dialogue, no different to how they may encounter the SDLP'. The Republican struggle, in brief, is one 'whose permitted visible structures and activity appear conservative, remote and steeped in the authoritarianism of our Catholic, military and oppositional culture'. The 'our' is a semantic device, for the analysis is Baron Cohen's. It is a reductive and simplistic analysis by an outsider of a complex and heterodox movement, which contained many powerful liberatory voices, such as those of Reid and Wilson, but it was an analysis which defined the company's political project. What was constructed as the insiders' 'resistance to liberation' was met by an outsider's *insistence on liberation*, which attempted to prescribe rather than co-facilitate collective solutions. While the company's attempts to unsettle the conservatism of Republican orthodoxy is to be applauded, there was an assumption that this was a unique enterprise, rather than one among a range of existing indigenous and progressive forms of political education. Laurence McKeown had organized classes on gender and sexuality in the H-Blocks long before Frontline first disembarked in Belfast in 1987. The concept of 'resistance to liberation' denied core historical realities, such as the role of Ireland in the development of anti-colonial movements during the long twentieth century. It equally elided or avoided critical questions raised by the post-independence realities of, for example, Zimbabwe and Ethiopia, or by the systemic homophobic oppressions in Cuba and Nicaragua. There is no evidence of *sustained* cultural action within any twentieth-century liberation struggle, though we can point to an indigenous and uneven flowering within sections of these movements. In brief, Irish Republicanism was found wanting when measured against achievements for which history offers no compelling evidence.[42]

Derry Frontline's most important achievement was its contribution to exposing to critical debate the hidden and brutal treatment of women under the surface of the war. The company showed courage in confronting the Republican community on issues such as homophobia, domestic violence and the Church's systemic misogyny. The focus on young unemployed people was another defining element of the group's political value, and the early work in Manchester remains an important example of theatre as cultural and political education. What made the work possible and valuable, however, were not methods, which can themselves become a subtle form of coercion, but the presence in the company of people who lived the reality of the war, and who had suffered the effects of the counter-insurgency and its many violations. Jim Keys, Declan Nelis and Mary Gallagher and the other local activists created, by their very presence, a space in Republicanism for what was at times an incisive critique of the political contradictions at the heart of the movement.

On Insiders and Outsiders

One trope of Baron Cohen's writings since 1994 has been that the Derry company were faced by the constant threat of sectarian assassination and state violence.[43] However, in his comprehensive study of the IRA, Maloney notes that a ceasefire had effectively been established in Derry long before 1994.[44] By the late 1980s an experiment had begun in Derry to try and scale down the war. A Peace and Reconciliation Group, which included former paramilitaries from both sides, mediated between the IRA and the British forces. At the centre of it were two Quakers, Diana and John Lampen. The group achieved a significant downgrading of the conflict. It is these facts that make Baron Cohen's claims in several essays that the Frontline company were under constant threat either from Loyalists or from counter insurgency forces, rather mystifying. Maguire notes this claim.[45] However, the idea that the company's vulnerability was a rare case of the repression of a theatre group is not borne out by the facts on the ground, or by comparison with other groups or individuals in this study. Baron Cohen's account, for example, also reported by Pilkington, that the company felt impelled to bury scripts and related documentation for the *Threshold* project in the Irish Republic, has not been corroborated by ex-members of the group's board to whom I have spoken.[46] The war continued, and individual members of the company were vulnerable to state violence, but this was because they were indigenous Irish political activists, not because they had written a play. Or, more precisely, they were political activists who had also written a play. When we place ourselves deliberately in dangerous situations we need to be very precise about our belonging, and the necessities which define our engagement. Ethnographer Alexandra Jaffe has written: 'My outsider status gave me the upper hand in the production of knowledge that was inherently political ... I could pretend to belong and to be involved, but the fact remained that I could leave ... my experience of powerlessness was situational not structural.'[47] This was my experience in Belfast, and it is the experience of many practitioners and academics in war zones. The temptation to project oneself as a cultural or intellectual adventurer must be resisted out of a basic human respect for those who really are in danger, and who really do suffer in wars and civil conflicts.

'Only Catholics Combine'

Loyalism and theatre

Loyalism did not produce autonomous community theatres to compare with those which evolved within the Nationalist and Republican communities. The Protestant tradition has produced accomplished playwrights such as Gary Mitchell, Marie Jones, and Michael Hall, but not a *community* theatre tradition, and certainly not a political community theatre tradition. Academic David Grant:

> Marie Jones sees historical reasons for this reluctance to join with others in a theatre group. Protestants she argues, grow up with the ethos 'The State is Ours'. Any gathering is seen as dangerous to the leaders. So we end up sticking to our own wee square. Only Catholics combine.[1]

Tom Magill believes that this cultural division was exacerbated by discriminatory employment statutes that excluded Catholics from technical and engineering work. Consequently, he says, 'Catholics have been associated with arts and humanities ... the overriding perception is that the arts, and particularly theatre, is a Catholic concern'.[2] Marie Jones agrees, noting that 'It is easier for a Catholic to identify with Sean O'Casey than for a Protestant to identify with Shakespeare. Theatre culture seems more immediate for Catholics.'[3] The Shankill born actor David Calvert, noting the defensiveness of Protestants about their culture, says that community drama is seen in the north as 'the kind of things priests do'.[4] Calvert was embarrassed when his family came to see him perform; an emotion he says was sourced in a 'Puritan suspicion of fun. Theatre is suspect because it is seen to produce nothing.'[5] There is a consensus among those who have made theatre, or who have tried to make theatre in Loyalist communities, that it is difficult to originate and to sustain. However, there were two initiatives within the Loyalist communities which, while they cannot compare in scale or duration to the Republican theatres, deserve attention. The central figure in the first was Michael Hall, and in the second Tom Magill.

Expecting the Future

Michael Hall was born and raised in the heartlands of East Belfast
Loyalism, 'in the shadow of the Harland and Woolf shipyards'.[6] His
working-class household was, he says, uniquely defined by a 'secular
humanism': and while his relatives included members of the Orange Order
and the B-Specials, he had no strong sense of a Protestant identity. His
grandfather was the shipyard poet Robert Atkinson, and he came from
a genealogy which, on his father's side, included Betsy Gray, one of the
leaders of the United Irishmen. A Presbyterian from County Down, Gray
famously led the attack on the English forces at Ballynahinch on 13
June 1798, and was killed in the rout that followed. Sent to traditional
Irish dancing lessons, Hall recalls being asked 'Are you a Protestant or a
Catholic?' Unable to give a definite response he was told, 'Oh, you must be
a Protestant then, for a Catholic would know'. Radicalized by the student
movements of the 1960s, he was one of the founding members of People's
Democracy, and was present at the infamous attack on civil rights marchers
at Burntollet Bridge on 4 January 1969. It was Hall who led the battered
marchers into Derry city centre beneath the flag of the Belfast Anarchist
Group. In common with many young radicals, the eruption of violence
in the north had taken him by surprise: 'our attention had been focused
almost exclusively on events abroad, especially the tragic war in Vietnam
and the worldwide student revolt, which revealed its revolutionary potential
during the May events in France, 1968'.[7] A socialist and internationalist
who felt no affiliation with Loyalism, Hall believed the conflict to be a
war between two versions of authoritarian nationalism, Irish and Ulsterite,
and he rejected both.

In the following decade he qualified as a social worker, and spent seven
years with the NSPCC, where he met Dr Ian Adamson, a community
paediatrician and historian, with whom he worked to develop community-
led support structures for victims of domestic violence and abuse. His
unorthodox methods led him to resign after conflict with NSPCC managers,
but they also led him to a fruitful relation with other community activists
in Belfast, including Des Wilson and Noelle Ryan at Springhill Community
House. These relationships gave the lie to a commonly held belief that the
two communities were incapable of dialogue, or of finding a ground for
common purpose. On the contrary, there were throughout the war many
inter-communal dialogues on a range of issues, including education. It was
while he was facilitating a community discussion on the emotional impact
of the conflict that the inspiration for his first play, *Expecting the Future*,
came. Its source was a comment made by one young woman to another:
'How would you know? It's alright for you to talk; you don't know what
it feels like.' The play would, says Adamson, engage with the silence that
surrounded 'the terrible anguish this violence leaves in its wake'.[8]

Expecting the Future is set in the TV lounge of a maternity hospital and focuses on the relationships between five women as they wait to give birth. Their talk is witty, their subjects husbands, lovers, their children, birth, and hope. Betty, the eldest, and a wit, dreams of escape from Belfast:

> BETTY: I'd like to make a clean break. You know what I mean? Just me and Danny and the kids. To be honest he's always at odds with the in-laws anyway, and even his own lot. No, I'd love to escape Belfast. Them flats is no place to rear kids.[9]

Sally is having her first child, but there are complications. She is in a mixed marriage, whose specific difficulties become a symbol for the larger crisis: how do you even agree on the child's name? When her child is stillborn, the symbolism is painfully underscored. Lilly is a poet, who performs an eight stanza celebration of doctors, drink and end of pier antics at the hospital knees up: hers is another repressed creative voice. The dramatic focus, however, is on Anna and Mary, two young mothers to be. Mary's husband has been arrested for suspected membership of the IRA, while Anna's policeman husband is dead, his head blown apart in an IRA attack. When she first enters the ward Anna is reserved, a fact heightened by the easy banter between the others and she is seen as stand-offish. When she attempts to leave the room after Lilly's poetry reading, Mary challenges her:

> MARY: I mean, you hardly say one word to any of us. Like we're all in the same boat, you know, aren't we? But you act as if you can't wait to get away from us and back to your wee hubby.
> ANNA: (*staring at Mary, not malevolently, but almost resignedly*) My husband's not long buried. He was a policeman. The IRA shot him in the back of the head.

She leaves. Later, in a long peroration, Anna tries to communicate to Betty the meaning of the death, an experience for which 'There are no words. It has nothing to do with words.' Pain is accentuated by a community which finds it difficult to deal with her grief; which talks *about* her but not *to* her. Repressed emotion issues as trauma and panic attacks, in which

> Your whole being feels as if it is sliding into itself, in a sickening confusion of jumbled emotions ... your body seems like a blanket wrapped too tightly around you, suffocating you. A terrible, tight shell that your ... your what? your heart? ... your breath? ... your pain? ... is straining to break free from.

How is she to help the children through this? For there is a terrible contradiction at work, between the finality of a father and husband's death, and the seemingly infinite expansion of a grief which reaches out 'beyond today, into your very future'. A grief which is felt to be universal: she cried, she tells Betty, not only for her husband, and for her children, but for '*all* grief, *everyone's* grief'.

Betty is the emotional fulcrum of the play, and Mary later talks to her about the loss of a husband and father who is locked away for life, and, to all intents and purposes, is 'dead' to his children, who will never know him. She tells Anna that they are both victims of 'this stupid bloody country', that both must survive without husbands. She anticipates the war continuing endlessly, bringing more deaths, and more pain for mothers on both sides. Lily sums up the dominant emotional register when she cries out: 'This bloody country doesn't deserve children.' At the close there is a reconciliation of sorts between Anna and Mary, who will give birth to babies whose lives are predefined by the war, by death and incarceration.

Expecting the Future was first performed by a makeshift community theatre group in West Belfast in 1983, and has been performed since in Farset, Larne and, in May 1998, in a professional production at the Lyric Theatre, Belfast, directed by Patricia Downey. However, it was not originally intended for performance, but was seen initially as what Hall calls a 'Reading Play', written to stimulate debate among young people on the emotional consequences of the conflict. Ian Adamson believes that

> Young girls reading it in Springhill Community House, Ballymurphy could identify without hesitation with the grief expressed by the policeman's widow, just as teenagers from nearby Shankill community project could relate to the feelings expressed by the IRA volunteer's wife.

Its success, he believes, lies in the fact that it is able to 'transcend political differences and touch that sense of compassion which was common to all the young performers'.[10] *Expecting the Future* was an attempt to dramatize the often invisible and inarticulate grief brought by the conflict, to yoke together childbirth and death in a plea for a human solidarity. His next play would draw on 'hidden histories' of a different kind.

Loyalism in Crisis

It was said that when Republican POWs first entered prison they went straight to the library, while Loyalist prisoners went straight to the gym. It was a caricature of the reality, but it had enough of truth in it to capture a critical fault-line between the two traditions. When, in 2002, the Linenhall Library was asked to catalogue the respective libraries from the H-Block wings, the IRA's was found to contain a vast selection of political, philosophical and historical texts, as well many of the world's literary classics. There was little on the Loyalist side, some say no library, but certainly nothing comparable in scope. Nor was there a comparable system of education and cultural production within the Loyalist cells. There was no prison theatre, no *An Glór Gafa* or *The Crime of Castlereagh*. These differences reflected differences in perceptions within the two communities about their prisoners. Jonathan Stevenson:

> Loyalists concede that the Nationalist community is better able to certify its ex-paramilitaries as political leaders because that community subsumes a prison community that the Unionist community has never had. In the Protestant community, ex-prisoners are commonly ostracized.[11]

The critical disconnection was social class. The Republican Movement was working-class, and its intellectuals and leaders all came from the same streets. There was no such fit between Unionism and Loyalism, whose nomenclature signalled the separation between a largely middle-class leadership and a working-class 'force'. The play *This Is It!* would explore this gap, and its consequences for the cohesion of Loyalist political culture in the early eighties.

An Idea for a Play – Ian Paisley and the 'Third Force'

In 1984 Sam Duddy, Public Relations Officer for the largest of the loyalist groupings, the Ulster Defence Association (UDA), published a small volume of poetry entitled *Concrete Whirlpools of the Mind*. It was an evocative title which seems to speak at once of historical stasis and spiritual turbulence. While some of the poems 'reflected all the self-certainties of an indignant defender of Ulster', says Hall, others spoke emotionally about the waste of a generation. The poetry complicated the 'monolithic stereotypes so beloved of the media.'[12] Heartened by what he felt was evidence of progressive thinking within the UDA, Hall arranged to meet with UDA chair Andy Tyrie. Tyrie was raised in Ballymurphy, close to the home of Sinn Féin leader Gerry Adams, and, like Adams, had become a political figurehead for his community. He had helped to organize the successful loyalist strike which brought down the Sunningdale Agreement in 1974, but he shared with the Sinn Féin leader a belief in a political solution, and in 1978 he founded the New Ulster Political Research Group (NUPRG).[13] In 1979 NUPRG produced a report proposing an independent Ulster, the greatest barrier to achieving which was not Republicanism, but internal dissension. Hall:

> The most paradoxical aspect was that not only were these internal tensions and contradictions mostly hidden from the general public, but even within the Protestant community they had never been fully

aired or explored. This was partly a legacy of the violence, which had forced many ordinary people to keep their heads down and their mouths shut, but also because there were no forums to carry forward any public debate.[14]

It was Andy Tyrie who suggested that theatre could provide a way to take the debate into pubs and clubs, 'in a less threatening, more entertaining and hopefully more thought-provoking manner by presenting these contradictions in a play'. It was also Tyrie who suggested that the drama be set in 1981 at the inception of the Reverend Ian Paisley's 'Third Force'.[15]

On 6 February 1981 Ian Paisley had led 500 men up a hill in County Antrim, where they were filmed waving legal fire-arms certificates above their heads. This *coup de théâtre* was meant as a warning to the British and Irish governments, who were then engaged in dialogue. At a rally in Belfast City Hall, a mass gathering was invited to sign a version of the 1912 Covenant, the founding document of the Orange State. Over the following months Paisley would address many such gatherings, culminating in his call on 2 September for the establishment of a 'Third Force', which could engage the IRA. The call came in the context of a year in which the hunger strikes had enabled the Republican Movement to dominate global perceptions of the war. Feeling threatened from within by a resurgent IRA, and from without by the ongoing dialogue between England and Ireland which would lead to the 1985 Downing Street Agreement, Unionism was convulsed by a passionate internal debate, of which Paisley's demagoguery was only the most audible aspect. It was this crisis which *This Is It*, written by Michael Hall with Andy Tyrie and Sammy Duddy, took as its starting point.

In the introduction to the published version of the script Hall offers a summary of the authors' intentions:

> The play centres on a young working-class Protestant, who, despairing of Ulster's continuing political crisis, eagerly participates in the massed display of the Rev Ian Paisley's 'Third Force' in Newtownards in November 1981. Through the play the authors endeavour to explore the diverse attitudes and contradictions which exist within Northern Ireland's Protestant working class.[16]

The young man in question is called Billy, and his journey becomes the dramatic mechanism through which the debate is opened up. Before the play proper opens, a roll-call of deaths in the year 1981 is read out:

> VOICE: September 1981
>   5th Off-duty soldier shot dead in University area of
>   Belfast.

6th Detective fighting for his life after being gunned down leaving Mass in Armagh.

7th Two teenage policemen on first patrol blown to pieces in 700lb landmine explosion.

13th UDR man fatally shot in back, Maghera.

14th RUC Reservist murdered after seeing his wife (who had just had their second child) at Mid-Ulster Hospital in Magherafelt.

19th Catholic man murdered on Ormeau Road, Belfast. UFF claim responsibility.

22nd Two soldiers seriously injured when terrorists fired into their Land Rover ...[17]

This is another battlefield text, and the stark enumeration reinforces its urgent argument that political events are out of control, and that Paisley's dangerous demagoguery is filling the vacuum. For Billy, Paisley's call to arms offers a solution, clarity of purpose amid the drift of state action. The play begins in his home as he prepares to make his journey to meet the great man. The stage directions are very precise: it is Sunday 22 November 1981, the eve of the Newtownards demonstration. It is lunchtime, and Billy is agitated as he packs his overnight bag. His father and mother's indifference to events and their inability to recognize the historical meaning of this moment anger him:

MOTHER: Where are you off to then, Billy?
BILLY: Newtownards, ma.
MOTHER: What for, son?
FATHER: 'Cause the Big Man's holding a rally there.
MOTHER: You going to watch it?
BILLY: No, ma, I'm going to be in it! (*Then, with determination*) I'm joining the Third Force!
MOTHER: But, for why, Billy? (*Then, to her husband*) Could you not put the paper away for just once when we're sitting down to a meal?

(*Father sighs in resignation and folds up the newspaper*)

BILLY: Ulster has taken enough from the IRA. All the killings, the bombings – it just goes on and on. There has to be an end to it! 'Cause, if we don't put a stop to it, Ulster will be destroyed.
FATHER: That's what the IRA want.
BILLY: Well, it's not what we want, so why do we let them get away with it! Somebody has to stop them!
FATHER: Billy, the police and the Army are ...

BILLY: ... are just piddling about like toy soldiers! Their hands are tied behind their backs! Anyway, I don't think Britain even wants to stop it – she doesn't give a damn about us! No, the only ones who can defend Ulster are Ulstermen!

Rejecting his parents' fatalism, Billy leaves, saying he is not sure when he will be back, as he is to be a soldier in Ulster's new army, and he could be sent anywhere. The following scene finds him in a bar in Newtownards, several hours before the demonstration. Dave, a UDA sergeant, and Tommy, a right-wing Loyalist, are discussing football when Billy enters with James, a shopkeeper and member of the Democratic Unionist Party (DUP). The talk turns to Paisley, whom Dave sees as a demagogue who fears to fight, a general who retreats once his foot soldiers move forward. His ability to mobilize and then abandon his people was protean, and part of the ideo-pathology of the conflict, and of Unionism's moral crisis over physical force. For Dave the critical issues are class, political cowardice and hypocrisy:

DAVE: Haven't we seen it all before? Think of all the men 'inside' now. How many of them are politicians? Well? Not fuckin' one of them! Those ones on the platform do all the mouthin' – "Ulster will fight and Ulster will be right!" – but who is it does the fightin'! Us! The ordinary Prods! That lot keep their noses clean. None of their families has to worry about gettin' a bloody mini-bus up to see them at visitin' times! Oh, no, they're too smart for that. But what really gets up my nose is that after havin' goaded us into action, they turn around and disown us! They don't wanna know us then!

When he finds that, notwithstanding Paisley's record, many of his local UDA company are joining the march, he is nonplussed. Tommy goads him as he leads Billy out:

TOMMY: Come on, Billy, let's leave this nest of turncoats. God love them! (*As he passes DAVE he leans drunkenly close to his face*) Well, Dave, when the Third Force clears out the IRA all by itself, people will look at you lot in the UDA and say: 'Where the fuck were you!'
DAVE   (*angrily*): Get stuffed!
TOMMY: Come on, Billy, let's go. (*He leads BILLY to the door, then turns around*) This night'll go down in history, you'll see. The Big Man said it's now "a do or die situation". This is it, lads! This is it!

(*Tommy and Billy depart. Everyone else stares after them. Lights fade.*)

Before the next scene documentary footage of the Third Force demonstration is played. Scene three is set in the same pub, but it is now December, three months after the rally. Billy has come back to Newtownards to see Tommy. Stirred by Paisley's promise to take apart the IRA, Billy had returned home to await the call to arms, but in vain. Bitterly disillusioned, he has come to Tommy for advice, only to find the UDA man had missed the September rally after nipping into a pub to get warm. Tommy reacts angrily to the idea that his action demonstrated a lack of commitment:

TOMMY (*angrily*): When the time comes I'll bloody fight alright!

DAVE: But wasn't that the time?

TOMMY: How could it be! Sure all the speeches the week leadin' up to it were so bloody contradictory! One minute they're talkin' about 'exterminating' the IRA and warning the IRA that the Third Force wasn't 'politically restrained' – and the next they're reminding us that we're 'law-abiding' people. You can't friggin' have it both ways!

DAVE: You can surely.

TOMMY: You friggin' can't!

DAVE: You can have the politicians remaining law-abiding, and the Maze filled with those who went outside the law. Isn't that the score now? Only the politicians will disown the ones inside. I've seen it all before. I don't trust any of them any more.

It is at this point that an older man, Sam, intervenes and offers a radical rethinking of their history:

SAM: You're talking here as if we are two completely separate communities in Ulster. Republicans talk the same way.

TOMMY: Well, aren't we?

SAM (*pointing to his forehead*): Up here we are, but that's about all. Oh yes, I've just remembered: some of us attend different churches ... those that bother to go.

ALAN: Come off it, Sam, there's more than that separates us.

SAM: You couldn't be more wrong. We have far more in common than you think. Both communities here come from ancient roots, roots that long predate the coming to Ireland of the Anglo-Normans, or the Vikings, or even the Celts. We're much older than all that.

Tommy responds with the orthodox analysis, namely that the Ulster Protestants are a distinctive cultural group who migrated from Scotland, and that the act of Plantation marked the beginning of modern Irish history and the struggle between distinctive and irreconcilable identities. Pointing to the geographical proximity of Ireland and Scotland and the likelihood of many centuries of migration and re-migration, Sam puts forward an alternative analysis. We are asked here to accept a rhetorical coherence, an intellectual drive which pushes against the naturalistic dialogue that has preceded it.

SAM: The Romans called the people in this part of Ireland the 'Scotti', and when some of these 'Scotti' migrated across the water they united with the local people to form what became known as 'Scotland'. They took the Gaelic language with them and it spread throughout the Highlands. But the links don't stop there. Even before the 'Plantation' the Irish chieftains imported thousands of Scottish mercenaries – the galloglass – to help them in their battles against the 'English'. They even crowned a Scotsman King of Ireland, because as far as the Irish chieftains were concerned the two peoples were one and the same. (*Sam looks around the gathering.*) So whether you like it or not, and whether the Republicans like it or not, the peoples of Ireland and Scotland have a continuous, shared history – possibly even a shared kinship. Both communities in Ulster have a right to be here. Certainly we have done great wrongs to each other in the past but we must accept that what's done is done, and we should be looking to the future.

DAVE: But we look at the future differently: we want to be British and they want to be Irish.

SAM: Whether we are prepared to accept it or not, we have an Irish part to our heritage, and they have a British part to theirs. There's no escaping that reality, for any of us. We're a mixed people here: look at the 'Planter' surnames among Sinn Féin – like Adams and Morrison. Or the Gaelic surnames among your crowd – Murphy, Doyle and Duddy. And I'll tell you another thing: when you lot go on about defending the 'heritage of your forefathers', half your forefathers probably fought for King James!

And, he might have added, Irish mercenaries fought for King Billy. Sam is here projecting Adamson and Hall's thesis, that Scotland and Ireland were originally peopled by one tribe, the Cruthin, and that Scottish plantation was not an act of colonization, but of reclamation: the assertion of an ancient, historical and shared ownership. Against the Republican analysis, which focuses on the similarities between the Irish experience, and the colonial and post-colonial experiences of Africa and Asia, Hall privileges a theory in which Ulster becomes, 'part of a story of ever shifting patterns of culture, language, religion and rule across these islands ... a story not only of heterogeneity but of hybridity'.[18] This hybridity obtained not only in the early modern period, but has characterized the complex history of nationalism. It is worth noting that, in making his point, Hall does not refer to those incidents in Irish history when Catholics and Protestants made common cause. Why not Tone and Davitt? Why not emphasize those moments in twentieth-century Irish history when both communities joined in class struggle, exemplified in the internationalism of Connolly and Larkin? Precisely, I think, because they have been appropriated so powerfully into the narrative of Republicanism. In a bold intellectual move, Adamson and Hall's theories elide post-Ascendancy Irish history with its dominant narrative of the struggle for Irish nationhood. In its place is the 'archipelago' analysis, whereby Loyalism and Republicanism are explained as historical diversions, which have obscured a longer and more durable shared history. What Ulster needs, in Sam's vision, is not people with the courage to kill, but a people with the courage to recognize a commonality based on this history: he is asking his audience to accept the historical and difficult challenge of creating a 'completely new society' alongside the Catholic working class. Even as he asks, he affirms the possibility: he is one of them, and he calls for solidarity from the ground of a shared political and cultural history. *This Is It!* is a play about migrations, and the last scene take us back to Billy's home. Billy is lost. He is an ideological migrant, whose move from the known community of home to the imagined community of the 'Third Force' has brought an inner dislocation and alienation. Disillusioned, at the play's close he decides to emigrate to Australia. But Australia does not want an unskilled working-class lad, and he is refused a visa. He is trapped, and so also are his people, unless they can open up to a different conception of their political and cultural identity. In a powerful image which closes the penultimate scene, Sam makes a plea for dialogue with the Catholic working class: he asks of his friends, and then of the audience: 'Are you brave enough to talk to them! Or maybe you wouldn't want to bother!' Just as the play's analysis opens up history, so here it opens up its form to allow for dialogue. 'And what about you lot? Any of you think it's high time we got together?' Hall's dramaturgical intention was to allow for, to encourage, contributions, to bring audience and stage, political vision and practical thinking, together. The difference between Republicans and Loyalists such as Tyrie, it is suggested, was not a difference over class (after all the IRA claimed as its central aim the creation of a socialist republic of Ireland), the difference was over whether it was to be a united working class in an independent Ulster, a United Kingdom, or a united Ireland.

This Is It! was tragically prescient in its call for class unity. In the years that followed the play, the number of sectarian killings would rise exponentially, as an impotent Loyalism reacted to the inexorable rise of Sinn Féin. The killings accelerated, tellingly, after Tyrie was removed from the UDA leadership following an attempt on his life.

The Writing Process

Although the text is jointly credited to Tyrie, Hall and Duddy, Hall wrote the script. He summarized the creative process in an email to the author:

> First of all we explored the range of attitudes prevalent in the Protestant community, and, in the process of this exploration, we imagined 'characters' who would best represent these diverse trends in a theatrical way. If I recall, the three of us almost role-played how these characters might respond to the main theme of the play – i.e. Paisley's Third Force. I then went away and endeavoured to capture in a script all that had been said in the course of our discussions. Then, the three of us went over it and made further suggestions and amendments.[19]

This approach gave an aesthetic coherence to the text, and allowed Hall to demonstrate his facility with the distinctive rhythms and inflections of east Belfast speech. His role as a writer was to facilitate, rather than determine, the play's arguments. Tyrie's main objection to the final draft was not the political analysis, but the amount of swearing in the text, though he agreed that for the sake of authenticity some needed to be retained. The original version of the play also included songs and poems which, Hall suggests, were put in without consideration for length or possible performance contexts. These were later cut away to leave a trimmer, more compressed, and hopefully, performable text. It still had ten characters, a fact which added to the problems of getting it staged. However, the main obstacle was, says Hall, 'the dearth of community drama groups within Belfast's Protestant working class' who could produce the play. Tyrie's solution was as surprising as it was pragmatic: 'He asked if I could muster a cast from my contacts in Catholic West Belfast. "Tell them I will guarantee their safety in Protestant areas".' Fr Wilson and members of the People's Theatre were very supportive, as was Joe Reid, and valiant attempts were made to put together a company and a viable rehearsal schedule. In the end these efforts came to nothing, and the play has never been performed. Given that the UDA's internal newsletter regularly called for the assassination of Des Wilson, an issue on which Hall successfully intervened with Tyrie, it is striking that the curate even considered involvement. Nonetheless there was, for a brief moment, and in the context of intense sectarian violence, the prospect of a drama written by leading figures in the UDA being performed by a Roman Catholic priest and his Nationalist theatre company in the heartlands of

Loyalism. A drama, moreover, whose central concern was the identity and future prospects of the Ulster state.

Although it never received a public performance *This Is It!* was, and remains, an important text in the history of the Troubles' theatres. In the period after 1984 the play script received numerous community group readings, and the issues it raised were discussed. In 2003 Hall decided to print a shortened version of the original text in the Island pamphlet series: a decision taken he writes, 'Because the need to contribute to the community debate is more pressing than ever – and the same tensions within Loyalism and Unionism have resurfaced in the wake of the recent Assembly elections when Dr. Paisley's DUP emerged as the largest Unionist party'.[20]

The failure to mount a public performance of *This Is It!* was due in large measure, as Hall acknowledged, to the absence of a theatre tradition within the Protestant community. It was only in the post-ceasefire period that community theatres began to emerge, the most significant being the Shankill Community Theatre, which was created as a response to one of the Troubles' final and most terrible incidents.

The Shankill Community Theatre

On Saturday 23 October 1993 a young IRA volunteer named Thomas Begley detonated a bomb in Frizzell's fishmongers on the Shankill Road. The bomb fuse was meant to be long enough to allow time for the shoppers and Begley to get out, but it had been cut too short, and the device exploded prematurely. Begley died together with nine local people, including two children. The IRA's target had been the leadership of the UDA, which met each Saturday in a room above Frizzell's. That Saturday the meeting had been moved to another venue. The IRA attack had been planned in response to a wave of sectarian attacks by the UDA and Loyalist Volunteer Force (LVF) during the previous month, in which three Catholics had died and a dozen more had been injured. However, the Shankill bombing simply intensified Loyalists' paramilitary attacks, and the following six weeks would see another sixteen Catholics murdered in what journalist Ed Maloney calls 'a period of unprecedented terror'.[21] The authorities' response to the terror was to seek to divert energies and emotions into creative outlets. A series of community regeneration programmes were funded under the auspices of 'Shankill '94', including one devoted to cultural work. Tom Magill was approached and asked to set up a community theatre project. He was aware of the potential difficulties, noting that there had been other theatre initiatives in the community, 'but none of them had amounted to anything'.[22]

Magill began by selecting a play for the putative theatre company, and had settled upon Frank McGuinness's *Observe the Sons of Ulster Marching Towards the Somme*, when he was given a copy of a play by a local writer.

The play, *Somme Day Mourning* was the first work of Brian Ervine, whose brother, David Ervine, was the leader of the Progressive Unionist Party (PUP), the political wing of the UVF. Ervine's play is set in 1914. Magill:

> The central character, Rab, a shipyard worker and socialist tries to resist the tide of opinion sweeping him to war on England's behalf – his war is in Ulster, against the social deprivation of the Shankill. Despite his own better judgment, he caves in and joins up, but lives to regret his decision, returning to the same desperate conditions on the Shankill: not a 'land fit for heroes'. The play is epic in style, using a chorus of women and songs to comment on the action. Other characters in the play represent different shades of what it meant being a Protestant in Belfast, from one extreme of being in favour of an Independent Ulster, through insisting on being British, to the other extreme of flirting with being Irish. The play is also a discussion on cultural identity from a Protestant working-class perspective.[23]

Magill brought in local poets Rene and Denis Grieg who ran Lapwing Publishers to help develop the project. He was keen to avoid simply recruiting members from the Orange Flute bands, and wanted a young cast which was representative of the different ideological perspectives in the community. The first task was to find such a cast, and, after one initiative involving a pastiche of a 1914 recruiting poster failed, they decided on a more direct approach, by engaging with young people on the streets and in locals clubs and pubs. They were met, says Magill, mostly with patience, but 'sometimes with amazement, scorn, ridicule, disbelief, scepticism, puzzlement, suspicion, hilarity etc.'[24] They were careful to avoid the nomenclature associated with theatre, such as 'rehearsal' or 'audition', and instead invited the volunteers to 'meetings' about a play. The approach yielded a dozen volunteers, five men and seven women. The production would demand the development from scratch of a company with its own methods, social and political relations, and rehearsal ethos. Magill:

> None of these twelve future players had had any previous experience of performing on stage. We had to create new habits of attendance, participation, co-operation, trust, commitment and creativity in order to transform formerly passive spectators into active performers. Getting them to believe in themselves was the single most difficult task that faced me ... The play with its original songs meant that we had to learn to play our instruments in a new way, breaking out of the mould of the past by playing new tunes.[25]

As the group's confidence grew Magill introduced them to Boal's image theatre exercises, and to more challenging voice and movement exercises.

When the time came to stage the play, the local Woodvale cricket team gave over their hall:

> We transformed the bleak hall into a theatre with rostra, seating, lighting, sound, and a wooden set representing the shipyard and the trenches. From initial cynicism the cricketers turned to amazement when they saw the team effort we had put into our collective transformation of their empty hall.[26]

Securing an audience was less easy, and the turnouts for the performances were small, despite the provenance of the text and the fact that this was a local theatre group. The local media were heavily represented however, as a production of Ervine's play by a Shankill-based theatre was extremely newsworthy. The production opened with the potent image of an actor striking 'the big drum of the Shankill Protestant Boys ... stained into its skin was the blood from the knuckles of the drummers of the past: the symbol of Ulster's blood sacrifice'.[27] Perhaps tellingly, when the media exposure led to invitations to tour the production, the invitations came not from Loyalist communities, but from the Irish Republic and from An Culturlann on the Falls Road. It was one more instance of a bifurcation in historical energies. Magill offers the figure of Janus as symbolic of this difference, with Loyalist and Republican facing away from each other, the one focused on the past, the other turned towards the future.

In *This Is It!* one of the characters, Dave, asks rhetorically: for whom did Protestants die at the Somme or on the beaches of the Dardanelles? He asks because those sacrifices for the Mother Country did not bind the English to them. Loyalists and Unionists may have been 'our' Paddys, but they were Paddys just the same, and the English were always even-handed in their racist reception of Unionist incomers, Catholic or Protestant. The central question asked by both *This Is It!* and *Somme Day Mourning* is: who defines us, and in whose interests?

The company were proud of their first production, and Magill felt that the project had been a great success. Theatre, he wrote later, had offered the possibility of creating 'new rituals' to challenge a patrimony which celebrated sameness, and had created a space in which Protestants could forge a unified vision of the future based on a re-imagined past. Magill was interested in how theatre was inherently subversive of the core values of Protestantism, which Ian Paisley had defined as 'characterized centrally by individualism and self sufficiency'. Theatre, by contrast, says Magill, is a resolutely social practice, a labour to shape images of reality which is defined by 'dialogue, team work, collective creativity and mutual trust'.[28]

Figure 10, A and B.
Somme Day Mourning
by Brian Ervine, Shankill
Community Theatre, Belfast,
1994.

The White In Between

In 1995 Magill wrote a play called *The White In Between*. The text, he told me in an email, was influenced by the work of the Nobel prize-winning Italian playwright, actor and activist, Dario Fo.[29] His hope was that it would be staged by the Shankill Community Theatre as part of that year's Belfast Festival programme at Queen's University. Instead the production would bring about the embryonic company's demise. *Somme Day Mourning* had been what Magill calls a 'comfort play', which had explored the ideological confusions of Loyalism from the safe ground of a known history. He felt that the community needed to move to a more politically reflexive examination of their cultural identity, and he proposed *The White In Between* as the vehicle for this examination. The title of the play refers to the Irish tricolour, and the semiotic ambiguity of the white stripe that lies between the orange and the green – does it conjoin or separate the two traditions? Magill offers a synopsis of the play:

> My central character is a Black English soldier by the name of White. He comes to Northern Ireland under the command of Major Ramrod, thinking he is helping to restore peace to the troubled

Figure 11. Rehearsals for *The White In Between* by Tom Magill, Shankill Community Theatre, Belfast, 1995.

province. But gradually seeing what is going on around him, he discovers his identity and his roots in Africa. He casts off his uniform and rejects the army. Again with the help of song and dance, it was my intention to explore concepts of 'otherness'.[30]

The *Somme* company worked on the text for six months. Then, as the first night approached, there was a critical meeting at the Woodvale Cricket Club rehearsal room which was attended by the cast and Magill. In a letter to the former chairperson of Shankhill '94, the ex UDA leader Jacky Hewitt, Magill described what happened:

> In last Sunday's *Sunday Life* (enclosed) there is an article implying that I walked away from the production of *The White in Between* written by me and for performance by Shankill Community Theatre Company. This is simply not true. There was a vote of the company on Monday October 16th (3 weeks before the opening of the play which is advertised in the Queen's Festival) in Woodvale Cricket Club – 9 people voted not to do the play (regardless of cuts or additions) because they considered it 'Too controversial', and 3 people (including myself) voted to do the play with certain cuts and additions. After a read-through of the play in May the company decided it should be the next production for the Shankill. At a later date the play was vetted by 'local powers' to ensure that any contentious material could be negotiated. While I have been Artistic Director of the company the ethos has been democratic – so I agreed to stand by their decision.[31]

Magill was dismayed and shocked by this collective act of 'self-censorship', although he immediately identified the cultural factors which had contributed to the decision. This was a white community, with little historical experience of Black or Asian people, and dominated by paramilitary groups who have strong links to British and European neo-Nazi movements. Magill's play was asking this community to recognize itself and its crisis of identity through the eyes of a black soldier. White was not only black, he was the vehicle of a trenchant anti-militarism in a drama which also criticized religious institutions. It is difficult to imagine a play which could have represented a more provocative challenge to the belief systems and reflexive politics of the Loyalist community.

Conclusion

To understand why the Shankill community read *The White In Between* in a way which subverted Magill's intentions we need, as ever, to focus on the immediate political context. The IRA's 1994 ceasefire had inaugurated an embryonic but powerful pan-Irish Nationalist bloc embracing the USA and the Irish Republic. In 1995 Unionism again felt itself to be on the back foot, and, in this context, White's desertion was not read by the Loyalist working class as an example of self-liberation, as an affirmative assertion of identity. On the contrary, he was a British soldier posted to Ireland to protect *them*, to secure *their* heritage from the final working out of the 1916 rebellion. Why would they *not* see his action as abandonment, or the affirmation of his African culture as an act of treachery (reinforcing an historic racism), rather than as a symbol, a liberatory example? So, while I can see the thrust of Magill's thesis, that we either define ourselves or we are defined by others, I can also see how the Shankill group came to reject a play which, in that moment, would be read as an endorsement of the Republican version of recent history. The white in between was not, they were saying, a meeting ground, but a necessary barrier.

This was not, however, as in the case of Baron Cohen in Derry, an example of an outsider misreading a community. The failure to mount the play was not a failure of understanding, or of practice politics. On the contrary, this was a play mounted from within a community by someone who knew it, and insisted on pushing it as hard as he could towards a more complex understanding of the war and its legacies. *The White In Between* was a play made for the Falls Road, where it would have been readily absorbed into a confident historical project. But Magill chose to play it on the Shankill and therein lay his political courage and intellectual daring.

For both Magill and Hall, theatre's openness, and its capacity for generating and holding in creative tension contradictory readings, makes it the supreme art for the practice of change. But they also recognize that conservative elements in the Loyalist community intuitively knew this, and resisted the imaginary enactment of change as surely as they resisted its enactment through politics. The tragedy is not that there are no progressive and visionary voices within these constituencies, for these plays are about those voices; it is that they have not prevailed. Here is political commentator John Coulter writing in 2005:

> What unionism needs is a new ideological direction; one which will unite rather than divide all shades of Unionist, Protestant, Orange and loyalist thinking in the North. The last generation has witnessed unionism indulge in the luxury of internecine fragmentation to the point that some groups are reduced to 'fringe' status, such is their insignificance. What unionism needs is a political revolution. It needs a new sense of destiny in a technological world which is rapidly seeing the evolution of something approaching a European state.[32]

These texts and theatres were contributions towards that needed political revolution.[33]

PART THREE

CASEBOOKS (2)
STAGING THE PEACE

The 'Long Peace'

The final chapter of Marc Mulholland's short history of Northern Ireland is called 'The Long Peace'.[1] The title is a neat nod towards the concept of the 'Long War', elaborated by Gerry Adams and his circle in the cages of Long Kesh in 1976, and which had defined the IRA's military and political strategy in the following decades. It was a strategy founded upon historical certainty and infinite tactical patience, and these qualities defined Sinn Féin and the IRA in the post-Good Friday period. The Peace Process proved as complex, and as defined by dead ends and diversions, as the war had been. Maintaining the unity and cohesion of the Republican Movement taxed Adams' legendary political skills to the full, though splinter groups such as the Continuity IRA and the Real IRA emerged to claim the mantle of Connolly and Pearse, and to continue a low-level bombing campaign against state forces. To a minority of Republicans, including ex hunger strikers such as Brendan Hughes and Anthony McIntyre, the accommodation with Unionism was an act of political surrender, a betrayal of the legacy of the 1916 Rising, and of the sacrifices of generations of IRA volunteers and their families.[2] But the majority stayed with Adams, who is the most important politician to have emerged from within Republicanism since Michael Collins. Adams is a pragmatist, and a skilful and ruthless tactician, whose instincts have always been political rather than militaristic. In the early seventies he had been drawn to the Marxist Cathal Goulding's conception of a National Liberation Front with the Communist Party and the Marxist Connolly Association as a means to achieve a united Ireland. A political activist from an early age, Adams had cut his political teeth in campaigns around bread and butter issues such as housing and employment and civil rights. What led him to reject Goulding's call for a political front with the Loyalist working classes was that he could not see how any unity could be achieved until Ireland's political institutions had been normalized and partition ended. Ed Maloney: 'Adams had a foot in both Republican camps ... he liked much of Goulding's political approach but deplored his failure to defend Belfast's Catholics.'[3] It was Adams' skill in mobilizing popular mass protests against British troops in Ballymurphy which was credited with politicizing the community, and creating the political infrastructure and ideological ground for the Provisional IRA. For many in the pre-1976

IRA military force *was* the strategy, but for Adams it was always only a tactic, however critical. Recent history has shown that he had begun to steer the movement towards the Long Peace soon after the hunger strikes. By the mid-1980s, says Maloney, 'There was broad acceptance of the leadership's assertion that the movement alone was not strong enough to bring about the conditions necessary to end partition and that allies were needed.'⁴ By the early 1990s the view had been formed within Adams' circle that a National Liberation Front in all but name was possible. A combination of revolutionary Republicanism, Constitutional Nationalism and US emigré economic and diplomatic muscle could, it was felt, deliver a political structure defined by north-south structures and devolved powers, as an interim step to full unification. Adams' success in convincing his own people delivered the first IRA ceasefire on 31 August 1994. Based on a new IRA policy, the Tactical Use of Armed Struggle, or TUAS, the ceasefire depended upon a speedy and positive response from Britain and the Republic of Ireland.

Progress was slow as Unionists, unnerved by the developments, called for a period of 'decontamination' of the Republican movement. It was a telling adjective, redolent of an ancient loathing. At Westminster John Major's Conservative Party, who were kept in power by the support of DUP and UUP members, hoped to secure the peace while holding out on meaningful political dialogue. The decommissioning of IRA arms was a critical stumbling block, which was solved by the creation of a twin-track process whereby Sinn Féin committed to political dialogue, and the IRA committed to decommissioning in parallel talks with a specially convened international verification body. Major sought to calm Unionist outrage at this accommodation by calling for new elections to determine who would enter talks. This was portrayed as a democratic lock on Republicans, but was a step too far for hard-liners within the IRA who, on 6 February 1996, and in a direct challenge to the Adams' strategy, detonated a devastating bomb at Canary Wharf, which killed two and injured another hundred. Notwithstanding the revulsion the bombing caused, when the elections for the Forum for Peace and Reconciliation were held on 30 May, Sinn Féin achieved their best ever results, with seventeen seats and 15.5 percent of the overall vote. More significant, perhaps, was the manner in which the DUP overtook the UUP as Unionism's dominant party. The next decade was the story of how the two 'extremes' of northern politics were brought into alignment.

It was the British Labour Party's landslide victory in the general election of 1997 which left Tony Blair free to take risks, and created the conditions for the 1998 Good Friday Agreement. Britain promised to cede its political claim on the north of Ireland if and when its people voted freely for union with the South. The latter ceded, in turn, its historic constitutional claim to the north as an integral part of the Republic. So-called 'North–South' and 'East–West' bodies were established to facilitate commerce, culture, and civic and political ties and legislation was promised to end a hundred years of discrimination in the north's civic, commercial and political institutions. A significant element of the Agreement concerned cultural rights, with the Irish language granted enhanced status, alongside a speedily resurrected and little-practised Ulster Scots, to ensure balance. Educational provision would provide scope for bilingual schools. However, the single most critical decision, and the one which would have most impact on the development of political community theatre, was the staged release of Republican and Loyalist prisoners.

The impact of the Agreement on Loyalist communities was, generally, negative, with many seeing it as a significant step towards a united Ireland. While courageous and visionary paramilitaries-turned-politicians such as David Ervine and Billy Hutchinson sought to use the process to advance their community's agenda, and to create a more sophisticated and cohesive vision of unionism's future, the differences at grass-roots level ignited a series of internecine turf wars over control of drug trafficking, prostitution and protection rackets. The release of prisoners simply exacerbated these crises. At old flashpoints along the inaptly named Peace-line, sectarian violence continued unabated, and the 'peace' was for many Republicans and Unionists in those first five years simply a less intense and visible form of war. There was suffering and hurt on both sides in this period, and it was mainly the young, raised during the war, and lacking political sophistication, who caused it. Unionists were correct in their assessment that the Good Friday Agreement, while it seemed to have copper-bottomed the Union by getting Sinn Féin to sign up to the principle of consent, had created the political and cultural institutions which would bring a united Ireland closer. The proponents of the Long War are masters of the long political game. While Unionists hoped the Good Friday Agreement would mark the endgame of the historical forces set in motion by the 1607 Plantation, for Republicans it was just one more move in a very long and very slow game of political chess.

The 'Force of Argument' and not the 'Argument of Force'

As the Peace Process made space for new political alliances, so it also created space for the emergence of a vast post-Troubles literature encompassing autobiography, biography, memoir, novels, poetry, social research, historiography, and life histories. Academic Stephen Hopkins sees such writings, regardless of genre, as fulfilling several important functions: first as contributions to historical, social, and cultural knowledge; second as acts of personal or historical justification which attempt to define the historiography of the Troubles; and thirdly as a way of continuing the war by literary means. He writes:

For those authors/subjects who have played an 'active' role in the conflict, and belong to or have belonged to paramilitary organizations, this can serve as a means of conducting the battle by force of argument, rather than by the argument of force.[5]

The founders of *An Glor Gafa* were part of this phenomenon. A compilation of Republican prisoners' reflections was published in 1994, edited by Brian Campbell, Laurence McKeown and Felim O'Hagan. *Nor Meekly Serve My Time – the H-Block Struggle, 1976–1981* was compiled while the editors were still in Long Kesh, and smuggled out in two green-bound volumes. Explaining the motivation for the publication, the editors wrote:

> Just as the forces of Irish history produced the hunger strikes, so they in turn have affected subsequent history … the participants in those events are the witnesses best able to leave an historical record. This book is the Blanketmen as historians, people who not only changed history but were themselves changed by it.[6]

In 2001 McKeown published *Out of Time, Irish Republican Prisoners Long Kesh, 1972–2000*, a study of the 'social construction of an Irish Republican prisoner community as understood by the prisoners themselves'. Based on the thesis which had gained him his doctorate from Queen's University in 1998, McKeown saw the research as 'the continuation of a political education process which began in the H-Blocks of Long Kesh', and hoped that the book would be 'of value to Republican ex-prisoners in terms of understanding where they have come from and where they can go to in the future'.[7] Theatre also offered a space in which the three functions identified by Hopkins could co-exist, through productions in which the historical, political, religious and moral questions raised by the conflict would be explored. This phenomenon is most apparent in the work of Amharclann na Carraige/Theatre on the Rock, home to Ireland's DubbelJoint Theatre, a theatre whose production processes constitute a microcosm of the social, economic, political and cultural relations of the post-Agreement Nationalist and Republican communities. Loyalism has no equivalent space.

DubbelJoint at
Amharclann na Carraige

A Brief History of Amharclann na Carraige

Situated in a wing of the Belfast Further and Higher Education College on the Whiterock Road, Amharclann na Carraige/Theatre on the Rock, is the home of DubbelJoint Theatre. It is a unique theatre space where the cultural impulses set in motion by the 1981 hunger strikes have found a stage. Its director is Pam Brighton, an important figure in the history of political theatre in post-1968 Britain and Ireland. Brighton has also worked as a director in Canada, Scotland and Australia. Her work in Britain included periods with CAST, the Royal Court Theatre, 7:84 England, and the Half Moon Theatre, before she became one of the leading producers of new plays in Ireland. She was a director for Belfast's Charabanc Theatre, and Commissioner for Radio Drama with BBC Ulster, before founding DubbelJoint with Marie Jones and Mark Lambert in 1991. The ethos of the West Belfast audiences reminds Brighton of the Half Moon Theatre in London's East End, where she worked as a director: 'People here come to the theatre because they want to see *that* play, not because it is a social habit', she told me, and this creates a 'very particular type of audience', one which assumes an ownership of the theatre.[1]

February 1994 had seen the premiere of Marie Jones's adaptation of Gogol's *The Government Inspector*, also at the Féile an Phobail, beginning a relationship with the playwright which was to define the first years of the company's work. The Brighton/Jones partnership provided DubbelJoint with a sequence of acclaimed productions which brought a sharp humour and popular theatre forms to bear on Irish history and contemporary concerns. In August 1994, the same month as the first IRA ceasefire, the company premiered Jones's *A Night In November* at the West Belfast Festival. Based on events surrounding the 1993 World Cup qualifying match between the Republic of Ireland and Northern Ireland, the play was a smash-hit across Ireland, and toured to London and New York. It was followed by *Women on the Verge of HRT* (1994), *Stones in his Pockets* (1996), and *Eddie Bottom's*

Dream (1996). All three transferred to London, with *Stones in his Pockets* becoming an international hit in the late nineties.[2]

In the following decade DubbelJoint would continue to stage a series of works which placed the company as Ireland's foremost company for new writing. DubbelJoint's name, a conflation of Dublin and Belfast, signalled its intention to create a national theatre based in the north, and speaking from the heart of the Nationalist experience. The new writing included Peter Sheridan's *Mother of all the Behans* (1998) and Pearse Elliot's *A Mother's Heart* (1999) a powerful and controversial study of four mothers' attempts to come to terms with the loss of children killed during the Troubles. In 2002 the company staged *Working Class Heroes*, an adaptation by Ballymurphy writer Brenda Murphy of Robert Tressell's *Ragged Trousered Philanthropists*. Further new work followed, including Joe Mulhern's play *Peadar O'Donnell*, a celebration of the novelist, union organizer and Republican volunteer, who served on the IRA Army Council between 1924 and 1934, and had been an editor of *An Phoblacht/Republican News*. Two thousand and two also saw the premiere of Brian Moore's *Black Taxi*, a celebration of the remarkable people's transport system which developed during the Troubles. The *Irish Times* described *Black Taxi* as 'a comedy, a musical, a lecture on a successful commercial venture, a history of the Troubles, and a portrait of West Belfast'.[3] Moore would contribute three other plays to the company's repertoire: *Paddy on the Road* (2002), a tribute to singer and songwriter Christy Moore: and two musical comedies, *The Session* (2005) and *The Ballad of Malachy Mulligan* (2006). This is a considerable body of work. But it is the sequence of plays which arose from within the community, and which connect DubbelJoint directly to the radical grass-roots tradition defined by the People's Theatre, Belfast Community Theatre and the H-Block theatres which are the focus of my interest here.

JustUs and the Community Shows

In 1995 Brighton was approached by a group of local women who asked for her help in developing a piece of theatre for International Women's Day. The women had set up a company called JustUs, whose aim was to present plays which reflected women's experience of the conflict. The collaboration was significant in helping DubbelJoint develop their ties with the West Belfast community. The resulting play, *Just a Prisoner's Wife*, was the first to deal with another hidden narrative within Republican experience and was a hit at the 1996 Féile an Phobail, before touring through Ireland. Former prisoners who saw the piece commented that the theatre had helped them, for the first time, understand the reality of their families' experiences. In common with future productions, the theatre operated as a form of community therapy and political education. The success of the collaboration with DubbelJoint led to the new company being awarded the Belfast City Council Best Arts Partnership Award for 1996. In a company document written in 2000, the collective wrote of their work that 'JustUs exists to empower the community to tell their own story, in their own words, through the medium of the dramatic arts'.[4] The company's productions would, the document said, focus on 'reflecting the politics of our community' and would seek to contribute towards 'healing and conflict resolution'. The company also wanted to develop a training programme which would foster the development of women writers and performers. In 1997, JustUs again collaborated with DubbelJoint on what would become one of the most iconic and controversial productions in the post-ceasefire period, *Binlids*, which was premiered at Féile an Phobail on 5 August 1997. Directed by Pam Brighton and designed by Dan Devenny, *Binlids* was written by Brenda Murphy, Christine Poland, Jake MacSiacais and Danny Morrison, former IRA and Sinn Féin publicity officer, novelist and journalist. As with *Just a Prisoner's Wife*, *Binlids* takes as its central theme the experiences of women in the battlefield, but its historical scope and epic structure distinguish it from the earlier work. Tracing the evolution of the struggle, from Internment without trial, which began on 7 August 1971, it concludes in the late 1980s as the Republican community comes to terms with the execution of three IRA volunteers in Gibraltar and its violent aftermath, which included Loyalist Michael Stone's gun and grenade attacks on mourners at Milltown Cemetery.[5] At the funerals of those killed by Stone, two British Army intelligence officers drove into the cortege and were captured, interrogated and then executed by the IRA. It was a terrible sequence of events which offered a microcosm of the Troubles. *Binlids* does not attempt to justify the IRA actions, but to explain them. The argument that IRA violence was rendered objectively necessary by history, was always essentially reactive, and a response to British or Unionist state oppressions, would become a central theme in later works staged by the company. The play had two interdependent aims. The first was to allow the community to tell its own story to itself. The second was to tell the story to outsiders in order to challenge the negative view of Republicans in the world outside Ireland. Talking about how the 400 victims of the British state's forces were rarely mentioned in the media, while the IRA's victims were visibly and loudly mourned, Murphy told a reporter:

Ordinary people were dying every day and that was never broadcast. This is a chance for people to hear a story of the other side. We were described in the papers as animals, scum. We're not animals. We're not scum. We're resilient people, and we are here, and we survived it. And we're just telling our story.[6]

As with the H-Block Theatres and the work of Belfast Community Theatre and People's Theatre, *Binlids* was a testament to a community's endurance.

Brenda Murphy had been imprisoned, beaten and strip-searched, and like Paula from Belfast Community Theatre she saw it 'like being raped, daily, you know'. Acting was 'like a therapy'.[7]

Binlids is composed of forty-two scenic elements, including songs and choruses, reportage, verbatim dialogues, speeches, newspaper reports, and devised or written naturalistic scenes. It is less a montage than a rich, formal bricolage, whose final form was dictated by the practical political purpose of telling, as fully as possible, a complex twenty-eight year history. In his study Tom Maguire points to the relationship to Living Newspaper forms, and quotes Alan Filewood on documentary theatre: 'It is a genre of performance that presents actuality on the stage and in the process authenticates that actuality, and it speaks to a specifically defined audience for whom it has special significance.'[8] Filewood's definition helps to explain the powerful reactions to the production, both positive and negative. For, if you did not belong to that 'specifically defined' audience, or did not have a detailed understanding of the history which was its content, then the significance of *Binlids* might well evade you. Two narratives dominate the play: the first is that of the Westrock massacre of 9 July 1972, the second is that of the interrogation, torture and imprisonment of internees. The Westrock massacre, in which five people, including two children and Fr Wilson's fellow curate, Fr Noel Fitzpatrick, were killed by British soldiers during indiscriminate firing into the streets, is recreated here through small scenes and verbatim reportage. Happening so soon after Bloody Sunday, the massacre marked a significant hardening of local support for IRA resistance. And, as they would during investigations into Bloody Sunday, soldiers lied about the context of the deaths. The speech by the mother of thirteen-year-old Margaret Gargan carries, beneath the surface ordinariness of the language and the simple and direct address, deep trauma and suffering:

NELLY GARGAN:

> She was 13 when she was murdered, only a child really, she was the type who loved to wear trousers. She was well thought of in school and it was the Head Sister who sent the only photo I have of her. On the day of the shooting she was down working in the community centre. She came in that night and asked me if I was going out but I said no. She asked why I didn't go round to St John's with Mary McGarry. I told her I had no money. She gave me a pound so me and Mary went round to St John's. Bernadette and Collette Tate were minding the kids. We were sitting in St John's having two bottles of Tuborg Gold and Tommy Best came in and said to me, 'Nelly, you better get home. There is shooting in your street.' The army said they done it at the inquest. They had tried to say she was a 21 year-old gunman

because she had jeans on her. There were no apologies or
nothing. In fact, I never even got her clothes back.

The play is an accumulation of such moments, scenes of interrogation and
torture, violation and sudden death, arbitrary brutality and humiliation,
the objectification and attempted subjugation of a whole people. Writing
in the *Irish Times* in response to criticism that the play was merely the
tired iteration of 'Republican *causes célèbres*', Brighton pointed to this
dimension, saying that: 'for the cast themselves it was, at times, an extremely
painful journey, remembering old traumas, talking to other people about
some of their most painful memories'.[9] In the same article Brighton talks
of the play as a 're-enactment of a community's trauma'. A common theme
of the criticism was that the play did not show Republican violence, and so
was not balanced. There was a common view in the media that the violence
visited on the Nationalist community, however undeserved (and the majority
of those killed or tortured had carried out no acts of violence), was at least
explained by IRA violence. Reflecting that he also had challenged Brighton
for a lack of balance, Tom Maguire notes: 'It was only on completing the
research for this paper that I began to see ways in which my own view was
the response of a cultural *evolue* conditioned to seeing the circumstances of

Figure 12. Rehearsal for *Binlids* by Brenda Murphy, Christine Poland, Jake
MacSiacais and Danny Morrison, DubbelJoint Theatre, Belfast, 1997, directed by
Pam Brighton.

Republicans as self-inflicted and their strategies of resistance as barbaric.'[10] Maguire's intellectual honesty is rare, and for the most part critics continued to see torture and state violence as necessary evils, and the deaths of ordinary Irish non-combatants as a kind of moral collateral damage. The problem for Republicans was that they were forced to protest their humanity from within a war which had deepened a reflexive anti-Irish racism. The atrocities committed by the IRA against civilians at Enniskillen, or the Birmingham pub bombings, were indeed terrible. And they were described as such in the media. But the deaths of Irish men, women and children, which were often just as terrible, were not. This was an issue of power, and not morality. In response to critical reaction to *Binlids* Pam Brighton wrote that the play was not 'seeking a balance in itself' but a balance across a range of political and cultural writings.[11] This is a proper aim for any political play. Where in *Mother Courage* does Bertolt Brecht make the case for capitalism, or for the necessity of war? *Mother Courage* is inserted into a world already out of balance; it is a piece of ideological ballast on behalf of the drowning. While *Binlids* was conceived as an attempt to counter the negative social construction of Nationalists, it was also, like *The Crime of Castlereagh*, an act of commemoration and celebration.

Constructing the Text

The text of *Binlids* evolved from story-telling sessions in local women's houses. It was while exchanging accounts of their experiences that the JustUs group conceived the idea of creating a drama documentary based upon the Ballymurphy community's experience. The first step was to settle on the overall narrative, and to select the themes and incidents which would form the basis of the history. This process was followed by extensive research, involving interviewing local people, including relatives of those who had died, for example, in the Westrock massacre. Sections of the text were prepared in advance by the writers, other sections, mainly the second half of the play, were developed through improvisation in rehearsals under Brighton's direction, and were then written up. It is a collective script founded on collective research. The cast spent a great deal of time ensuring that the play's account of a shared history was authentic, and scenes, once rehearsed, were shown to neighbours to make sure that they were 'right'. It was, paradoxically, because they came from the Ballymurphy community that the company paid such critical attention to the representation of communal experience. Those who have endured oppression know that its effects are always specific, embodied in personal and deeply traumatic experience, and that this particularity must be respected, and not subsumed in generalized accounts.

Binlids was a promenade production, with scenes enacted on five stages which surrounded an open area in which the audience gathered.

Periodically stage actions would take place among the spectators, for example a funeral procession or a fire-fight. These scenic arrangements were intended to construct the audience as participants in, or witnesses to, the history. This proximity also generated resistance from spectators who preferred the role of judges. The loose episodic structure allowed the company to compress a complex history into a (relatively) short drama. The stages were rarely used simultaneously to generate a montage effect. The power of the images is cumulative rather than synchronic. The stages' primary role was to allow scenes to be set in advance, ensuring a swift transition from episode to episode. *Binlids* also saw the continuation of one of DubbelJoint's defining methods, namely the use of casts composed of a mix of professional and amateur performers. Besides Brenda Murphy and Christine Poland the cast included also the actress Mairead Ui Admaill, wife of the IRA volunteer Felim Ui Admaill, and Jim Doran. Brighton had first used a mix of professional and local performers in *Just a Prisoner's Wife*. She told me that she had been concerned then that the local women would be overawed by working with professionals, but it turned out to be the other way round. Brighton thinks the tradition of the *meitheal* has a beneficial effect in theatre making: 'They don't allow any kind of hierarchy in their heads, and yet they're absolutely respectful of people's skills.' Members of JustUs would later act in Brighton's production of Pearse Elliot's *A Mother's Heart*.

'Distasteful' and 'Exploitative' – the Arts Council of Northern Ireland and Republican theatre

The critical and political controversy generated by *Binlids* was as nothing in comparison with the impact of JustUs's next and last work, *Forced Upon Us*, written by Brenda Murphy and Christine Poland and premiered at An Feile Phobail on 28 July 1999. The play dealt with the foundation of the Unionist state. A generally sympathetic review in the *Irish Times* offers a gloss of the plot:

> *Forced Upon Us* is classic left-wing agit prop theatre – told sharply from the point of view of a marginalized and brutalized Catholic working class in north-east Ulster in the period 1912 to the foundation of the one party state and the RUC in 1922. The re-enacted incidents and proclamatory [verbatim] speeches of the time sketch a clear line from the mass singing of the Ulster Covenant, through the arming of the UVF – many of whom joined the B-Specials to the eventual formation of the Royal Ulster Constabulary in 1922. The controversial raw style of the JustUs company hits you in the teeth from the start. A young Catholic woman shrieks down the ramp followed by a Protestant workman who rapes her, and this is followed

Figure 13. Forced Upon Us by Brenda Murphy and Christine Poland, DubbelJoint
Theatre, Belfast, 1999, directed by Pam Brighton.

by the burning alive of a Catholic shipyard workman by a gang of
Protestants after the sinking of the Titanic.[12]

Problems began when, under the regulations of the Lottery New Work
Funding scheme, from which DubbelJoint received parts of it funding,
officers at the Arts Council of Northern Ireland (ACNI) requested a copy
of the script. Senior Drama and Dance Officer Imelda Foley, later the
author of a study of the politics of gender in Ulster's theatre, then sent
the script to three external assessors for consideration.[13] Their responses
were summed up in an article by the ACNI director Brian Ferran, who
told journalists that 'the script had been deficient in three main ways – its
characters were wooden – "cardboard", I believe, was the word used. It
was also deficient in structure, and the quality of writing was as bad as
anything the assessors had ever read.'[14] In view of these 'deficiencies' the
ACNI froze the £20,000 allocated to the production in DubbelJoint's
budget projections, even though the play was already halfway through its
run. The magazine *Fortnight* ran a long feature as part of its 'Reader's
Forum'. Author Ian Hill had managed to secure copies of the readers'
reports, and offered more examples of their views on *Forced Upon Us*:
it was, they had written, 'a propagandist play which could only serve to
deepen existing prejudices', 'distasteful', 'exploitative', and 'very poorly

realized'. While Hill agreed that it was 'propagandist in the extreme' he added that 'it is not theatre's business to be fair'. Moreover, reading a script was not the same as seeing it staged, and Hill felt that in Brighton's hands the draft had been realized as a compelling production. Written by working-class Republican women and from women's perspective, the play was, he believed, an important dramatic and historical document.[15] In the same forum, Malachi O'Doherty disagreed, arguing that Brighton had failed in her creative editorial duty by allowing the script ('a shapeless piece of work') to go forward.[16] The controversy would draw in opinion from both sides of the community before settling into a predictable political stand-off. *An Phoblacht/Republican News* pointed out that the ACNI had, only months before, declared that DubbelJoint had met their Standards for Excellence, while Gerry Adams upbraided the council for presuming to tell the Nationalist and Republican communities what they could and could not write plays about.[17]

The Arts Council's actions were defended in a fluent and combative article in *Fortnight* by the public affairs officer, Damian Smyth. In the article Smyth accused the ACNI's detractors of having 'push button agendas', and insisted that the Arts Council has been a consistent friend of a pluralist culture. Indeed, he noted, DubbelJoint had been funded when many people would like to see their 'artistic practice cease for good'. ACNI's detractors, he continued, were using censorship as a distraction from the real issue, namely the Arts Council's duty to make a judgment on artistic standards. Simply put, the play was not a good play, regardless of its content. Even as the arguments over censorship and artistic policy raged, Chris Patten's impending report on the future of policing in the north of Ireland was creating the political context which helps to explain the ACNI's actions. Published in September 1999, Patten's central recommendations, which included a new name and badge for the RUC, a change to the oath of allegiance, and a positive recruitment policy towards Catholics, were greeted with a deep and visceral anger by Unionists. For Unionists, as for Republicans, the RUC and the Unionist state were synonymous: they were its guarantors and guardians of the 1912 Covenant. As late as November, as the government absorbed the implications of implementing Patten's report, written questions about the withdrawal of funding from DubbelJoint were raised in the House of Commons by MP Kevin McNamara, who sought reassurance that neither the 'RUC, the Police Authority nor any other public authority' had intervened in the decision to withdraw funding for the production.[18] The government response iterated the official line, namely that the Arts Council had determined that the script fell 'below the threshold of artistic acceptability', and it denied that the ACNI officials had engaged in any correspondence with the RUC, or any other relevant public bodies, in coming to their decision. What is clear is that the play's subject matter could not have been more contentious in that moment, or its trenchant ideological

Figure 14. Forced Upon Us by Brenda Murphy and Christine Poland, DubbelJoint Theatre, Belfast, 1999, directed by Pam Brighton.

bias more unwelcome to the state authorities. The problem with *Forced Upon Us* was not that it was a bad play (a matter of judgment) but that it was the wrong kind of play (a matter of politics).

Forced Upon Us was JustUs's last production. The controversy over the script overshadowed and drew attention away from the wider significance of the work, namely that this was a theatre created by women, and offering women's perspective from within a traditionally patriarchal community. Pam Brighton argued that, far from being an assault on the Peace Process, plays such as *Forced Upon Us* facilitated reconciliation by allowing the community to articulate its own history on its own terms: 'It is crucial that this history is looked at squarely. You've got to have an analysis into why and how this state began, because the only way you can understand why people are who they are is by understanding what they've experienced. There is a genuine desire for peace here.' In the coming years plays would be written which were less obviously controversial, and which offered, without compromising historical commitment, a more nuanced and open analysis of the political situation of Republicanism.

'All Arts is Politics, and Especially Drama'

In 1994, while *The Government Inspector* was playing at Amharclann na Carraige, Pam Brighton was invited out for lunch by Gerry Adams, the Sinn Féin president:

> This was before the Good Friday Agreement, and he said 'I want to put no pressure on you at all, it is entirely your decision, but I think that what you have started here in the community is fantastic, and the only thing I ask is if you see any way of involving ex-prisoners? Because I think there are some ex prisoners who should be involved in it, as writers and so on.'[19]

In the following decade DubbelJoint would draw many former POWs into its creative orbit, although not because Brighton acted directly on Adams' suggestion, but rather she says because, 'the ex-prisoners are probably the most creative, confident part of the community in a way, people who would get involved in something like this'. A good example of this was the 2006 production of Laurence McKeown's *The Official Version*. In addition to the playwright, two of the four actors, Gerry Doherty and Rosena Brown, were former POWs, as was designer Danny Devenny and stage-manager Gary Kearney. As a consequence, although the company cannot afford to maintain an ensemble, it can draw on a talented production team which has evolved organically and is deeply committed to the theatre's role. In this sense, DubbelJoint manifests Eoghan MacCormaic's vision of a professional theatre that could draw amateur and local performers into a shared cultural and political project. Jake Jackson, a former writer for the company:

> To me at a personal level, all art is politics, and especially drama. If you go back to the great plays of Aristophanes in the 420s in Greece, where the heart of drama was to engage with the big ideas and the political discourse of the day. When Aristophanes put on a play, he was satirizing Aristotle and the ideas of Aristotle. I think that's the kind of work DubbelJoint is in.[20]

A Writing Partnership

In 1999 Brian Campbell and Laurence McKeown approached Pam Brighton seeking her professional advice on a film script they were developing. Based on their experiences in the H-Blocks, *H3* uses fictional characters to retell the story of the hunger strike from the prisoners' perspective. Brighton was already an admirer of the two writers' poetry and prose, having read editions of *An Glor Gafa* during research for a proposed BBC Ulster programme on Republican prisoner writing, and she immediately agreed to look over the script and offer advice. The meeting was to provide DubbelJoint with a seminal work, and launch the playwrighting careers of the two writers. Brighton:

> At the time we wanted to do a play about Des Wilson ... this had been on the cards for about two years. It had taken me ages just to persuade Des to let me do it, and the two writers who were meant to do it fell through. I had already programmed the production, so the problem had to be solved. I was talking to my son and asking who could write this play, and he said, 'Brian Campbell could write it'.

The outcome was *Des*, first performed on 29 March 2000 at the Amharclann na Carraige. The production was directed by Pam Brighton and starred Jim Doran as the eponymous 'hero'. The writing posed Brian Campbell with two problems. The first was that of creating a play about a person who was still very much alive, and who was a legendary and popular figure throughout the Republican community. The second challenge was formal: how to compress a life that had spanned 75 years, including a central role in one of the most complex political events in the twentieth century, into a short drama. Fr Wilson was a man who had not only written a great deal himself, but about whom a great deal had also been written. Campbell's play would draw on these writings, which included Joseph Sheehy's biography of the West Belfast radical.[21]

The working relationship Brighton and Campbell established at the beginning has characterized Brighton's career. Brian Campbell and Laurence McKeown would join Marie Jones and Gary Mitchell in a growing list of Irish writers whose scripts were developed through an open and critical creative dialogue in and out of the rehearsal room. She is, in this sense, closer to Joan Littlewood in her methods than any contemporary. When Campbell began work on the script, his instinct was to portray the epic quality of Fr Wilson's life through the deployment of a large cast of some forty characters. When he showed his outline to Brighton, she suggested that he have just one character, Des, who would play all the roles. Campbell remembered the moment: 'I couldn't see how it'd work. She just said, "write". Then she demanded a change of tense, bringing the narrative into the present and the play burst into life.' It would take four drafts before Campbell was able to hand the script to a performer. He reflects: 'I always write crap first drafts; for me writing is rewriting'.[22] When he heard actor Jim Doran's first read through, he decided to rewrite the second half, and the rewriting continued during the month-long rehearsal process. It was a testing experience for a new playwright, but Campbell's experience in the H-Blocks had left him with a healthy and productive attitude to criticism, indeed he thought writers should 'hunt it out', in order to test their ideas. He advised young writers to 'get your work to practitioners in the field for advice. Indeed, get your work out there full stop.'[23]

Playing *Des*

Campbell created a dramatic monologue, which told the story of Fr Wilson's life up to the critical point in 1975 when he resigned his curacy, and became the 'People's Priest'. *Des* is a skilful piece of dramatic compression, peopled with characters from the curate's early years in Ballymurphy, and it was performed with great technical facility by Jim Doran, a professional actor who had performed in *Binlids*, and was another member of the company's virtual ensemble. Like many monologues it inevitably sits heavy on the page, and it is only in performance that the careful construction, the shifts in emotional register, and the physical actions become palpable. Doran's charismatic priest is also an actor, a ventriloquist who conjures figures from the past and makes them present, who reinserts himself and others into a shared history. It was a virtuoso performance, and, as with all fine acting, was achieved with what Dario Fo, the great master of this form has called *supplesse*, a state of intense relaxation; the epic actor is first and foremost a story-teller. The early scenes of the play trace Fr Wilson's arrival at his new parish, a revelatory education in the fact of poverty, domestic violence, loan sharks, internalized violence and systemic state oppression, and a reminder that the Troubles arose in a context of great deprivation which they effectively disguised. Against the spiritual resignation and endurance of the laity, Campbell counterpoises the duplicities of the senior clergy, their complicity in oppression, their uncritical support for the state and its repressions, and their attempts to undermine any and all signs of popular organization and resistance. Against the hierarchy's conservatism we witness the evolution of an Irish liberation theology defined by praxis, the practical work to create education and work. In one scene we see the young Fr Wilson divest himself of his soutane in a (presumably deliberate) echo of Torres's famous remark, cited above, namely, that 'I took off my cassock to be more truly a priest'.[24]

The production utilized a single, simple set. A large and squat wooden cross dominated the stage, and was set on a plinth which rose through two levels. The back drop was sacral red, the floor a cardinal purple. Against this dominant symbolism was the priest, dressed simply in black. The play is about the meaning of the cross and the role of the Church in history. The great historical and public moments of the early Troubles are domesticated, brought into focus through the response of an individual. We witness Fr Wilson's deeply emotional response to the news of the death of Fr Hugh Mullan, who was shot by soldiers as he ministered to a dying resident during an army assault on Springhill Park on 9 August 1971. We observe his deep public anger at the violence visited on the community: 'I have seen enough to make me angry for a lifetime. And sad and weary for another lifetime.'[25] Both public analysis and private reflections are found in Fr Wilson's writings, and the play rubs them up against each other. Brighton's insistence that the text be written in the present tense was, as Campbell notes, the key that unlocked its energies. It also helped to focus its central dramatic and political purpose, for *Des* is above all a play about the process of conscientization. What we witness is the reflexive and painful coming-into-being of a radical view of the world, a view which was not achieved through intellectual conversion, but through praxis, that process of reflection-action-reflection which Laurence McKeown has argued is the basis of a radical politics. The play dramatizes, and this is the considerable achievement of both text and production, the life-process by which Fr Desmond Wilson, theologian and spiritual advisor of Maynooth, became Des, the priest of the poor and embodiment of radical hope. The focus on an activist epistemology is powerfully expressed through the play's treatment of Des's theological justification of armed resistance, a theological position which is born out of engagement with the realities of his people's suffering. At one point Des leaves a local defence meeting organized in response to recent attacks by B-Specials and Loyalist paramilitaries at which a call had been made to arm the people.

> DES: I walk out of the estate and down the Whiterock Road back to the parochial house. Burned-out shells of cars and lorries are everywhere. Occasionally a car will pick its way up the road and every time one passes I find myself on my guard. Two Protestant men were shot last night in North Belfast; a Catholic man two nights before that. Today there was rioting which ended in an exchange of gunfire not half a mile from here. We have come to this, and it is not the fault of the ordinary people. It goes against all I stand for, but who am I to tell the people not to get guns to defend their areas?

When Bishop Philbin issues a pastoral letter, one of many, condemning IRA violence but not the violence of the British Army, Wilson visits a conservative and respected theological mentor for advice. The theologian tells him that the only condition for a 'just war' which the IRA have not satisfied is that which says that there must be a chance of success. Otherwise, he continues, 'I believe that, given the conditions in these last five years, they have just cause, that it is a last resort, and so on'. It is clear that *Des*, a play written by an ex-IRA volunteer about a priest who believed armed resistance was theologically justified is, beyond its other merits, a central text in the construction of a Republican historiography.

The play was well received within the Republican constituency, but received no reviews in the mainstream press. In a letter to the author, Des Wilson distinguished between its effects on younger and older witnesses: 'It brought back memories which we have quietly set aside to some obscure part of our heads ... for the young ones these things are a look at a history which they do not know much about, but for us older ones it means the retrieval of painful memories.' Having his life placed on stage had been a powerful but sometimes difficult experience, he told me, noting, 'I found it hard to look at the Des play, naturally, enough', and then, with typical humour, 'Although I did see it three times!'[26] One of the most perceptive and interesting reviews of the production came from academic Dr Anthony McIntyre, himself a former IRA volunteer and survivor of the 1981 hunger strikes. In an obituary for Brian Campbell, who would die from a heart attack in 2005 at the age of forty-five, McIntyre wrote:

> I attended a showing of his first play *Des* about one of the few great Irish priests, Des Wilson. Although it was favourably reviewed, I came away thinking that the Des I knew was a much more laid-back personality than the passion driven character that Brian had produced. I felt that he had taken his own passion and put it into the character he had created. There was so much energy in the play that at times I was left pondering if I was watching Brian or Des ...[27]

Was the energy in the text, in the production, or in the performance? It was in all three. Campbell's *Des* is a man who feels and expresses great anger and emotion. It is a bravura performance of the text, but does it matter if it is not an accurate performance of the man? No, it does not. On the contrary Campbell's interpretation offers a useful distancing mechanism. These are Des's actions and ideas, but they are sufficiently removed from the reality of the man to allow for contemplation and judgment. In the following five years, before his sudden death in 2005, Campbell would author, or co-author with Laurence McKeown, a sequence of important plays which reflected the challenges and crises of the Long Peace.

The plays of Laurence McKeown and Brian Campbell

Following the success of *Des*, and with the twentieth anniversary of the hunger strikes due in 2001, Pam Brighton approached Brian Campbell and Laurence McKeown to ask if they wanted to contribute a play for the commemorations. Despite being intensely busy with the *H3* film, they co-wrote the musical, *Laughter of our Children*, which explores the impact of the hunger strikes on a small rural community. The title was taken from Sands' famous comment that, 'Our revenge shall be the laughter of our children'. The production programme offers a summary of the play's plot:

> The play is set in a small village in the North of Ireland in 1981, where Mary and George try to come to terms with their son Peadar's decision to volunteer for the hunger strike. The local schoolteacher decides to take a lead role in organizing a local campaign. Two old school friends of Peadar, now at Queen's University, must try to come to terms with where they stand. Myles, the GAA coach, wants to keep his head down and ignore the situation and Father Boyle, the local priest, struggles to control his parishioners.[1]

Laughter of our Children is a musical, although of a very particular kind. Brighton says of it: 'It is an incredibly sad play, but as it explores the deaths of the ten men it also deals with the optimism that they bequeathed'. The performers included Jim Doran and Brendan 'Bik' McFarlane, an accomplished musician and songwriter, who had been the officer commanding the H-Blocks during the 1981 hunger strike. It was McFarlane's smuggled communications to Gerry Adams which formed the basis for the most visceral and vivid of the histories of the crisis.[2] Another talented Republican performer, Terry 'Cruncher' O'Neill, who would later star in the Brian Moore musical trilogy at Amharclann na Carraige, performed the songs with McFarlane. The rural community is used as a microcosm of the larger society, and autobiographical material is woven into a public story set in 1981. A student, Liam, is moved by the hunger strikes to join the IRA, and this had been Campbell's path. He had been an engineering student in

Liverpool in 1981, and had joined the IRA on his return to Ireland before being arrested for possessing explosive in 1986. In another important autobiographical reference, Peadar's father is absolutely opposed to his son joining the hunger strike, just as McKeown's own father had been. In reflecting on his experience, McKeown writes movingly of rare visits by his father, who never accepted his son's Republicanism, and whose ambitions centred on seeing Laurence getting a 'respectable job' and settling down. Of his mother he notes that 'she was the one most in contact with me ... she was not a Republican and I wondered how she now felt being to the fore in this form of Republican struggle.'[3] In the fictional world of this play the hunger strike also impacts on everyone, from the local teacher, who comes into conflict with the authorities for supporting the H-Block campaign, to the parish priest who, following Catholic Church policy, attempts to undermine his parishioners' support for the ten men. For actor Terry O'Neill the play succeeded in placing the 'sacrifice and commitment of the hunger strikers into a very positive context'.[4] *Laughter of our Children* opened at Amharclann na Carraige on 2 May 2001, directed by Pam Brighton, assisted by Terry O'Neill. The play's production was part of a wider and conflicted debate within Republicanism about the political and cultural legacy of the hunger strikes. For Sinn Féin the hunger strikes were part of the Long War, and the ten men's sacrifices had helped to create the conditions for the move to a purely political and democratic engagement. For dissident Republicans, most notably Sands' sister, Bernadette Sands McKevitt, the political process was a betrayal of that sacrifice, and of the many sacrifices made for a united Ireland. The issue of why the hunger strikers died, then, has become central to Republican self-conception, and Laurence McKeown would return to it in his 2006 play *The Official Version*.

'To the Heart of our Difficulties'

In a review of the DubbelJoint production of Brian Campbell and Laurence McKeown's *The Cold House*, *Irish Times* critic Roy Garland noted: 'In our communities we are not dealing with forces fairly remote from our existence – like the IRA or the British Army – but rather with neighbours estranged by generations of mistrust and pain who now have got to make space for each other. The play illustrated how painful this can be.'[5] First performed at Amharclann na Carraige on 3 June 2003, directed by Pam Brighton, and featuring actors William Hoyland, Susie Kelly and Vincent Higgins, *The Cold House* was described by Brighton as 'a very important play, possibly the most important DubbelJoint has ever done'.[6] It was also she says the 'least popular'. This had nothing to do with its quality, but with the decision by the authors to present a human, rational and complex picture of the 'old enemy', the Royal Ulster Constabulary. It is a play which faces hard questions about the possibilities for reconciliation in a post-Troubles Ireland.

In a press release the company writes:

> *A Cold House* is about what happens when war ends and people are
> forced to drop the convenient stereotypes that conflict fosters and
> recognize a more complex humanity in each other. Whatever name
> one gives the other, terrorist or state terrorist, each is compelled to
> recognize the human across the kitchen table and see themselves in
> the other's eyes. Each character must confront their actions, or even,
> in Helen's case, her lack of action in accepting the status quo.[7]

The drama takes place in the home of ex-RUC Special Branch detective David
and his wife, Helen. When their old boiler breaks down one midwinter, a
plumber arrives from Henderson's, an established Protestant firm. His name
is Peter. Peter had been a member of the IRA, and spent 15 years in Long
Kesh, and, released under the Good Friday Agreement, has taken a job under
the nominally non-sectarian firm. He has come to a house which is both
literally and also metaphorically cold. In Belfast argot 'a cold house' denotes
any unwelcoming situation. In the opening scene we learn that David and
Helen are conflicted about their immediate future. Helen, a teacher, wants
to stay in Ulster, whilst David, still concerned about his safety, and angered
by the ramifications of the Good Friday Agreement, wants to sell up and
move to Yorkshire to be near their daughter and grandchildren. Helen sees
David's desire to move as an evasion, a refusal to accommodate the new
political realities. When Peter arrives to attend to the boiler, Helen leaves to
go shopping. Peter works on the boiler while David sits at the table, doing a
crossword. The two men discuss the cold, the firm, and the possibilities for
the boiler. Their innocuous sounding conversation is, on closer inspection,
defined by evasions, by a learnt and reflexive refusal to let the other, in the
words of another stock saying, 'know which foot you kick with'. Where did
Peter train, David enquires:

> DAVID: Round here?
> PETER: Aye, well, near here.
> DAVID: And then what?
> PETER: Aye, this and that. I've tried my hand at most things.
> DAVID: And have you always worked around here?
> PETER: No, I was away for a while.
> DAVID: Right. Where at?[8]

Peter had been in London for fifteen years he says, but he could not stay
away any more: 'You grow up somewhere, it's more than just a place, it's
everything about it, the people, the land, you know what I mean.' Even so,
he commiserates with David about his planned move to England, as change
is always difficult. Both men share a love of children, and of football. When

Figure 15. A Cold House by Brian Campbell and Laurence McKeown,
DubbelJoint Theatre, Belfast, 2003, directed by Pam Brighton.

Peter tells David that his four-year-old boy is called Pearse, the former RUC
man's suspicions are confirmed. Why would a man in his mid-forties have
such a young child unless he had been locked away? When Peter goes to
collect a screwdriver from his van, David rings his former colleagues in the
RUC. He is urgent:

> DAVID: Listen John, the guy is in my house ... I just need a favour. I
>   need to know if he is who I think he is. (*pause*) He's in my
>   fucking house. Right now ... All I need to know whether he
>   is who I think he is, and whether he is still a player.

As he talks on the telephone, he removes a gun from a cupboard. He puts
the phone down and hides the gun behind a box of cereal on the counter.
Peter returns with his screwdriver. He is affable and chatty. The phone rings
and David talks briefly and then rings off. He is trying to hurry Peter out
of the house when Helen returns. David angrily demands that Peter patch
up the boiler and leave, but Helen insists that he stays and does it properly.
As she goes to put away her shopping, the gun falls from the counter to the
floor. David moves to pick it up. Questioned by Helen, he reveals that Peter
is an IRA member, jailed for 15 years for the murder of their close friend,
a young RUC man called Stanley Moore. In a long speech, Helen describes

the death and its terrible impact on his young family. She asks Peter if he is sorry for his action. He replies: 'I'm sorry it had to happen.' Later he will tell David: 'I'm not justifying anything. I don't have to justify anything.' Helen's demand that he repent is a trope, as is his attempt to get her to realize that the death was part of a broader historical conflict which, while a personal tragedy for so many, had been objectively necessary. Later he will offer a more detailed context for his actions:

> PETER: It's not about seeking forgiveness, Helen. (*pause*) Maybe I'd
>   ask her to try and understand where I was coming from, why
>   I did what I did. That it wasn't personal against her – against
>   Jane Moore – or her husband or what religion they were or
>   anything like that. It was just simply that he was on one side
>   in a war and I was on the other. He did what he felt was
>   right and so did I.

At one point Helen asks why he had made choices which had led to prison, and which had 'ruined your life'. Peter's reply would also be McKeown and Campbell's: 'Well, I wouldn't say ruined my life. Changed it.' While Helen invites reflection and presses for a human closure, David and Peter hurl competing versions of history at each other. The IRA was to blame for stirring up Nationalist unrest. On the contrary Peter argues, the IRA did not produce the Troubles, the Troubles produced the IRA. The dramatic image is a potent one: a Unionist holds a Republican at gunpoint while he accuses him of being a 'terrorist in my home'. Later David will make this explicit, implying that Catholics had no place in Ulster. The play's dramatic and intellectual force (and it is a play about ideas) works by interweaving David's and Peter's competing interpretations of history with Helen's pragmatic demand for explanation and expiation. David reflects mainstream Unionism's perception of the new realities. Accused of complicity, he tells Peter that his best friend in the RUC had been a Catholic called Noel, who was blown up by an IRA landmine in Crossmaglen. He was, he tells him, 'As much an Irishman as you are'. Not all RUC men were sectarians, he tells the plumber. Indeed many had joined because they wanted to be good policemen and civic servants. The set-piece debates between the two men which are the play's dramatic fulcrum allow each to rehearse the grievances and pain of their separate communities. Between them they rehearse the great narratives of the Troubles, and of the irreconcilable views of Irish history which have defined their life choices. It is Helen who breaks the circle: who pleads for her husband to (actually and symbolically) lock the gun away, and who, in an action whose very homeliness becomes, paradoxically, an historic disruption, makes tea and sits them down together. The talk turns to cake. They break, if not bread, then cake together. It is a temporary reprieve, a peace hollowed out of memory and a circular justification. Peter goes, leaving the two (the Unionist Family) to resolve how to respond to him. David repeats his lament about 'terrorists in government'. For Helen, it is not an issue of revenge but of somehow finding the courage, and the hope, necessary to engage. She accuses David of running away from the challenge of creating peace, a charge he denies. There is no resolution. The play's tensions cannot be resolved in the aesthetic space; the challenges it poses are posed to the space of politics.

Although the production was favourably reviewed by *An Phoblacht/ Republican News* and *Andersontown News*, Brighton told me that many in the community were deeply angry about the fact that the two writers had interviewed ex-RUC officers, and had given the enemy such powerful arguments on stage. Yet Campbell and McKeown knew that dialogue has to happen if the society is to move forward. When Peter says to Helen of Jane Moore's suffering that many have suffered on both sides, but that 'there comes a time when it is more damaging to stay in the past', he is addressing the Republican constituency. Garland, whom I cited earlier, and who had criticized earlier DubbelJoint plays for reinforcing 'communal myths', felt that *A Cold House* had done what 'a play should do – stimulate thought and hopefully move us to action'.[9] He continues, 'the dialogue was deeply moving and most of those listening found the experience deeply moving. In this situation there can be no cheap grace and no easy reconciliation.' Referring to Helen's offer of a cup of tea, he comments: 'As one friend put it, we need to do unexpected things because it is only the unexpected that breaks the logjam'. Co-author Laurence McKeown told *An Phoblacht/ Republican News*: 'It is a play which asks the hard questions and confronts its characters with the uncomfortable truths that must be faced if people are to go forward in a society living with conflict. It is a deeply human drama which tears apart any cosy notions of what conflict resolution and reconciliation mean.'[10] A review on BBC Ulster's Arts Extra called the production 'an amazing experience ... compelling from start to finish ... one of the most important plays to come out of the north of Ireland.'[11] Seth Linder in the *Irish News* commended an 'excellent cast', and congratulated the writers for the play's 'authenticity', and its refusal 'to go down the easy path'.[12] It is a text that met Tom Magill's call for dramas which were more critically reflexive, and which faced up to the complex problems posed by the peace. So also did Brian Campbell's next play, *Voyage of No Return*.

Voyage of No Return

The flag of the Caribbean island of Montserrat has a blue background and a small Union Jack in the top left-hand corner. On the right is an image of Erin, female symbol of Irish freedom, who has long fair hair and holds a golden harp. The emblem of Montserrat is the shamrock, and her national holiday is St Patrick's Day. Until 1900 Irish was the first language of the island. Montserrat's first settlers were Irish, deported to the Caribbean as slaves, 50,000 of them, in a cruel footnote to Cromwell's subjugation of the recalcitrant colony in the years from 1649 to 1652. Exiled by colonizers, the Irish settled in Montserrat and were closely followed by African slaves. The enslaved Irish became themselves overseers of the black slaves, a mistrusted intermediary between English and African. The Seven Years War with France and the Jacobin rebellions which followed in England and Ireland rendered them, as ever, potential subversives. However, it was the black slaves who, on St Patrick's Day in 1768, rose in rebellion. The rebellion was betrayed, and then savagely put down by the English garrison with help from Irish planters and their overseers. Nine of the insurgents were hanged in public executions. Montserratians are the descendants of this enforced collision between Ireland and Africa, white slave and black slave. Each year on St Patrick's Day the two histories are remembered:

> The result is a Caribbean amalgam of colonial culture and African pride – a week long fete with islanders dancing Irish jigs one night, then mocking their one-time masters the next by cracking whips and masquerading in tall hats like bishops' mitres. 'We are celebrating the rise of the African freedom fighters', said historian Howard Fergus.[13]

The history of Montserrat was one axis of the new play. The other was provided by contemporary events. Throughout early 2004 newspapers in Belfast were dominated by stories of racist attacks on ethnic minorities. On 10 January 2004 the *Guardian's* Angelique Chrisafis reported:

> Northern Ireland, which is 99% white, is fast becoming the race-hate capital of Europe. It holds the UK's record for the highest rate of racist attacks: spitting and stoning in the street, human excrement on doorsteps, swastikas on walls, pipe bombs, arson, the ransacking of houses with baseball bats and crow bars, and white supremacist leaflets nailed to front doors. So-called peace walls between Protestant and Catholic communities are graffitied with swastikas and signs that read 'keep the streets white'. Both local Unionists and Sinn Féin warned this week that someone is likely to be killed or burned alive in their home if the campaign does not stop. But there are no signs of it abating.[14]

Brian Campbell's *Voyage of No Return* takes these two historical junctures as the starting point for a play which explores issues of racism and identity, and questions the simplistic binaries of colonizer/colonized, oppressed/oppressor which have defined Republican history. The past is brought into sharp focus and placed against the present as a warning and a challenge. Campbell's play is set on Montserrat, and interleaves past and present through two narratives. Narrative one tells the story of tourism consultant Gerard, a young, aspirational, working-class Catholic who is visiting Montserrat. There he meets and falls in love with Clarissa Sweeney, a black woman, and a primary school teacher. He tells her he is a 'taig with attitude', a member of a generation who have faced down history, and won. His vision is simplistic. He persuades Clarissa to come and live in Belfast, to be at the centre of the world, which means for Gerard the cosmopolitan centres of the West and America. Instead she finds herself at the social margins of a society struggling to find its identity. She faces racist abuse from the Irish, and is lonely. When the island's volcano erupts in 1997 they return to Montserrat, where she finds that her community has been devastated. Gerard mortgages their lives in a deal with American investors in order to create a new eco-tourist industry on the island. Global warming will bring more eruptions, tsunamis, and hurricanes: tragedy will become the new spectator sport as American tourists, encased in bullet proof glass, watch natural disasters from safety. She cannot accept his vision and leaves him.

Counterpoised with this story is a narrative set on the eve of the 1768 rebellion, and which concerns the relationship between Irishman Aloysius Daly, indentured servant, now overseer, and Bridget, a slave who keep his home, and is kept in a condition of sexual slavery. Aloysius wants to borrow money to buy a plantation. Like Gerard he has energy, and works hard. He senses the incipient rebellion, and tries to force Bridget to tell him what is happening. She refuses. He warns her that the planters will torture her for information, and they will accuse him of collusion. If she betrays her people they will both be safe:

> DALY: You can come home to Ireland with me. You'll be my woman
>   in Ireland. What do ya think of that? It's like nowhere else
>   on earth, Bridget. Outside our cottage on a summer's day
>   and the hawthorn white in the hedges and the birds singin'.
>   Would ya like that? Would ya?

She will not betray the plot, and he flogs her into unconsciousness. When the rebellion fails he taunts her:

> DALY: What were you expectin'? That the black man could rise
>   up and the Irishman would be beside him? I heard of it
>   happenin' but those days are long gone. We're not among the
>   slaves now, Bridget. We've learned to be cute.

Being cute requires the erasure if history. Gerard also wants to escape responsibility and 'getting rich' is also an act, the play implies, of self imposed exile, a corruption of the ethics of the *meitheal*, an abandonment of family, place and class. Gerard will be the midwife of a new wave of economic colonisation.

The authenticity of Daly's speech patterns derived from Campbell's discussions with Queen's University's Jonathan Skinner, an anthropologist whose research into Montserrat's Black Irish people was an important source for the play. Skinner: 'I provided the playwright with background information on the geography, characteristics and traditions of the Irish descendants on the island. Also, during the readings, I advised the company and cast on the dialect and expressions of the islanders.'[15] The authenticity heightens the play's focus on the historical continuities of racial and ethnic oppression which is the play's core dramatic theme. The dramatic structure is precise and economical, and is organised to force the historical comparison. The play deconstructs the monolithic myth of the Irish-as-historical-oppressed or liberator. Daly is a classic example of Fanon's *pied noir*, oppression's middleman, whose introjected violence is visited on those weaker than him. Despised and rejected by the English, 'treated like shit', he has, through his own prodigious efforts, bought two estates. His interests and values have changed because his material standing has changed. In a powerful speech Bridget reminds him of his own people's suffering:

> BRIDGET: You don tell me stories. You don told me about the ships
> were bring ya here. You remember? You come in a slave ship
> what bring the slaves from Africa. Same ship. You told me
> these stories about what it was like. Your friend don die on
> that ship. Your friend don die in your arms. You tell me this.
> They beat you. Many were sick. Many don die. 'We were the
> white niggers, no better'. You say. White niggers … White
> niggers … White niggers.

Her call is for an historically aware solidarity, a plea for a common humanity which transcends colour, gender, nationality. Her words are echoed and ironised in Gerard's description of himself as a 'taig with attitude'. Clarissa could, with little change, make Bridget's speech to Gerard. Daly wonders in 1768 at how his neighbours in Ireland would respond if he returned with a black woman, and so too, in 1997, does Gerard. Racism in Belfast made Clarissa wish she could be invisible. She tells of being accosted by youths who spat on her and told her 'go home monkey woman', a term Daly will use to describe Bridget. Gerard's response is an evasion: 'I can't stop people shouting at you in the street. I can't stop the door being covered in shit. I could go to the cops again. Useless.' He cannot offer what Clarissa needs more than statutes or legal protections – an empathy with her experience, the human solidarity which Bridget had demanded of Daly.

Voyage of No Return was a powerful challenge to its audience's self conception. The Irishman in this history is not a Wolfe Tone or an Emmet.

Aloysius is the Irish man as victim turned oppressor, torturer, rapist, and midwife for England's colonial interests. The Irish language is not the language of the violated, but of the violator. Daly's virtues, not least of which is his prodigious energy and capacity for work, are turned against the enslaved. The gap between Gerard and Daly is not so very great, as both see others as commodities, and their powerlessness as an opportunity for exploitation and self-advancement. Writing about the place of theatre in the post-conflict situation, Laurence McKeown emphasized its role in teaching history: 'Those who aren't aware of history don't know where they are in the present and certainly don't know where they are going in the future'. Those who do not learn from history are condemned to repeat it, and the play's final potent image focuses the theme. On the day of the executions the slaves are forced to go and watch the rebels die. Daly orders Bridget to put his coat on for him. She hesitates:

DALY: Do ya want Paddy Nine Tails to spake to ya?

After a few beats she puts his coat on him.

DALY: Cailin maith. Cailin maith.

He puts on his cocked hat and admires himself. He goes to leave and then stops.

DALY: And here. O'Sullivan was telling' me ya were makin' spells for an end to slavery. Hah! Ya'll be a long time at that game, Bridget. A long time.

It is a hard and uncompromising analysis, and one reinforced in the play's programme, which quotes former slave and abolitionist Frederick Douglass on the treatment meted out by Catholic Irish immigrants to their fellow black workers in New York and Detroit:

Perhaps no class of our fellow citizens has carried this prejudice against color to a point more extreme and dangerous than have our Catholic Irish fellow citizens, and yet no people on the face of the earth have been more relentlessly persecuted and oppressed on account of race and religion than have this same Irish people.[16]

Voyage of No Return was premiered at the Amharclann na Carraige on the 30 July 2004 and was directed by Brighton, with Peter Ballence as Daly, Ide Chiahemen as Bridget, Andy Moore as Gerard and Shereen Patrice as Clarissa. Played in the round, with a simple set decorated with wall banners, the production was commended by *Irish Times* reviewer, Aisling McCrea, who wrote: 'seldom has a play been so perfectly timed as the DubbelJoint production of Brian Campbell's new work *Voyage of No Return*'.[17] Noting that, 'racism is about power, domination, rape, violence, denial of the other's humanity', *An Phoblacht/Republican News* considered both play and production to be 'brilliant' and the best play by Brian Campbell to date.[18] It would also be his last. On 8 October 2005, Campbell died from a suspected heart attack. He was forty-five. It was one mark of his growing status as a writer that, as well as tributes from the Irish media, the former IRA volunteer received obituaries in the *Observer* and *The Times*. It was in the latter that his long time friend, comrade, and writing partner, Laurence McKeown was quoted as saying:

> For Brian there was no distinction between art and politics, each was the other, and his application of both was seamless. For him art existed in the real world. It was all around him. He did not have to invent it or distort reality to create it. 'What is more dramatic than the lives of people in struggle?' he would say …[19]

The Official Version

In 2005, as the twenty-fifth anniversary of the hunger strikes approached, there was talk of reviving *Laughter of our Children* with a group from Donegal, and performing it at the Long Kesh site, but health and safety issues prevented the production from going ahead. In any case, says Pam Brighton, Laurence McKeown was ambivalent about a revival of the play. Instead, they agreed to stage a commemorative evening of rehearsed readings from Sands' writings. Shortly after, McKeown contacted Brighton to say that he had an idea for a new play. The initial draft of what became *The Official Version* was developed through a creative and practical dialogue with director Pam Brighton. She was able to secure funding to workshop McKeown's initial ideas with the actors and production team. The workshops were invaluable for writer and performers, says Brighton:

> The first draft was quite short, and in the workshops we were able to unpick it and develop it. For example, the most underwritten character, and I think she works now, just, is Theresa, the daughter, who we felt was very underwritten … all that stuff about her having some resentment of Gerard and never having told her mum … all that came from the workshops.[20]

McKeown took away the ideas and redrafted the play. Brighton:

> Every draft I would pick over and go through with him. It was a fairly lengthy process, but the jump from the fourth draft to the fifth was astonishing. He had finally got the emotional centre of the play, and

Figure 16. Laurence McKeown and his sister on the opening night of *The Official Version* at Amharclann na Carraige, Belfast, 2006.

so we changed very little when we got to rehearsal. The workshop had been phenomenally useful. One of Laurence's great qualities is the ability to respond to criticism. He has absolutely no ego about that. He is more than happy to rewrite.

Brian Campbell had said that writers must open themselves to critique, and McKeown told *An Phoblacht/Republican News* that as he wrote the new play alone, he could hear 'his friend's gentle criticism and encouragement in his head as he worked on specific scenes'. He regularly attended rehearsals, and would phone Brighton each evening to discuss the progress of the production. He was, she says, 'very engaged'. When I asked him why, given his other commitments, plays were so important to him, McKeown replied: 'Because they are public, they get tested there and then with the community ... and because I enjoy the buzz of the theatre!'[21] *The Official Version* would represent McKeown's third attempt to retell the story of the 1981 hunger strike, and to make sense of its role within Republican history. In the context of the Peace Process, and the growing tensions within Republicanism over the direction Sinn Féin leadership were taking the Movement since 2000, it is also, perhaps, the most important.

Performance

On 19 September 2006 I went to Amharclann na Carraige to see the DubbelJoint production of *The Official Version*. My companion was Joe Reid, and the date marked twenty-one years almost to the day since we had first met at Springhill House and began a relationship which had defined our separate practices. As we walked up the Whiterock Road the walls bore witness to the dangers facing the Republican leadership from within: 'Remember Michael Collins' said one piece of graffiti; 'Not a Bullet' said another, referring to decommissioning. When we entered the lobby of the Amharclann na Carraige to collect our tickets people were milling around, most middle aged like us, but with a sprinkling of young people. We entered the auditorium, which is large, high and rectangular, reflecting its previous life as a college hall. To the left the walls were covered in a series of panels and poster displays on the history of the hunger strikes and of Long Kesh/Maze prison. The production programme provided a space for personal reflection on the meaning of a site which affected the lives directly, or indirectly, of some 200,000 people. Together with grainy photographs of the prison, were pieces by, among others, academic Ms Mick Beyers (Laurence McKeown's partner), singer Frances Black, Ian Milne an ex-prisoner, Brian Campbell's wife Grainne and Mary Nelis of the Bogside, Derry, mother of three prisoners, and a formidable activist and politician. In one article Mike Ritchie, director of the ex-Republican prisoner support network, Coiste na n-Iarchimi, wrote about the proposed museum at the site, and an International Centre for Conflict Transformation which will ensure that 'reflection and education could be associated with the site'.[22] Coiste offer guided tours of the Long Kesh site, another way in which the Republican story is enacted and embedded in the new order. The play takes the idea of such tours as its starting point, except that, in a neat reversal of reality, the tour guide is Robert, an official in the Northern Ireland Office and a former deputy governor at Long Kesh. Robert has agreed to show single mother Julie around the prison site as a favour to a mutual friend. Julie, a mature student, has embarked on research into the conflict. Raised in a Unionist community, it is her interrogation of Robert, and through him of recent Irish history, which provides the intellectual bedrock of the play. Meeting at the same time for the Coiste tour with a guide who, intriguingly, does not arrive, is Annie, 62, mother of a former POW, Gerard, now dead, and her daughter Theresa, an up-and-coming Sinn Féin politician. *The Official Version* is a play concerned with personal memory and historical 'truth', and the complex relationship between them. It is also a drama about revelation, about politics and intimacy, public resistance and private suffering, collective action and personal feeling.

The stage for McKeown's play had been positioned at one end of what is a genuinely 'empty' and flexible performance space. This flexibility was in part the result of a poverty of resources which prevents the company investing in decent seating. The audience occupied plastic chairs which were set in rows. Some rows had tables in front for drinks, and families or groups of friends gathered around them. The set consisted of an imposing white/ grey washed concrete wall which towered above the stage. Grass and weeds hugged its base. It conveyed an air of neglect, and of nature reclaiming and reabsorbing the land on which so many historic events had been enacted, a warning to those watching that the past can be quickly overwhelmed by the force of the present, and its essential lessons lost. Later, a single bed will denote the hospital cell where the hunger strikers died. The two pairs of visitors criss-cross the open stage in the shadow of the prison wall, talking, reflecting and arguing: indeed, thinking and remembering constitute the play's defining actions. Around this simple dramatic rhythm McKeown weaves his arguments.

As the play opens, Annie and Julie enter from opposite sides of the stage. Annie is a warm and open matriarch, whose assumption of a shared community with everyone she meets drives much of the play's humour. She is waiting for her daughter Theresa. Julie is in her thirties. She is intense, smart, polite, intrigued, and is waiting for her guide, Robert. Through their conversation we learn that Annie's son, Gerard, had served nine years in the prison, including the period of the Blanket protest. When Julie commiserates with her, Annie waves her away. Echoing McKeown's non-dramatic writings, she tells Julie that, though difficult, the experiences had been positive too: 'They turned a prison into a home and a community ... It's the place he grew up in. The place he learnt about the world. Where he made great friends. Had happy times.'[23] Now he is dead, killed by a cruel irony not in prison, but in a car accident as he explored Ireland for the first time. Annie is intrigued when Julie says that she also is waiting for someone. The exchange causes knowing laughter:

ANNIE: Someone who's been inside?

Julie gets a little anxious.

JULIE: Ah ... Yes, he spent some time here.
ANNIE: Wonder did he know Gerard?
JULIE: Maybe.
ANNIE: I always like to hear from others who knew him.

They leave, and Robert enters. He is a big man; tall, broad, imposing and smartly dressed. He conveys the impression of being on permanent duty. As we will discover, he too is a man with deep emotional ties, though his are to a different community, and his loyalty is to a different conception of place, state and land. As with David in Campbell and McKeown's *A Cold House*, he views the Unionist state as a given, its hierarchies and punishment systems a bulwark against anarchy and criminality. He is proud of the state's efficiency and durability; it has been tested by the IRA and not found wanting: 'Throughout all the bombings and killings your electricity went on at the flick of a switch, water came out of the taps, the buses and trains continued to run. And, the prisons functioned too of course,' he tells Julie in their first conversation. In Robert's world view IRA men such as Gerard, detached from a validating historical narrative, are simply common thugs and murderers. Like the great walls whose supposed impregnability he will later celebrate in loving detail, Robert's belief system is also rigid. The world contains good and evil, and he is on the side of the dutiful and the good. Yet he also has dreams, and memories of innocence and childhood. Faced with Julie, whose studies have opened up a new perspective on her Protestant heritage, he is nonplussed: 'That's the thing about research,' she tells Robert, 'you don't know where you might end up.' Uncertainty frightens him, and so when Julie tells him she wants to talk to former prisoners he warns her, without a hint of irony, against listening to people who 'are running around these days thinking they know what happened in places like this … when they really don't have a clue'. Subversives subvert truths, and it is better that she listens to him.

They go and Annie and Theresa re-enter. The dramatic movement is circular, in and out of the past. Theresa has been chosen to stand for Sinn Féin in the coming elections, and Annie will be her election agent. History is moving implacably forward. Theresa: 'We all have stories to tell … but things change and move on'. One of the stories they share is the story of the relatives visiting sons, fathers and brothers who stank from sitting in their shit and piss all day, unwashed and naked. In fact Gerard's father had found the visits difficult, as McKeown's father had. He should have come on the Coiste tour with Annie, but he cannot allow himself to do it. Annie sees the prisoner experience differently, feels that it had made her son, or that he had, more accurately, made himself through it. The exchange contains one of the play's pivotal lines. Theresa is challenging her father's understanding of what happened to his son:

> ANNIE: He relives the jail experience more than Gerard ever did. And
>   it's not a good experience. All he can see are the conditions
>   Gerard was in.
> THERESA: But he needs to realize those conditions changed mammy.
>   The prisoners ended up getting what they wanted.
> ANNIE: I know that.
> THERESA: Sorry mammy I know you know but daddy needs to accept
>   that.

There are, as I have noted, many Republicans, including former POWs and leading IRA figures, who do not believe that 'The prisoners ended getting what they wanted', because what they wanted was a British withdrawal, the end of partition, and a united Ireland. This simple exchange is weighted with the authority of McKeown's experience. It is not only 'Daddy' who is being addressed, but the Republican family.

Amidst the intellectual debates and reminiscences *The Official Version* has moments of great comedy, which derive primarily from Annie's initial ignorance about Bobby's relation to the prison. On the first occasion when the paths of the two 'tours' cross, Annie reveals that Theresa is standing for election:

> JULIE: Lovely. And for which party?
>
> ANNIE: Well there's only one party a young woman would want to represent. Sinn Féin of course. (*Turns to Robert*) Changed times Bobby, isn't it? (*Smiles*) Just shows you, what youse did in here created a whole new generation of activists.
>
> (*Robert looks shocked. He looks at Theresa. Julie is aware of the tension. Robert moves away a little.*)
>
> JULIE: That's great. Well, eh ... (*Looks after Robert*) ... I think we're moving on. Need to see a bit more. OK? Maybe catch you later.
>
> ANNIE: OK love. Bye Bobby.

The exchange caused loud laughter on the night I watched the production. Julie and Robert walk off. Their relationship is key to the play's ideological purposes. Long Kesh is at once a symbol of the failure of Partition and of the power, legitimacy and longevity of the Republican vision of a united Ireland. Annie assumes Robert shares that vision, because History has tested it and judged it to be correct. For Annie the future of Ireland and Sinn Féin policy are now coterminous: 'There's only one party a young girl would want to represent'. McKeown's view is more complex. He and Campbell faced sharp criticism from the Republican community for their determination to recognize the complexity of Loyalist experience, including the trauma and suffering caused by IRA actions. In *A Cold House* Unionism and Republicanism confronted each other directly through David and Peter: the historical conflict was played out as a verbal duel. In *The Official Version* the conservative and radical wings of unionism, represented by Robert and Julie, are engaged in an internal debate. Naturally it is McKeown's version of both perspectives that we get, but the dramatic device is critical to our reception of the piece, and to its symbolism. The lesson Julie has taken from her research into Irish history is that Long Kesh is a symbol of failure: that you cannot use the penal system to solve a political crisis. Hers is McKeown's voice, and he would later say that he related most strongly to her. And indeed, this is the great technical problem at the play's heart;

for it is only through a performance of intense emotional commitment (paradoxically) that actress Maria Connolly prevents Julie's relentlessly radical intellectual analysis from becoming unbelievable.

> JULIE: This was never a normal prison. Anyone with half a brain can see that. And once you start to deny that you get into all sorts of silly and ludicrous arguments that just don't stand up to scrutiny. I've no political axe to grind. I've never met any of these prisoners but I hope to. And I know I'll find them articulate, they'll be able to explain totally their rationale for everything they did. I don't have to agree with their politics or reasons for doing what they did but I do have to accept their version is true to them and makes total sense to them and their community.
>
> ROBERT: I thought you were studying history, not teaching it.
>
> JULIE: I'm saying I'm no expert on Irish history but even from the little I've learned you just wonder does no one ever learn from history? Like, who drew up these policies? Who thought it a good idea to open this prison as an internment camp? Who thought internment a good way to deal with political issues? I mean, Britain in the 1970s interning its own citizens without trial for anything up to four years! That was only supposed to happen behind the Iron Curtain. In Russia or China. That's what I was always told. But not here, not on the edge of Western Europe in a supposed democracy. And thankfully someone decided to end internment, must have seen it was making a bad situation worse, but then what? Someone else designs these H-Blocks and we're back worse than ever.

This tension between character and analysis, which is brought off just, and would in the hands of a less experienced performer not work, is necessary to McKeown's political aims. Julie is less a character than a dramatic device to allow McKeown to do on stage what it would be difficult to do in life, to debate history with a real life Robert. Julie's is the Unionist voice which Republicans could engage with, the voice that Republicans need Unionism and Loyalism to hear. Making the link with other struggles she asks rhetorically:

> JULIE: Who decided that from March 1 1976 political prisoners would suddenly become criminals? Or turn it the other way round. Take it away out of this country. At what point did Nelson Mandela become a political prisoner? On what day in prison did he stop being a criminal and terrorist and from

then on become a political prisoner? He spent his early years breaking rocks in a quarry, his last years being visited by Presidents and financial leaders. Was that because the man changed? His beliefs were as strong the day he walked out of prison as they were when he went in. What changed was the political situation in his country.

The insistent point is that these were not normal prisoners and this was not a normal prison because this was not a normal state. The hunger strike was another of the many potent confluences, like the Easter Rising, which had defined that history. Her argument is not that Robert has to *accept* what was done, but that he needs to understand *why* it was done. The hunger strike, she tells him as they stand in the prison hospital, changed Irish history and it changed Robert's history, and the history of Unionism and Loyalism, and it needed to be understood and absorbed in its all its historical complexity, and not simply dismissed as a criminal aberration.

While, perhaps paradoxically, the Unionists debate public history, the Republican visitors, who have absorbed that history into a political purpose, address the personal traumas of the hunger strikes. For Annie and Theresa the visit is a process of revelation and discovery, addressed to the issue of the war's consequences for intimacy and for personal relations. They talk about the 'coms' and equipment that were smuggled in and out of the H-Blocks in mouths and vaginas:

ANNIE: There must have been millions of those wee notes went back and forth but the only ones you hear of are about the protest and the politics. The everyday lives of people behind them are missing.

THERESA: I suppose all our lives took second place then. There was always something more urgent to be done. Something against which to measure our own needs.

ANNIE: Walls and barbed wire and searches ... Still the wee notes went in and out. And then the wee radios they had smuggled in. Well, actually they weren't so wee. Did you ever see the size of them?

We discover that Theresa had lost her maidenhead through secreting a radio in her vagina. This is felt as another violation, chosen but unnatural: one of the many psychophysical scars left by the war. This revelation leads to others, such as her jealousy of the attention Gerard received, her sense of anger at the IRA failure to capitalize on the hunger strike to drive the British out, and how this disillusionment led her to leave home. Later Annie will apologize for all the times that activism took her away from Theresa, and Theresa in turn will reveal that she and Gerard were eventually reconciled, though Annie never knew this. The war had created a paradox, an intense sense of communal purpose which had overlaid and damaged personal relations. Repression of emotion is a survival reflex, but it comes with a heavy price. Bernadette Devlin McAliskey:

> Thirty years we stood at gravesides with our chins up and our backs straight. Men, women and children, holding the line in a public display of strength that masked pain. And it has always struck me as we went through those years that that is part of how we survived, that is part of how the community survived with the press watching us, with the police surrounding us, having to go through military roadblocks to get to funerals. We all toed the line and although every heart in the cemetery might have been breaking, there scarcely was a sob ever heard. Now that the war is over, won or lost or in transition, at least now that that period is over, there is a sense of the depth of that pain that still has to find some form of expression, and that is only at a communal level.[24]

In one compelling image they circle the simple iron bedstead on which a hunger striker had died. There is a single dead lily on it, which Annie picks up and then lets fall gently. It is here, as they sit on the bed, that she reveals to Theresa that Gerard had signed up for the hunger strike, but that Annie had prayed for him not to be picked. Gerard had belonged to two families, his own and the Movement, and sometimes the needs of the two had conflicted. Annie, like many mothers, had been drawn into the struggle through her children, even at the point that they lost them to the prisons. The moment is the play's emotional core, the counterpoint to its intellectual debates.

> ANNIE: It's a sacred place.
> THERESA: Don't let the Unionists hear that. They say that's the only reason we want to preserve the prison – to turn it into a shrine to the hunger strikers.
> ANNIE: There's a difference between a shrine and a holy place.
>
> *Theresa turns to Annie.*
>
> ANNIE: Places where you feel something significant occurred. Not thoughts about the place and what happened and how, but … the feelings you get. (*Annie looks around*) And it's always a peaceful feeling. It's as if you want to speak in whispers, not make noise, walk softly. (*Pause*) It's where the human spirit rose above physical conditions. It's free. And has left its imprint on the walls, more lasting than the paint or plaster.

Figure 17. The Official Version, DubbelJoint Theatre, Belfast, 2006, directed by Pam Brighton.

A little later they will laugh about a memory of Gerard and then check themselves:

ANNIE: We shouldn't be carrying on like this here.
THERESA: Why not?
ANNIE: Well, it just doesn't seem right.
THERESA: To laugh? Do we have to be solemn when we remember? Would they want us to be solemn? What was it Bobby Sands wrote? 'Our revenge will be the laughter of our children.' I'm sure Bobby would be happy with the laughter of women also.

Annie nods.

ANNIE: You're right. I'm sure he would. (*Pause*) That's an idea. Why don't we bring children in here so that Bobby and the others can hear the laughter?

Annie's vision is of people coming together not as votaries of a secular theology, but in an act of celebration and historical confirmation and affirmation. They leave and Julie and Robert enter, and, in an important dramatic counterpoint to their dialogue, we hear Robert tell the story of an uncle paralyzed by IRA volunteers, his spine and life shattered.

> ROBERT: My uncle Billy was left crippled by those bastards. Worked all his life, raised his family, never did anyone any harm. Treated everyone equally. And just because he was a prison officer they tried to kill him. Nothing to do with the Maze. He never worked in it, wasn't even near it, but that didn't matter. No. He was a target like all the rest of us. Ambushed as he was leaving work at Belfast Prison. Got out of his car and tried to escape but they chased after him. Tripped and fell and they shot him where he lay – on the ground. He hadn't a chance. A bullet lodged in his spine. Crippled for life. But still alive. Alive to tell the story that no one wants to hear.
>
> JULIE: I'm sorry, I didn't know.
>
> ROBERT: No, of course you didn't know. Sure no one wants to know. All they want to hear about is the scum who waged murder and destruction.

The last scene brings the four together in a tense stand-off as Annie realizes that 'Bobby' had known her son, but as a guard, not a comrade. Robert storms off. 'His wee world's collapsing around him', Annie says. Julie stays, and the symbolism is important. Robert belongs to Unionism's past, Julie to the future. She joins with them in a final affirmation; indeed she is given the last word, a neat theatrical choice:

> *Annie walks to the front of the stage and speaks to the audience.*
>
> ANNIE: Our sons and daughters made history ... and so too did their mothers and fathers.
>
> *Theresa walks to the front of the stage.*
>
> THERESA: So there's a need to tell that history, talk about it, write about it.
>
> *Julie steps forward.*
>
> JULIE: So that we can discover it. So that we all can learn from it.

The applause on the night I saw the play was warm and prolonged. Although it is a play about ideas, in fact there was a great deal of humour, and of knowing digs at Gerry Adams and the Sinn Féin leadership. Indeed Adams, who came to watch the first half, stayed to the end, preferring to miss a plane to the USA, and it is easy to understand why, given the importance of this play as an historical intervention into the debate about the legacy of the hunger strikes. More than any other Republican work, *The Official Version* is an attempt to gather the hunger strike into a coherent and justificatory narrative and to project that narrative firmly into a future which will validate the suffering and sacrifices of the past. And while anti-treaty Republicans disagree profoundly with McKeown's position, none, presumably, can deny his right to his own version of collective history.

'There is No Official Version'

On the day after the performance, I met Laurence McKeown at the offices of Coiste na n-Iarchimi where he works. I had contacted him by email, requesting an interview, and had received a courteous and positive response. Coiste's office is in a converted shop on Beechmount Avenue, a side street off the Falls Road. When I arrived, I was shown to a small reception area. McKeown was busy with a television crew from the Basque country, and when he arrived he apologized for the brief delay before leading me up a set of narrow stairs to his office. As soon as I had sat down he asked me if I had seen the production of *The Official Version* and I said that I had, and I began to talk about the quality of the performances. He smiled and nodded towards the wall behind me. 'Go and have a look next door', he said. I got up, and, as it was a small office, was able to turn and look around the corner into the next room. Seated at the desk was Rosena Brown, who was playing Annie in the DubbelJoint production. Brown is a professional actress, and had been a regular performer with Charabanc theatre from the mid-eighties onward, and had credits for roles in TV and film, including Ken Loach's *Hidden Agenda*. A mother of seven, who hails from the Republican Twinbrook estate, she had been arrested and imprisoned on explosives charges in 1993, and was released under the terms of the Good Friday Agreement. Her first appearance for DubbelJoint had been in 1999, in the Pearse Elliot play *A Mother's Heart*. I congratulated her on her acting and we chatted briefly about the play. McKeown told me that without Brighton and DubbelJoint he and Campbell might never have begun writing plays. The encouragement had been a critical factor in overcoming their lack of experience. Comparing *The Official Version* with *Laughter of our Children* he said that the latter dealt with the hunger strike at a more visceral level, whereas the new play was as attempt to place those events within an historical frame, to get a purchase on them through reflection. The need to move on is a central theme of his and Campbell's dramatic works. He sees himself, and other former hunger strikers, as an example of the danger of stasis. 'It was 25 years ago, yet people still see you first and foremost as an ex hunger striker.

Well, I've moved on, and the movement must move on.'[25] Staging the play's actions in Long Kesh was part of this process. It is being redeveloped, but Coiste has lobbied for a section to be preserved as a centre for education and commemoration. Talking about the play in an interview for the *Irish Times*, McKeown said that he identified himself most with Julie: 'I would generally be very optimistic, and the researcher is open to alternative views. I always believe that engagement does not mean endorsement.'[26] *The Official Version* reprises central themes from the earlier plays, and especially *A Cold House*. One of these themes is that conflict resolution does not require people to accept each other's views, but to accept that others were motivated by a coherent politics rooted in historical and objective conditions. McKeown rejects the idea that the play's title is a claim on the 'Truth'. In an interesting gloss on Julie's character, he told the same reporter:

> People ask is this the official Republican version, it's not. The person who uses that term is the character of the researcher, Julie, who in a sense bought into 'the official version' of events. In a sense there is no official version because everybody has their own truth about what happened. The more of those truths we can hear, the better we will get a more complex tapestry.

Nor were the survivors, however defined, untouched by the experiences: 'People did come through it, but they didn't come through unscathed, they were scarred. They are survivors in that sense and they have a hope for the future.'[27] Parts of that complex tapestry are the narratives of those who did not emerge with hope. Pam Brighton:

> Prison has two effects on people. Either they come out with such a lust for life, and a sense of how valuable life is, like Laurence McKeown or Gary Kearney, the stage manager, who is upbeat, optimistic: or they're wrecked by it. And the play we're doing next summer, a big community play which we haven't done for a couple of years, is going to be about the effects of prison ... Laurence and I are going to structure it ... but I think some of it is going to be written by people directly out of their own experience, some of it will be improvised ... it's not going to be just about the upbeat. There are a lot of alcoholics out there created by Long Kesh ... families have been split and wrecked, and it's a side we don't look at enough, that the movement doesn't look at enough ... a terrible sense of abandonment.

Bernadette Mc Aliskey has pointed out that there was never a necessary correspondence between activism and its consequences: 'There is a connection between our resistance and the price that we paid for it. And the price was not shared out equally. That's not our fault, but it's a reality that the price for resisting was not shared out equally by those who resisted. In many cases the price of resisting was paid by those who did nothing.'[28] The proposed community play is an attempt to address this, to add to the sum of understanding.

During my conversation with McKeown he indicated that he was unhappy with the way the actors were playing the moment in which Theresa tells her mother how she had lost her maidenhead. It was 'getting laughs' and he felt that was inappropriate, that the violation should be felt as just that. He had written a new, shorter version he said. Would I look at it and let him know what I thought. Later that evening an email arrived with the new version. One critical line he had removed had Theresa say: 'For my mates it happened round the back of the club or in the rear of a car, but for me it was smuggling a radio in!'[29] It was true that the night before the audience had laughed at this line. I replied to McKeown saying that I thought the cuts would help, but that it all depended on how the actors played the revised scene. The next day he wrote again saying that Pam Brighton had decided the changes were not necessary, and that they would play the original differently in order to avoid the laughter. He ended his brief note with the laconic, 'What would I know, I'm just the writer!'[30]

Creating a Common Ground

Loyalist and Unionist communities also have to come to terms with the war's consequences, and Amharclann na Carraige's audiences have increasingly come from those constituencies. The production of Gary Mitchell's *Remnants of Fear* earlier in 2006 had strengthened these important links. Mitchell, who was raised in Loyalist Rathcoole, was forced out of his home by members of the UDA, and had to flee with his wife and seven-year-old daughter. He was forced to pay to relocate his family outside the city to keep them safe. *Remnants of Fear* examines the intra-communal violence which has convulsed the Loyalist areas of Belfast in recent years. Naturally such a play offered a version of Loyalism that would present no challenge to Republican beliefs. One way to see *Remnants* is as a companion piece to Campbell's *Voyage*, as important forms of internal political critique, though with the critical difference that Mitchell's play was not playing in front of a Loyalist audience. Challenged as to why he was showing the work at the West Belfast Festival, rather than in his own community, Mitchell has said that he would love to premiere his work in Rathcoole if a similar festival existed, but it did not. He also pointed to the absence of Loyalist working-class theatres that could perform his work. One consequence is that supporters of his plays have been coming over to the Ballymurphy theatre. Praise for *The Official Version* from the *Irish Times* and *An Phoblacht/ Republican News* was perhaps expected, but it was the presence of former

UDA members in the audience which gave the performance I saw a special political dimension. Brighton again:

> There were a few guys I was talking to last night. Both ex UDA men from the Shankill. And one was very quiet, but the other was saying 'This is fantastic … it's been a real lesson tonight, I've learnt so much.' He'd come here originally because *Remnants of Fear* was on. And he said, 'What you are doing here is fantastic. To have done *Remnants of Fear* about us, and now this, it's fantastic … we've all got to learn.' And he thought a terrific element was where the prisoner is telling his parent everything is grand, and that you never talked about the actual suffering involved … that the play really forced you to think about what you've been feeling and what people have been suffering.

McKeown has expressed a desire to build on this new relationship, and to see his plays performed in Loyalist areas. He was raised in a mixed community, and his work expresses a strong urge to create dialogue. There is little doubt that his and Brian Campbell's relationship with Pam Brighton and Amharclann na Carraige has been one of the most significant developments in Irish political theatre in the past decade.

Touring, Funding and Politics

The Official Version, like all DubbelJoint productions, toured the north of Ireland and the Republic. Touring is essential to the company's mission as a national theatre, offering 'critical, serious, progressive and entertaining theatre'.[31] Tours are expensive, and the company's funding means that it cannot subsidize them. Instead they have developed a circuit of venues which receive the shows, and which recoup their costs through ticket sales. The Community Relations Council and Children in Need have both funded specific programmes of work. The theatre needs resources to develop its building infrastructure, and to resource its community out-reach work. There is little doubt that a revived Stormont parliament will create the conditions for expansion, and, in order to develop both in-house and touring works, the company will require a significant increase in current funding. In the last financial year they received £76,000 from the Northern Ireland Arts Council. Box office receipts represented 40 per cent of all income in 2005–06, as against 12 per cent in 1999–2000, when the Arts Council gave the company £103,000. The sharp fall (when set against inflation) simply reflects how closely DubbelJoint's fortunes have reflected the ebb and flow of the Peace Process: 'There was a time, before the first government here, when everyone thought Sinn Féin were going to get the arts portfolio, including the Northern Ireland Arts Council … it was a period of about six months when they were unbelievably nice to us!' In 2005, following the IRA's Northern Bank Robbery, when £20 million was stolen, two theatre companies, DubbelJoint and the Irish language company Aisling Ghear, were audited by the Arts Council. They remain the only two companies to be treated this way in what was an unprecedented action. The presumption must be that the audit was carried out at the behest of the intelligence apparatus in order to ensure that proceeds from the robbery were not being laundered through the theatres' accounts. Aisling Ghear was audited for a second time in 2006. In 2005 the ACNI also withheld money which had been allocated to DubbelJoint, and released it only on a monthly basis after demanding additional information about company plans and finances. The action was again unprecedented, and seriously affected DubbelJoint's ability to plan effectively. These actions, together with the audits, are a gentle (compared with state violence) reminder to the West Belfast Republican community that it has still to learn to fasten its ideological shoes on the right side if it wants public funding. Brighton would like to see Sinn Féin take the arts portfolio in any future government, so that the skills, talent and expertise of the community can be harnessed to the task of developing a democratic political culture.[32]

Conclusion

Amharclann na Carraige is a unique popular political theatre of a kind not found elsewhere in Ireland. The closest contemporaneous comparison that can be made is with Dario Fo and France Rame's La Commune in Milan, Italy in the 1970s, or with the work of London's Hackney Empire under Roland and Claire Muldoon since 1986.[33] Its stage provides a space where the complex and ongoing debates within Republicanism about the meaning of the Long War, and the potential for a new polity, can be enacted. Pam Brighton is proud of DubbelJoint's achievements:

> I think our track record on new writing is beyond any other theatre in Ireland. We have created new audiences. But a lot of people have problems with us because they see us as Republicans, and they use that as a way of dismissing the work. I would make no apologies about being a Republican company and a Socialist company; I just wish we were taken a bit more seriously at an aesthetic level. This audience takes theatre seriously. You couldn't put on crap here, because they wouldn't accept it. The plays have got to be accessible and they have got to be about something ... even at £7 it's expensive to them and they want something to get their teeth into. I look around at all the plays we've done, and I'm proud of them. Proud of working with writers like Laurence, and Brian Moore, who has turned into a terrific writer. The talent around here is just phenomenal, colossal.

PART FOUR

'NOT A PROFESSION
BUT A MOVEMENT'

The Politics of Process

Insurgency, theatre and community

I want here to draw together the main themes of this narrative, and in particular to identify those characteristics which are specific to these theatres, and which derived from the historical and political circumstances of the Troubles. The great difference in both scale and forms of theatre as between Republican and Loyalist communities means that much of what follows relates primarily to the Republican and Nationalist theatres. Yet, despite these differences, there were important commonalities. The most obvious was that all interventions were defined by the Troubles and its aftermath. They were all battlefield theatres, and their styles, contexts, modes of organization, texts and performance strategies derived from the conditions of the war. They were organic interventionary theatres, based in and belonging to working-class communities. Even in those cases where theatre was initiated by a professional, for example Tom Magill in the Shankill, or Michael Hall with the UDA, the professionals came from *within* the community, and understood its history. They were *situated* theatres and derived their political authenticity from their relationship to a specific historical reality. While elements of such practices are transferable as technique, what is not transferable is the historical context from which these practices emerged, and the generative themes (regional, national and local) with which they engaged. In all cases the theatres belonged to, or sought to address, an ideological and political formation, though the specific relationship in each case to Republican and Loyalist parties and armed groups varied. Censorship was a shared experience. This ranged from the impact on all forms of cultural activism of the state's counter insurgency policies, to the intra-communal censorship exercised by the IRA and UDA/UVF within their respective areas: for example the withdrawal of the members of the Shankill Community Theatre from Magill's production of *The White In Between*. More normative forms of censorship, for example through the refusal or withdrawal of funding by the Arts Council of Northern Ireland (ACNI), were not significant in the conflict period, given that the ACNI was irrelevant to the production or maintenance of Republican or Loyalist cultural activism. All the groups' names denote a strong sense and allegiance to place: Belfast Community Theatre, Derry Frontline, Shankill Community Theatre, and DubbelJoint. They were also characterized by a commitment to inter-communal political dialogue, even though the exigencies of the war severely limited the possibilities for this. In brief, they were partisan political theatres, but they were not sectarian theatres.

'Not a Profession but a Movement'

Talking of his work in the slums of Calcutta and its environs, the Indian playwright and director Badal Sircar has written:

> Obviously such a theatre takes on the characteristic of a movement, and cannot be taken as a profession ... only those who feel the urge to change, and want to use theatre to contribute to the forces of change, can be in this theatre.[1]

Sircar's concept of theatre as a 'movement' rather than a profession helps to illuminate distinctive features of these community theatres, and in particular of the Republican models. His statement is echoed in an intriguing qualification made by Pam Brighton when talking to me about DubbelJoint's actors. 'Gerry Doherty is now a professional actor. Well, he is and he isn't, because he's an ex-prisoner ... Rosena's not ... [Meehan] Sorcha's not really ... she acts very little.'[2] Few of those who made these theatres conceived of themselves as theatre professionals. Laurence McKeown is first and foremost a political thinker and activist, whose concern with the future of Irish society is expressed in part through theatre. He is a playwright, but that is not all he is. Brian Campbell conceived of himself as a writer, but it was across a range of genres, and it was always writing in the service of a larger political project. Wilson is a priest, theologian, journalist, political thinker and a polemicist, for whom theatre assumed greater importance as a vehicle of political thinking and as an aspect of liberation praxis the more the war progressed. Michael Hall is, I think, a talented playwright, but again play writing was only a part of a broader political project and commitment, and one which the conditions of the war stymied. His collaboration with the poet Sammy Duddy and UDA leader Andy Tyrie was inconceivable outside the war. The testimonies of the IRA POWs who acted in *The Crime of Castlereagh* show that theatre was not chosen out of professional interest, but as a means to express a political commitment. Eoghan MacCormaic and Micheal Ghunna Giolla are cultural thinkers, writers, and academics who also acted. Joe Reid is a fine actor, a playwright, a director, a man steeped in modern theatre history, and an incisive theorist and thinker about culture and politics, but in his professional life he is now the Director of Learning and Teaching at Belfast Metropolitan College. Brenda Murphy, Christine Poland and the women of JustUs, whose theatre generated a critical and political crisis that reached the British House of Commons, now work outside the theatre. Jim Keys left behind a job in the building trade to throw in his lot with Derry Frontline, and developed into an actor, producer and facilitator, but he remains first and foremost an activist. To this list we could add the many fine performers, such as Marie McKnight, Pat McGlade, Declan Nelis, Sharon Reid, Ann and Carol Deehan and so on, who may, perhaps, in another history, have taken theatre as a profession. Many performers were also parents and carers. There are exceptions, such as Tony Flynn of Belfast Community Theatre, who did become a professional actor, and has appeared at the Abbey Theatre in Dublin. But for the most part Sircar's analysis holds, namely that acting in these theatres was an aspect of a larger political commitment. Performers belonged not to the theatre but to a *movement which included theatre*. A good example is Rosena Brown, who starred in McKeown's *The Official Version*, and who by day works for the cause of ex IRA POWs and Sinn Féin, and by night is an actress, and a very good one. What evolved in Ireland, as in African and south-east Asian anti-colonial movements, was not a theatre school, but a schooling in theatre. Ngugi wa Thiong'o is eloquent about this collective creation of artists:

> The Kamiirithu practice was part of education as a process of demystifying knowledge and hence reality. People could see how the actors evolved from the time they could hardly move their legs or say their lines to a time when they could talk and move about the stage as if they were born talking those lines or moving on that stage. Some people in fact were recruited into the acting team after they had intervened to show how such and such a character should be portrayed. The audience applauded them into continuing doing the part. Perfection was thus shown to be a process, a historical social process, but it was admired no less. On the contrary they identified with that perfection even more because it was a product of themselves and their collective contribution. *It was a heightening of themselves as a community.* (Italics in original)[3]

The experience or understanding of 'acting' within the *meitheal* theatres was similarly shaped by the 'historical social process' of the war in Ireland. We can see this if we compare remarks made by Badal Sircar with those of Pat McGlade of Belfast Community Theatre, where both speakers are attempting to describe what acting means in a context where what you are 'pretending to be', and what you 'are' cannot be easily separated by an appeal to technique. In Sircar's example, the play being performed was comparing the exploitation and oppression of the contemporary Indian working class to that of the Sathai rebels who took up arms against the British Empire in the nineteenth century. History is felt to be immanent as both warning and inspiration:

> All that happened to us is happening to us. Each of us was that young man, trying our best to deny the existence of the "killed man" in our midst. It is not a theatre one can perform by enacting. It can only be performed by *state of being*. (Italics in original)[4]

Pat McGlade made very similar comments when asked about how she experienced the role of Patsy in Belfast Community Theatre's *Sign on the Dotted Line*:

> How do I feel playing Patsy? It's a very emotional part. And people ask me how I can get into it so well. Well, some of my family and friends have come through all that. So when I'm on stage I'm thinking of what they went through and how would I feel if I were going through it. Could I stick it? Could I stand what they were doing to me? It's hard to do. It hurts while you're doing it. And each time you do it hurts even more. But I think that's maybe why we can portray it so well. *We feel it with so much of ourselves.* (Author's emphasis)[5]

The idea that a role 'hurts' is a striking one. A recurring theme in the reflections of the cast of *The Crime at Castlereagh* is that the work was 'emotionally draining', so much so that some prisoners felt unable to cope with re-enacting their life experiences. When Derry Frontline was working on the play *Threshold* they encountered a block which, while arising from the experiences of the Republican community, has resonance for all liberation theatres. The performers, Dan Baron Cohen recounts, found great difficulty in expressing emotion:

> First, the woman playing the freedom-striker had great difficulties with the role. She had difficulties with the idea of being vulnerable and emotional onstage when her own life – she has lost two brothers in the war – necessitated that she conceal all forms of vulnerability. That is normal in her community. It is a community that cannot risk a theatre of therapy. Performing vulnerability and tenderness was an enormous threshold we had to cross in rehearsal.[6]

Similarly, Paula from Belfast Community Theatre was struck during the company's tour of *Sign on the Dotted Line* to South Yorkshire in 1987 by the emotional, often tearful, response the play received. Her comments echo Baron Cohen's: 'In Ireland I tend to find that people tend to hold back a wee bit more because they've been hurt that often ... it's not that they've got used to it ... that's not true ... but what they have grown used to is holding back their feelings.'[7] The 'hold back a wee bit' is a recognition that, as with the activists in Derry, acting is a risk, because expressing emotion may endanger, or destabilize, community cohesion. Again it is in the plays of the post-conflict period, such as *A Cold House*, *The Official Version* or the proposed community play by DubbelJoint, that the impact of war on emotional health is being explored. Even as I write these lines in April 2007, the Northern Ireland Secretary, Peter Hain, is warning that the psychological trauma wrought by the Troubles may be so deep that it may yet undo political progress. Much work is being done to address the emotional impact of the conflict, especially on children, who were always the most powerless and vulnerable of the Trouble's victims.

Workshops and performances in war situations, therefore, are not confrontations with the limitations of natural acting ability (however defined), but a fraught engagement with the trauma of personal and collective histories. In themselves, such accounts raise many questions of profound importance about theatre and reality, about 'acting' and 'being', not the least of which is the distinction between a 'politics of acting' and the 'acting of politics', and how the two interleave in resistance and liberation theatres. These matters deserve substantive attention; an attention which is beyond the scope of this study.

Texts

The battlefield created the necessity for new texts. Franz Fanon has written how the urgency of the historical situation creates writers: 'a great many men and women who up till then would never have thought of producing a literary work, now that they find themselves in exceptional circumstances – in prison, with the Maquis, or on the eve of their execution – feel the need to speak to their nation, to compose the sentence which expresses the heart of the people and to become the mouthpiece of a new reality in action.'[8] The writings of *An Glor Gafa* and the prison plays fall within this axis: so too the texts of Belfast Community Theatre, the People's Theatre, Justus, and, to a lesser extent, those of Derry Frontline. It may be more accurate, given the manner in which texts were created, to talk of the creation of performance scripts, or 'scores' on which performances were based. The texts produced by the theatres were also felt to belong to a movement rather than to an individual or group. For example, *Sign on the Dotted Line* began as a smuggled fragment from the Long Kesh pageants, and was developed through collective work, individual authorship and improvisation into a unitary whole. *Binlids* and *Forced Upon Us* were created through a combination of individual and collective writing, improvisation and community research. *The Crime at Castlereagh* began as a poem, and was developed into a performance score through group work. Even when plays had been written by individual authors, for example Campbell's *Voyage of No Return*, McKeown's *The Official Version* and Des Wilson's sketches, they were given their final form through practical work and in dialogue with a director and actors. *This Is It!* may have been penned by Michael Hall, but its situation, plot, characters and central actions were determined in dialogue with Andy Tyrie and the UDA's leadership. Derry Frontline's scripts were created through workshops, and then written up by Baron Cohen, and their content and form depended on that collective work. Nowhere in this history do we find a script which left the rehearsal room exactly as it entered it. Writing involved a constant process of open rehearsal where scenes would be offered for scrutiny and feedback by neighbours. Indeed, what we find is authorship closer to medieval conceptions of transcription or mediation, a process of crafting and shaping communal experience. Scripts were felt to belong to a shared experience, and their creation was always a social act. This reflected in turn a reflexive respect for what was specific in experience. It was these *meitheal* values which connected theatres whose disparate forms embraced satire and farce, epic models and naturalistic dramas, docudramas and realistic plays, physical theatre and agit prop. One of the most interesting developments was Michael Hall's pragmatic use of 'reading plays' to overcome the difficulty of mounting productions. The 'reading plays' also fulfilled one of the central functions of a political theatre; which is to say that a political theatre should generate debate. In *The Aesthetic Dimension* Herbert Marcuse writes:

> The radical qualities of art, that is to say, its indictment of the established reality and its invocation of the beautiful image of liberation, are grounded precisely in the dimension where art transcends its social determination and emancipates itself from the given universe of discourse and behavior while preserving its overwhelming presence. Thereby art creates the realm in which the subversion of experience proper to art becomes possible: the world formed by art is recognized as a reality which is suppressed and distorted in the given reality.[9]

It was one of the functions of this theatre, within its aesthetic limits, to make possible such acts of recognition.

Resistance Theatres or Liberation Theatres?

In *The Wretched of the Earth* Franz Fanon offered the first primer of decolonization, and set out the political philosophy of liberation. Fanon was the first to define the psychopathology of colonialism, its racist rationalizations, and its dehumanization of the colonized. Fanon describes decolonization as a dramatic act, or a set of acts: 'Decolonization never takes place unnoticed ... It transforms spectators crushed with their inessentiality into privileged actors, with the grandiose glare of history's floodlights upon them.'[10] Certainly the Republican working-class communities of the north of Ireland occupied the spotlight of history for thirty years, utilizing both the theatre of politics and the politics of theatre to bring a united Ireland closer. The IRA was guilty of ethically indefensible actions during the conflict, for which they would plead the exigencies of war. Similarly, Republicanism in the 1970s was often the site of murderous internecine conflicts. But these facts do not alter the reality of the historical oppression of Irish Nationalists, the political legitimacy of resistance to a violent state, or the right of the community to talk of liberation. Many who made the theatres saw themselves as part of a liberation movement and the theatres as liberation theatres. Certainly Belfast Community Theatre and the H-Block Theatres saw themselves in this way, and the People's Theatre was powerfully inflected by liberation theology and a commitment to class-based activism. For Baron Cohen of Derry Frontline, however, the Republican movement was a resistance movement which lacked the cultural apparatus needed to instigate liberation, because it lacked the political awareness of the need for such an apparatus. We have seen, however, that this assessment was contradicted by the realities of Republican irredentism, and the alternative forms of social life, culture and education to which it gave rise. While cultural activity was uneven and was not underpinned by Sinn Féin in a systematic way, it was nonetheless palpable and significant, and the writings and philosophies of Freire, Fanon and Ngugi were absorbed into an indigenous praxis, particularly within the Springhill and Conway Mill networks.[11]

Ngugi's call for a return to the pre-colonial language, for a thousand 'centres', was effected through existing grass-roots cultural formations in Springhill and elsewhere, as well as in the prisons. Many of the themes of Derry Frontline plays had been anticipated by progressive elements in Sinn Féin, and in particular by the women's section. In educational and cultural thinking, far from being the backwater Baron Cohen describes, defined by an obsession with melancholic songs and leprechauns, the Republican communities could draw upon a patrimony from the 1890s onwards which anticipated and prefigured later debates about decolonization. If cultural development was uneven, at times spasmodic, that also was a function of the war. Joe Reid:

> Basically you've got to remember that you were in a political situation where activists were caught up in many situations. So what happened then was that something took over, and you were pulled away ... and so you never got the chance to stay with the theatre always ... you had to prioritize.[12]

The Dunlop Players, a workers' theatre based in Durban, South Africa during the apartheid era, also faced the practical difficulty of making theatre within a life defined by struggle:

> Despite all the enthusiasm, energy and the belief in the importance
> of their work, there are times when the obstacles, difficulties and
> problems facing creative workers seem insurmountable.[13]

With the exception of the African National Congress's cultural units,
and the Ethiopian cultural brigades, there is no evidence of any liberation
movement being sustained by the kind of programmatic cultural front of
the type Baron Cohen proposed. It was not that the Irish could not match
the Africans or Latin Americans; it was that all such movements face the
practical challenge of sustaining cultural work in a context of war.[14] Ngugi's
experiments in Kamiirithu lasted less than a year, for example, precisely
because the historical forces which generate these theatres also end them,
usually violently. Jane Plastow and Solomon Tsehaye's essay on the work
of the Eritrean Cultural Brigades during the war of secession with Ethiopia
depicts conditions of production that Irish Republicans would immediately
recognize. The essay describes a liberation theatre practice defined by the
immanence of death or violence: by a pragmatic attitude to forms: by the
collective and deeply political construction of texts: and by the political
relationship between performer and activist.[15] African theatre offers other
resonances. John S. Mbiti has stressed the relationship between the African
worldview and theatre processes as one in which 'whatever happens to the
individual happens to the whole group, and whatever happens to the whole
group happens to the individual'.[16] These are sentiments with which the
makers of the Republican theatres would absolutely identify. The emphasis
on the interplay of collective and individual, and of the relation of theatre
to fundamental issues of political survival, human rights, and national
identity, places these theatres firmly within the global liberation theatre
movement. The Republican theatres occupied a transitional ground between
the Western European agitational political theatres of the twentieth century
on the one hand, and the Freirean, process-based groups and liberation
models developed in the South on the other.[17]

  There is also in these theatres, as in anti-colonial theatres in a more
general manner, a deep sense of the immanence of history, of narratives
which press upon the living as warnings, imperatives and encouragements.
Franz Fanon has spoken about this as a necessary shift in the tense of a
people's narrative, in which the perspective, 'this all happened long ago' is
substituted by 'what we are going to speak of happened somewhere else, but
it might well have happened here today, and it might happen tomorrow'.[18]
Again this resonates with Sircar's comment, cited earlier: 'All that happened
to us is happening to us'. Campbell's *Voyage of no Return*, for example,
has this historical urgency, as do *A Cold House*, *Night before Clontarf*,
Crime at Castlereagh, *Forced Upon Us*, *Sign on the Dotted Line* and *Binlids*.

Within Loyalism, *Somme Day Mourning*, and *This Is It!* also carried this historical charge. These theatres were not dealing with possible dangers or crises, but were theatres in a dangerous war zone contesting the history and future of the state.

The Republican community theatres belonged to a movement whose goal was the overthrow of the Unionist state and the inauguration of a united Ireland. While their forms differed, they shared common values, and a common perception of theatre, of art, as inseparable from, indeed critical to, the achievement of a new form of society. They were the only radical theatres in post-'45 Britain and Ireland to meet Erwin Piscator's stringent criteria for a political theatre, which is to say that they demonstrated *immediacy* through the link to local events, *authenticity* through their class roots in socio-political reality, and above all, that they existed within, and were produced through, a *revolutionary or insurrectionary moment*.[19] We can also identify a shift in the function and complexity of dramas over the course of the Troubles and its aftermath. There was a movement from celebration and justification, through reflection, to texts which offered a more nuanced and historically objective assessment. It is clear that such shifts are historical in character, and that certain texts become possible only at certain points in a movement's or society's development. The career and writings of Brian Campbell and Laurence McKeown offer an instance of this trajectory in the Peace Process. However, it would be an error to view Republican community theatres as a coherent counter-institution, or to assume that they represented a conscious critique of bourgeois models of theatre making. For example, what deeply disappointed Tom Magill about the second performance of *The Crime of Castlereagh*, was that the group took the opportunity offered by the Féile an Phobail performance to reinsert all the panoply of the traditional theatre – proper costumes, lighting, a working set and realistic props. While the purposes and contexts of Republican theatres were revolutionary, what is notable here, and throughout this history, is how consistently the structures of the institutional theatre, with its box office and technical apparatus, would be replicated. 'Poor Theatre' was enforced by historical circumstances; and where it was not enforced, it was not chosen.

Coda

In March 2007 the DUP's Reverend Ian Paisley and Sinn Féin's Gerry Adams agreed an historic accommodation which saw the two parties come together to govern the north of Ireland. It is clear that, whatever the challenges and crises that inevitably lie ahead, the 'Long War' is over. While the Continuity IRA have continued their campaign of economic fire bombings and small-scale attacks on military targets, and remain a consistent if weak threat to the Peace Process, the vast majority of Republicans, including those who are against the Good Friday Agreement, are agreed that physical-force Republicanism, the Defender tradition, which had defined Irish resistance to colonial and neo-colonial occupation for four hundred years, has ceded its place to democratic gradualism.

The theatres in this study played a vital and complex role in those working-class communities which were the main sites of the war, and where the peace will now be shaped. They were profoundly important theatres, which is not at all an aesthetic but rather a political judgment, because those who made them were political actors in a conflict during which what was at stake was the survival of the state, and of the 1921 settlement.

The last words go to Belfast Community Theatre's Joe Reid:

> I think first we need to ask the question – what does the peace mean? What does it mean in bread and butter political terms? What does it mean in terms of non-sectarian working-class politics? That's one set of questions that need to be asked. But I think there's another set of questions as well. I think theatre's a big role to play in this whole police debate. A major role. There are bridges of understanding that need to be built, and theatre's a big role to play there. But a theatre of challenge, not a theatre of the forelock – of 'Let's get a group of Protestants, let's get a group of Catholics, and we'll all sit down and we'll come up with nice sketches about our experiences and understanding'. We've got to challenge each other's experiences. I think also that Ireland is emerging as a very self-confident economy, we need to challenge the basis of that. Because it doesn't matter what colour the flag is if there's still a boot on my neck – an economic boot, a military boot – I don't care. I think theatre's a major role to play in the debate within Republican politics. And I'm using Republican in its widest political context as a set of social values and rights. There's talk in the nine counties of the 'constitution': theatre needs to look at that. What do we mean by constitution? What's worked in the American constitution? What about the English radical tradition? Theatre's a role there, to start and make links. So theatre has more of a role to play, and a more critical role to play. But at the same time it's got to be hammering it out from a focal point of being here. Made by people who've a *right* to ask those questions. There are two kinds of people – those who have the right to ask those questions, and those who don't. And *we have that right*. End of story. (Speaker's emphasis) [20]

Notes to the Chapters

Notes to Acknowledgments

1 Raphael Samuel, *Theatre of Memory, Vol. 1, past and present in contemporary culture* (London: Verso, 1994), p. 8.

Notes to The Research Context

1 Raymond Williams, *Modern Tragedy* (London: Chatto and Windus, 1966), p. 61.
2 Cited in Declan Kiberd, *Inventing Ireland, the literature of the modern nation* (London: Vintage, 1996), p. 204.
3 Ibid., p. 204.
4 Himani Bannerji, *The Writing on the Wall: Essays on Culture and Politics* (Toronto: TSAR, 1993), p. 93.
5 Sole Purpose was formed in 1997 by actress/writer Patricia Byrne, and writer/director Dave Duggan. The company developed out of the Toxic Theatre Association, a loose collective of theatre activists based in Derry. The company aims 'to produce work relevant to communities in Northern Ireland [and] to produce interactive theatre and workshops which provide a safe space for all participants to explore sensitive issues, for example conflict resolution'. The company's work is presented in Loyalist and Republican communities, and in the years since their foundation they have earned an international reputation for their work in conflict resolution.
6 Lionel Pilkington, *Theatre and the State in Twentieth-Century Ireland* (London: Routledge, 2001).
7 See, for example: Lionel Pilkington, 'From Resistance to Liberation with Derry Frontline: an interview with Dan Baron Cohen', *Drama Review*, 38: 4 (1994), pp. 17–47; 'Theatre and Cultural Politics in Northern Ireland: the Over the Bridge Controversy', *Journal of Irish Studies*, 30: 4 (1996), pp. 76–93.
8 See, for example: Dan Baron Cohen, 'Listening to the Silences: defining the language and the place of a new Ireland', in *Ireland in Proximity, history, gender, space*, edited by Brewster, Scott and others (London: Routledge, 1999), pp. 173–88 and Derry Frontline, *Theatre of Self Determination, the plays of Derry Frontline Culture and Education, north of Ireland, 1988–1992*, ed. with an introduction by Dan Baron Cohen (Derry: Guildhall Press, 2001).
9 David Grant, *Playing the Wild Card, a survey of community drama and smaller*

scale theatres from a community relations perspective (Belfast: Community Relations Council, 1993).

10 Tom Magill, 'Between a Bible and a Flute band: Community Theatre in the Shankill and in Long Kesh', in *The State of Play: Irish Theatre in the Nineties*, ed. Eberhard Bort (Trier: WVT Wissenschaftlicher Verlag Trier, 1996), pp. 124–33: Tom Magill, 'Theatre as Democracy: Boal in Belfast', *Fortnight*, November (1988), pp. 21–2.

11 Tom Maguire, *Making Theatre in Northern Ireland* (Exeter: University of Exeter Press, 2006).

12 Ibid., p. 19.

13 For accounts of CAST's work and the development of the alternative theatre movement see – Sandy Craig, *Dreams and Deconstructions: Alternative Theatre in Britain* (London: Amberlane, 1980). Andrew Davies, *Other Theatres: the Development of Alternative and Experimental Theatres in Britain* (Basingstoke: Macmillan Education, 1987): Catherine Itzin, *Stages in the Revolution* (London: Methuen, 1980): Baz Kershaw, *The Politics of Performance – Radical Theatre as Cultural Intervention* (London: Routledge, 1992).

14 Sheffield Popular Theatre was based in the Darnall estate in east Sheffield. During its lifetime it would produce a series of community shows as well as launching the women's performance group The Chuffinelles. Our reason for leaving was based on a fundamental disagreement about the relationship between theatre and political movements in the city.

15 Bill McDonnell, 'Towards a Common Stage', *City Limits*, no. 6, June 1983.

16 In most research there are those serendipitous moments which alter our view of the field. One such occurred while I was researching sources for the Belfast People's Theatre, and came across the name of Michael Hall, whose Island pamphlet series (see bibliography) has been an important influence in the post-conflict period. When I mentioned that I was writing about Republican theatres, he asked if I would be interested in two plays he had written, one of which was the fruit of collaboration with Andy Tyrie of the Ulster Defence Association (UDA). It was these texts that led to my decision to include a section on Loyalist theatre.

17 Ibid., p. 34.

18 Hussein Abdilahi Bulhan, *Frantz Fanon and the Psychology of Oppression* (New York: Plenum Press, 1985), p. 4.

19 Himani Bannerji, *The Writing on the Wall*, p. 48.

20 See for example: Eugene van Erven, *The Playful Revolution: Theatre and Liberation in Asia* (Indiana: Indiana University Press, 1992): Rustom Barucha, *Rehearsals of Revolution: the Political Theatre of Bengal* (Hawaii: University of Hawaii Press, 1983).

21 All citations in this section are taken from: Stephen Howe, *Ireland and Empire, colonial legacies in Irish history and culture* (Oxford: OUP, 2000), pp. 7–9.

22 Jonathan Stevenson, *We Wrecked the Place – Contemplating an End to the Northern Irish Troubles* (New York: Simon and Schuster, 1996), p. 77.

23 Maguire, *Making Theatre in Northern Ireland*, p. 6.

Notes to The Historical Context

1 R.F. Foster, *Modern Ireland, 1600–1972* (London: Penguin, 1989), p. 61. Foster's study offers a vivid and scholarly introduction to the complexities of

Irish political history in the pre-partition period. See also Robert Kee's study, *The Green Flag, a history of Irish Nationalism* (London: Penguin 2000), for an accessible and admirably detailed narrative history of Irish nationalism.

2 Kee, *The Green Flag,* parts four and five.

3 These events are the subject of two important plays: Frank McGuinness's *Observe the Sons of Ulster Marching Towards the Somme,* and *Somme Day Mourning* by Brian Ervine, which is considered in the study of Loyalist theatre in Part Two, pp. 143–64.

4 Michael Farrell, *Northern Ireland: the Orange State* (London: Pluto, 1980), p. 19.

5 Cited in Foster, *Modern Ireland,* p. 466.

6 Ibid., p. 467.

7 Ibid., p. 467.

8 For a detailed and vivid account of the Rising see Kee, *The Green Flag,* chapters 14–18.

9 Cited in Foster, *Modern Ireland,* p. 487.

10 Simon Prince, *Northern Ireland's '68: civil rights, global revolt and the origins of the Troubles* (Dublin: Irish Academic Press, 2007), pp. 21–3.

11 Gerry Adams, *Before the Dawn: an autobiography* (New York: William Morrow & Company, 1996), pp. 93–4.

12 Prince, *Northern Ireland's '68,* pp. 2–3.

13 The most powerful and incisive account of the birth of the Troubles is Eamonn McCann's *War and an Irish Town* (London: Pluto Press, 1975).

14 For a detailed analysis of the attempts by Terence O'Neill, Prime Minister of Northern Ireland 1963–69 to modernize the state and tackle the sectarianism within its civil institutions, see Prince's study of the inception of the Troubles.

15 Jonathan Stevenson, *We Wrecked the Place,* p. 36.

16 Ibid., p. 22.

17 See for example: Kevin Toolis, *Rebel Hearts* (London: Picador, 1995): Kevin Kelley, *The Longest War – Northern Ireland and the IRA* (Co. Kerry: Brandon Books, 1982).

18 Kelley, *The Longest War,* pp. 131–4. Kelley offers an acute analysis of the ambiguities of the IRA's vision of a new Ireland, which was much closer to a social democratic model such as Sweden's than to any Soviet blueprint. The continued power of the Catholic Church within the movement diluted the more radical elements' egalitarian aspirations.

19 Ed Maloney, *A Secret History of the IRA* (London: Penguin, 2003), p. 84.

20 Ibid., p. 81.

21 Ibid., p. 363.

22 Gerry Adams, *The Politics of Irish Freedom* (Dingle, Co. Kerry: Brandon Books, 1986), pp. 63–9.

23 Foster, *Modern Ireland,* p. 106.

24 Cited in Farrell, *Northern Ireland,* p. 270.

25 Fr Des Wilson, *An End to Silence* (Cork: Royal Carbery Books, 1985), p. 100.

26 Foster, *Modern Ireland,* p. 31.

27 Liz Curtis, *Nothing But the Same Old Story* (London: Russell Press, 1985).

28 Article in the *New Standard,* 19 November 1980, cited in Curits, *Nothing But the Same Old Story,* p. 77.

29 Article in the *Sunday Express,* 29 January 1984, cited in Curits, *Nothing But the Same Old Story,* p. 80.

30 Article in the *Sunday Times*, 13 March 1977, cited in Curtis, *Nothing But the Same Old Story*, p. 79.

31 Kate Millet, *The Politics of Cruelty: an essay on the literature of political imprisonment* (London: Viking, 1994), p. 108.

32 Convention (IV) relative to the Protection of Civilian Persons in Time of War, Geneva, 12 August 1949.

33 Marc Mulholland, *Northern Ireland – a very short introduction* (Oxford: OUP, 2002), p. 76–7.

34 For a moving and powerful account of each of the 3000 deaths, see David McKittrick, and others, *Lost Lives: the stories of the men, women and children who died as a result of the Troubles* (Edinburgh: Mainstream, 1999).

Notes to 'Gentle Fury': Father Des and the People's Theatre

1 John Gerassi (ed.), *Camilo Torres, Revolutionary Priest, the complete writings and messages of Camilo Torres* (London: Jonathan Cape, 1971), p. xiii.

2 Ibid., p. xx.

3 Ibid., p. 31.

4 Fr Des Wilson, *The Way I See It*, an autobiography (Belfast: Beyond the Pale, 2005), p. 109.

5 Ibid., p. 121.

6 Ciaran De Baroid, *Ballymurphy and the Irish War* (London: Pluto Press, 2000), p. 197.

7 Gerassi, *Camilo Torres*, p. 5.

8 Fr Mullan and Father Noel Fitzpatrick from Ballymurphy were murdered by British army snipers while administering the last rites to parishioners who had been shot during two episodes in which soldiers fired indiscriminately into the streets around Springhill. Fr Mullan died on 9 August 1971, while Fr Fitzpatrick, a friend of Fr Wilson's, died on 9 July 1972. Fr Mullan's death was part of a case brought by the Irish government against the British government at the European Court of Human Rights in 1975.

9 Wilson, *The Way I See It*, pp. 130–1.

10 Ibid., p. 30.

11 Besides his theatre writings, monographs and pamphlets, Wilson was a prolific columnist, writing regularly for, among others, *Andersontown News, An Phoblacht/Republican News*, and the *Irish Times*. His weekly columns were a form of alternative pulpit, offering him access to a laity which was not permitted to hear him in a church.

12 Wilson, *The Way I See It*, p. 68.

13 Ibid., p. 78.

14 'Bloody Sunday' refers to the events that took place in Derry on the afternoon of Sunday 30 January 1972. A Northern Ireland Civil Rights Association (NICRA) march had been organised to protest against the continuation of internment without trial in Northern Ireland. Between ten and twenty thousand men, women and children took part in the march in a 'carnival atmosphere'. The march was prevented from entering the city centre by members of the British Army. The main body of the march then moved to 'Free Derry Corner' to attend a rally but some young men began throwing stones at soldiers in William Street. Soldiers of the Parachute Regiment, an elite regiment of the British Army, moved into the Bogside in an arrest operation. During the next

30 minutes these soldiers shot 13 men (and shot and injured a further 13 people) mainly by single shots to the head and trunk. 'This Sunday became known as Bloody Sunday and bloody it was. It was quite unnecessary. It strikes me that the Army ran amok that day and shot without thinking what they were doing. They were shooting innocent people. These people may have been taking part in a march that was banned but that does not justify the troops coming in and firing live rounds indiscriminately. I would say without hesitation that it was sheer, unadulterated murder. It was murder.' (Major Hubert O'Neill, the Coroner, in a statement issued on 21 August 1973.) Citations have been taken from the Conflict Archive on the Internet (CAIN) http://cain.ulst.ac.uk/events/bsunday/sum.htm. Accessed 12 March 2006. In 1998 the Labour government set up the Saville Inquiry into Bloody Sunday. It has sat for nine years and has yet to issue a summative judgment.

15 Operation Motorman sent 26,000 soldiers, plus tanks, bulldozers, helicopters and Saracen armoured cars into the streets of Republican communities across the north. For analysis of the human rights violations of the British counter-insurgency see: Alan Jennings (ed.), *Justice Under Fire – the Abuse of Civil Liberties in Northern Ireland* (Pluto: London, 1988), and Bjorn Funnemark and Arne Borg, *Irish Terrorism or British Colonialism? The Violation of Human Rights in Northern Ireland* (Norwegian Helsinki Committee, 1990).

16 De Baroid, *Ballymurphy and the Irish War*, p. 142.

17 Fr Des Wilson, *A Diary of Thirty Days, Ballymurphy July–December 1972*, edited by Joseph Sheehy (Springhill Community House: Local Heritage Series), p. 61. Eleven men were later found to have been subjected to inhuman and degrading treatment involving the use of torture, including 'white noise', beatings, sleep deprivation and being made to stay in painful physical positions. Many more reported violence against them. As IRA members were skilled at evading capture in mass raids, it was inevitable that the majority of those who suffered were not members.

18 Fr Des Wilson, *A Diary of Thirty Days*, p. 60.

19 Ibid., p. 21.

20 Ibid., p. 23.

21 Ibid., p. 33.

22 Ibid., p. 34.

23 De Baroid, *Ballymurphy and the Irish War*, p. 97.

24 The house was demolished in 1988 as part of the rebuild programme. The new Springhill is located nearby at 6–8 Springhill Close.

25 Wilson, *The Way I See It*, p. 68.

26 Michael Hall (ed.), *Grassroots Leadership (2): Recollections by Fr Des Wilson and Tommy Gorman* (Newtownabbey: Island Publications, 2005), p. 7.

27 Ibid., p. 10.

28 Wilson, *The Way I See It*, p. 106.

29 Joseph Sheehy, *Exile and the Kingdom, the authorized biography of Desmond Wilson, Ballymurphy Priest* (Belfast: Glandore Press, 1995), p. 142. Sheehy was a central figure in the education network, and in particular in the local history group, and his work constitutes a vital contribution to our knowledge of the history of the community in these years.

30 All quotations in this section are from Sheehy, *Exile and the Kingdom*, pp. 144–7.

31 Ibid., p. 143.

32 Ibid., p. 144. All quotations in this section are from ibid., pp. 144–7.

33 All quotations in this section are from ibid., pp. 144–7.

34 *The People's Theatre, Volume 1*, p. 6.

35 Ibid., p. 32–3.

36 Wilson tells an amusing tale in his autobiography of the time the group was due to appear at the Open College in Belfast city centre. It was the mid-seventies, a time when the war was especially intense. Nobody turned up. Undaunted, the company went onto the streets and found one surprised (and initially very alarmed) local man. 'He asked how long would it take. I told him and he said, "All right", and we had one man for an audience.' Wilson, *The Way I See It*, p. 80.

37 Internment: 'In a series of raids across Northern Ireland on August 9 1971 342 people were arrested and taken to makeshift camps. There was an immediate upsurge of violence and 17 people were killed during the next 48 hours. Of these 10 were Catholic civilians who were shot dead by the British Army. Hugh Mullan (38) was the first Catholic priest to be killed in the conflict when he was shot dead by the British Army as he was giving the last rites to a wounded man. Winston Donnell (22) became the first Ulster Defence Regiment (UDR) soldier to die in 'the Troubles' when he was shot by the Irish Republican Army (IRA) near Clady, County Tyrone. [There were more arrests in the following days and months. Internment was to continue until 5 December 1975. During that time 1,981 people were detained; 1,874 were Catholic / Republican, while 107 were Protestant / Loyalist. Internment had been proposed by Unionist politicians as the solution to the security situation in Northern Ireland but was to lead to a very high level of violence over the next few years and to increased support for the IRA.' Source: CAIN website. http://cain.ulst.ac.uk/events/intern/chron. htm. Accessed 10 March 2007.

38 Des Wilson, *The Soldier's Synge*. All quotations are taken from an unpublished copy held in the author's personal archive.

39 Declan Kiberd, *Inventing Ireland*. See particularly chapter ten, 'J.M. Synge, Remembering the Future'.

40 *The Soldier's Synge* was to bring about another of the many sometimes surreal intersections of theatre with the war. The story begins with the arrival of army chaplains in the community. At first they were treated like any clergy, and welcomed into local people's houses. It was in this spirit that the theatre group invited several of them to a performance of *The Soldier's Synge* in the church hall. The chaplains loved it and thought it would be great for morale if the 'ordinary soldiers' could see their superiors mocked in this way. Fr Wilson: 'They asked for the play to come to the local barracks: the cast politely declined the invitation'. Later the People's Theatre would be glad that they had refused this 'hand of friendship'. Over time it became clear that the chaplains were exploiting their position and were using their visits to gather intelligence: asking questions which 'only police and soldiers would ask'. For Fr Wilson and others this was a fundamental breach of sacred trust, and he made his feelings known publicly through the *Catholic Standard* for which he wrote a regular column. In his autobiography he notes: 'The chaplains were told by their authorities to back off and that was the end of the socializing and invitations to take part in workshop or theatre. Naiveté, hospitality and trying to love your military fellow Christians can be a dangerous mix'. Wilson, *The Way I See It*, pp. 102–3.

41 Sheehy, *Exile and the Kingdom*, p. 146.

42 Hall, *Grassroots Leadership*, p. 9.

43 Joe McVeigh, *Renewing the Irish Church: towards an Irish Liberation Theology* (Cork: Mercier Press, 1993), p. 47.

44 Ibid., p. 48.

45 David Tombs, *Latin American Liberation Theology* (Boston: Brill Academic Publishers, 2002), p. 127.

46 McVeigh, *Renewing the Irish Church*, p. 12.

47 Ibid., p. 27.

48 Ibid., p. 11.

49 Wilson, *The Way I See It*, p. 79.

50 Des Wilson, *You're Not Going To Like This!* All quotations in this section are taken from an unpublished copy of the Woman and the Bishop sequence held in the author's personal archive.

51 McVeigh, *Renewing the Irish Church*, p. 28.

52 Des Wilson and Joseph Sheehy, *The People's Theology at Whiterock College* (Heritage Series: Springhill Community House), p. 45.

53 McVeigh, *Renewing the Irish Church*, p. 93.

54 Cited in De Baroid, *Ballymurphy and the Irish War*, p. 285.

55 Ibid., p. 287.

56 Wilson, *The Way I See It*, p. 160.

57 De Baroid, *Ballymurphy and the Irish War*, p. 286.

58 Wilson, *The Way I See It*, p. 159.

59 Hall, *Grassroots Leadership*, p. 14.

60 Des Wilson, *An End to Silence* (Cork: Royal Carbery Books, 1985), p. 100.

61 McVeigh, *Renewing the Irish Church*, p. 143.

62 Des Wilson, *Damien Walsh Memorial Lecture*, <http://www.victimsandsurvivorstrust.com>. Accessed 17 April 2006.

63 Des Wilson, *Moneylender*. Unpublished copy held in the author's personal archive.

64 Des Wilson, *The Capitalist*. Unpublished copy held in the author's personal archive.

65 Des Wilson, *What Can Poor Rich People Do?* Unpublished copy held in author's personal archive.

66 Williams, *Modern Tragedy*, p. 61.

67 Des Wilson, *Focailin*. All quotations are taken from an unpublished copy held in the author's personal archive.

68 The Red Hand Commandos were a proscribed and small loyalist paramilitary group, often used as a cover for sectarian killings by members of the larger, legal, Ulster Volunteer Force.

69 Quoted in De Baroid, *Ballymurphy and the Irish War*, p. 162.

70 In the *People's Theatre, Volume 1*, the editor Joseph Sheehy adds an interesting footnote to *Focailin* which reads: 'The following sketch has taken on added significance in the light of revelations about "The Committee". Focailin the banker believes it is his duty to "remove" certain people for the "good of society". All it takes is a little word (*focailin*) with the Operator and it's as good as done. To sleep at night both cling to their tunnel vision, locking out doubt and self questioning. But can they withstand the Clown, traditional symbol of Conscience?' (p. 35). Sheehy is referring here to Sean McPhilemy's book, *The Committee: Political Assassination in Northern Ireland* (Colorado: Roberts Rinehart, 1998). McPhilemy's thesis is that during the Troubles a high level

committee, comprised of figures from the UUP, the RUC, Special Branch, MI5 and the banking and business sectors, met regularly to identify and sanction the assassination of senior Republicans and suspected IRA members. The book was banned from publication in Britain and Ireland. I was given a copy by Sister Noelle Ryan, which she had brought in from the USA. Philemy's thesis has been substantiated by revelations since 1998 of high level collusion between the Unionist State, the Security Services and Loyalist and free lance assassination groups such as the Red Hand Commandos. Among the assassinations being examined by a committee of enquiry is that of the lawyer Pat Finucane, who was murdered by Loyalist gunmen acting with the support of the British security services in 1989. Amnesty International has written of this case: 'In the aftermath of Patrick Finucane's killing, substantial and credible allegations of state collusion began to emerge almost immediately. Since then, prima facie evidence of criminal conduct by police and military intelligence agents acting in collusion with loyalist paramilitaries in the killing has emerged. In addition, allegations have emerged of a subsequent cover-up by different government agencies and authorities, including the police, the British Army, MI5 (the UK Security Service, officially "responsible for protecting the UK against threats to national security") and the office of the Director of Public Prosecutions in Northern Ireland.' Amnesty International's statement can be accessed on the Pat Finucane website at http://www.serve.com/pfc/pf/inqubill/040923ai.html. Accessed 23 June 2007.

71 Des Wilson, *Damien Walsh Memorial Lecture*.
72 Wilson, *The Way I See It*, p. 169.
73 Paulo Freire, *Pedagogy of the Oppressed*, trans. by Myra Bergman Ramos (Harmondsworth: Penguin, 1972), p. 64.
74 Wilson, *The Way I See It*, p. 174.
75 Fr Des Wilson. Undated letter to the author. 1996.
76 Ibid.

Notes to 'At the Heart of the Struggle': the plays of Belfast Community Theatre

1 Cited in Robert Kee, *The Green Flag* (London: Penguin, 1972), p. 493.
2 Joe Reid in a letter to the author, 15 July 1987, personal archive.
3 From an interview with Joe Reid, given to the author in Belfast, December 1998.
4 This type of relationship, which I will return to, is reflected across the spectrum of radical and liberation theatre activity. Indeed, liberation and resistance theatres would seem to arise (for example in the Philippines, Pakistan, India and Britain in the 1980s) at moments of acute historical crisis, when military repression, civil war, or right wing authoritarian regimes intensify existing inequalities and oppressions, and bring working class/peasants and radical professionals into new relationships. The same process can be identified in the global movement of worker theatres of the twenties and thirties, with the then nascent Soviet Union providing both the argument and the model for change. These are necessarily general observations, but they reflect an important theme in radical theatre history. In the case of Derry Frontline, whose work is explored in Part Two, the relationship was especially complex and problematic.

5   Gerry Adams, *Before the Dawn*, p. 5.

6   From an interview with Belfast Community Theatre given to the author, Sheffield, September 1987. All citations in this section are from this source unless otherwise indicated.

7   See Eugene Van Erven, *Playful Revolution*, chapters two and three.

8   This is a common phenomenon. Most of the members of the socialist theatres such as CAST and 7:84 were not affiliated to specific left political groupings.

9   The prisoners had five demands: 1. The Right not to wear a prison uniform; 2. The Right not to do prison work; 3. The Right of free association with other prisoners; 4. The Right to organize their own educational and recreational facilities; 5. The Right to one visit, one letter and one parcel per week.

10   *An Phoblacht/Republican News*, 27 October 1979.

11   Kevin Kelley, *The Longest War*, pp. 318–19.

12   Jane Ashley and others, Labour Party Research Department, *Breaking the Nation, a guide to Thatcher's Britain* (London: Pluto Press, 1985), p. 173.

13   Bobby Sands became MP for Fermanagh/South Tyrone on 9 April 1981 in a by-election. Following his death on 5 May, his election agent, Owen Carroll, was elected to replace him.

14   Paula was one of several members who, for reasons of political affiliation, refused to give their surnames in any interview, or reproducible material. I have respected that decision here.

15   From an interview with Belfast Community Theatre, given to the author, Belfast, 1986. The Supergrass issue is examined below.

16   Ibid.

17   Belfast Community Theatre, 1986.

18   Ibid.

19   Reid interview, 1998.

20   Sean O'Callaghan, *The Informer* (London: Bantam Press 1999), p. 177.

21   Ibid., p. 352.

22   Cited in Pilkington, *Theatre and Insurgency*, p. 138.

23   Reid interview, 1998.

24   Reid interview, 1998.

25   The Emancipation Act of 1829 had removed bars to Catholic participation in Parliament, the judiciary and the civil service, but at the cost of raising the property qualification for voting, thus disenfranchising the Catholic poor.

26   Eoghan MacCormaic, *Night Before Clontarf*, unpaginated script in author's personal archive.

27   A useful account of the critical early period in the Peace Process can be found in Eamonn Mallie and David McKittrick, *The Fight for Peace – the Secret Story Behind the Irish Peace Process* (London: Heinemann, 1996). Their latest work, *Endgame in Ireland* (London: Hodder & Stoughton, 2001), offers a fascinating insight into the making of the Good Friday Agreement, and details developments up to August 2001.

28   All citations from original hand written notes on the play script.

29   A Nationalist community celebration centred in the Falls and Ballymurphy areas, and made up of shows, workshops, children's activities, poetry and song workshops and so on. A genuinely grass-roots cultural phenomenon.

30   Reid interview, 1998.

31   Fr Raymond Murray, *State Violence – Northern Ireland, 1969–1997* (Dublin: Mercier Press, 1998), p. 34.

32 All quotations in this section taken from unpaginated copy of *Sign on the Dotted Line* held in the author's personal archive.

33 Under the provisions of the 1974 Prevention of Terrorism Act, suspects could be held without access to legal representation for a maximum period of seven days. See glossary, p. 8.

34 From an interview given by Belfast Community Theatre to the author, Sheffield, October 1987.

35 Belfast Community Theatre, 1987.

36 On Sunday 6 March 1988, three unarmed Irish Republican Army members, including Mairead Farrell, were shot dead by undercover members of the Special Air Service (SAS) in Gibraltar. The episode sparked intense controversy and began a chain of events that led to a series of deaths in Northern Ireland on 16 March 1988 and 19 March 1988.

37 Reid interview, 1998.

38 Belfast Community Theatre, 1987.

39 Ibid.

40 All citations, Belfast Community Theatre, 1987.

41 Bertolt Brecht, *Brecht on Theatre: the development of an aesthetic*, ed. and trans. by John Willett (London: Methuen, 1978), p. 277.

42 Uptal Dutt, *Towards a Revolutionary Theatre* (Calcutta: Sarkar, 1982), p. 15.

43 Finance also came from Yorkshire Arts, Sheffield City Council, Sheffield Trades Council, NALGO, AEUW, Troops Out Movement and Sheffield Centre Against Unemployment.

44 Manor Campaign Theatre, 1985–92, for example, was made up of local residents from the city's most deprived estate, and produced during its lifetime pieces on housing, poverty, unemployment, welfare rights and health.

45 Philip Andrews, 'All Quiet on the Western Front', *Sheffield Star*, 26 September 1987; Tony Benn, 'United Ireland is the Only Answer', *Sheffield Star*, 11 November 1987; Tony Mitchell and John Kelly, '"IRA link" Outburst', *Sheffield Star*, 28 November 1987.

46 In November 1974 following two bombings in Birmingham that killed twenty-one people and injured hundreds more, six Irish men were convicted of murder and sentenced to life. After a long campaign to establish their innocence, they were released on 14 March 1991.

47 Reid interview, 1998.

48 Ibid.

49 All quotations from *Ecce Homo*, unpublished script, author's archive.

50 Reid interview, 1998.

51 Reid interview, 1998.

52 Ian Steadman, 'Race Matters in South African Theatre', in *Theatre Matters*, ed. by Richard Boon and Jane Plastow, pp. 55–75, p. 65.

53 Pilkington, 'From Resistance to Liberation', p. 23.

54 From an interview given by Belfast Community Theatre to the author, Belfast, 1986.

55 Reid interview, 1998.

Notes to 'The University of Freedom': theatre in the H-Blocks

1 Bobby Sands, *Writings from Prison*, p. 228.

2 Sands became MP for Fermanagh/South Tyrone in a by-election on 9 April

1981. Following his death his election agent, Owen Carroll, was elected to replace him. Sands' success was a critical marker in convincing sceptics within the Provisionals that a dual strategy was feasible. However, it was clear that, up until the late eighties, politics was seen as supplementary to, rather than a potential alternative to, military action.

3 *An Phoblacht/Republican News* email summary bulletin service, 13/10/2006.

4 Laurence McKeown, *Out of Time – Irish Republican Prisoners, Long Kesh 1972–2000* (Belfast: BTP Publications, 2001), p. 180. McKeown's work is essential to understanding the paradigmatic shift in Republican thinking and organizational structures in the post-hunger strike period. It is also a considerable piece of political ethnography.

5 Kee, *The Green Flag*, p. 198.

6 Edmund Spenser, *A View on the Present State of Ireland*. https://scholarsbank. uoregon.edu/dspace/bitstream/1794/825/1/ireland.pdf. Accessed 4 October 2006.

7 McKeown, *Out of Time*, p. 68.

8 Ibid., p. 130.

9 Ibid., p. 131.

10 Both quotations from Laurence McKeown, 'Writing our own History', paper given at the *Prison Writings: Probing the Boundaries* conference held in Vienna, September 2002. Source held at http://www.inter-disciplinary.net/ Mckeown%20paper.pdf, p. 4.

11 McKeown, *Out of Time*, p. 144.

12 McKeown, *Writing our Own History*, p. 4.

13 McKeown, *Out of Time*, p. 181.

14 McKeown, *Writing our Own History*, p. 5.

15 Republican Prisoners, *Scairt Amach*, Spring edition (Long Kesh Prison: 1989).

16 Editorial, *An Glór Gafa/ The Captive Voice*, Vol. 1, No. I (Dublin and Belfast: Republican Publications, 1989).

17 Edward Daly, *Mister Are You a Priest?* (Dublin: Four Courts Press, 2000), quotation sourced on the CAIN website at http://cain.ulst.ac.uk/events/bsunday/ daly/daly00.htm#ch14, accessed 19/05/2007.

18 Paddy Devenny, 'Personal Thoughts', *The Crime at Castlereagh*, Féile an Phobail programme, September 1996, unpaginated.

19 Eoghan MacCormaic, 'Revolutionary People's Theatre', in *Iris Bheag* (Dublin: Sinn Féin Education Department), December, 1988, pp. 31–4, p. 31.

20 Ibid., p. 30.

21 Ibid., p. 31.

22 See Belfast Community Theatre, Part Two, pp. 67–8.

23 Tom Magill, 'Between a Bible and a Flute band: Community Theatre in the Shankill and in Long Kesh', in *The State of Play: Irish Theatre in the Nineties*, ed. Eberhard Bort (Trier: WVT Wissenschaftlicher Verlag Trier, 1996), pp. 124–33, p. 124.

24 Ibid.

25 Interview with Tom Magill carried out by the author, Belfast, September 2006. All quotations in this section are from this source, unless otherwise indicated.

26 Magill, 'Between a Bible and a Flute Band', p. 130.

27 Dan Kelly, 'Diary of a Drama Project', *An Glór Gafa/ The Captive Voice*, Vol. 8, No. 1 (1996), pp. 11–18, p. 11. All quotations in this section are from this source unless indicated otherwise.

28 Paddy O'Dowd, 'Festival Drama in the Blocks', *An Glór Gafa/ The Captive Voice*, Vol. 8, No. 1 (1996), pp. 18–19, p. 18.

29 Dan Kelly, 'Diary of a Drama Project', p. 11.

30 Micheal MacGiolla Ghunna, 'Cultural Struggle and a Drama Project', in *Journal of Prisoners on Prisons*, Vol. 7, No. 1 (1996), pp. 71–4, p. 74. This volume was edited by Republican prisoners, and provided another forum in which a sophisticated intellectual analysis of the war and of the role of the penal system as a tool of counter-insurgency could be argued.

31 Author interview, 2006.

32 'Personal Thoughts', *The Crime of Castlereagh* programme. All quotations in this section are from this source unless indicated otherwise.

33 Author interview, 2006.

34 P. Devenny, P. Fox, E. Higgins, S. Jamison, D. Kelly, M. MacGiolla Ghunna, M. Og Meehan, F. Quinn, M. Morris, J. McCann, 'Personal Thoughts', *Crime of Castlereagh*, Féile an Phobail programme, September 1996, unpaginated.

35 Ibid.

36 A. Fugard, J. Kani and W. Ntshona 'The Island', in Fugard, Athol, *Township Plays* (Oxford: OUP, 1993).

37 Ibid.

38 Kelly, 'Diary of a Drama Project', p. 12.

39 Brian Campbell, 'Power and Confidence in Outstanding Drama', *An Phoblacht/ Republican News*, 19 September 1996, p. 10.

40 Ibid.

41 O'Dowd, 'Festival Drama in the Blocks', p. 18.

42 Sands, *Writings from Prison*, p. 104.

43 O'Dowd, 'Festival Drama in the Blocks', p. 18.

44 Author interview.

45 O'Dowd, 'Festival Drama in the Blocks', p. 19.

46 All quotations from 'Personal Thoughts'.

47 O'Dowd, 'Festival Drama in the Blocks', p. 19.

48 Quotation taken from notes on the draft chapter made by Tom Magill, May 2008.

49 Brian Campbell, 'Power and Confidence in Outstanding Drama', p. 13.

50 Micheal MacGiolla Ghunna, 'The Politics of Cultural Struggle', *An Glor Gafa*, Winter (1996), pp. 10–11, p. 10. Magill's work had introduced the Republican POWs to the basic principles and methods of Boal's 'poetics of the oppressed'.

51 Ibid., p. 11.

52 Eoghan MacCormaic, 'Revolutionary People's Theatre', in *Iris Bheag* (Dublin: Sinn Féin Education Department), December, 1988, pp. 31–4. All quotations in this section are from this internal Sinn Féin document.

53 For example within the British Workers' Theatre Movement of the 1920s and 1930s, or the cultural brigades of the ANC in 1980s South Africa, during the struggle to end apartheid.

54 See Part Two, casebook on Loyalist Theatres, for an account of the Shankill Community Theatre's work.

55 Tom Magill, 'Between a Bible and a Flute band: Community Theatre in the Shankill and in Long Kesh', in *The State of Play: Irish Theatre in the Nineties*, ed. Eberhard Bort (Trier: WVT Wissenschaftlicher Verlag Trier, 1996), pp. 124–33.

56 Author interview.

57 Patrick Magee, *Gangsters or Guerrillas? Representations of Irish Republicans in 'Troubles Fiction'* with a Foreword by Danny Morrison (Belfast: Beyond the Pale Publications, 2001).

58 MacGiolla Ghunna, 'The Politics of Cultural Struggle', p. 11.

Notes to 'Only Catholics Combine': Loyalism and Theatre

1 Edward Daly, 'A Defining Moment, chapter 14 of his autobiography', *Mister, Are You A Priest?* (Dublin: Four Courts Press, 2000), published on the CAIN website page 'Personal Accounts of the Northern Ireland Conflict' at http://cain.ulst.ac.uk/othelem/people/accounts/index.html

2 Paul Bew and Gordon Gillespie (eds), *Northern Ireland, a chronology of the Troubles, 1968–1993* (Dublin: Gill and Macmillan, 1993), p. 45.

3 Daly, 'A Defining Moment', CAIN.

4 De Baroid, *Ballymurphy and the Irish War*, p. 288.

5 Derry Frontline, 'Threshold' in *Derry Frontline: Theatre of Self-Determination, the plays of Derry Frontline Culture and Education, north of Ireland, 1988–1992*, ed. with an introduction by Dan Baron Cohen (Derry: Guildhall Press, 2001), pp. 25–6.

6 Ibid., p. 5.

7 Ibid., pp. 13–14.

8 'Frontline: Culture and Education', unpaginated document, written 1987 (FA: WCML).

9 Maureen O'Connor, 'In the Frontline', *The Guardian*, Tuesday 30 June 1987, p. 11.

10 'Struggle for Freedom: the life and work of Len Johnson, Manchester Schools Project May 15–24 1987', Frontline: Culture and Education, 1987, unpaginated programme for the project (FA: WCML).

11 Dan Baron Cohen, 'Staging Struggle for Freedom', *Red Letters*, 21: December 1987, pp. 15–32, p. 24.

12 Jim Keys, email to the author, 8 September 2006.

13 'Short Strand Visit added to Frontline Itinerary', *Andersontown News*, Saturday 3 October 1987, p. 8.

14 Jane Plunkett, 'A Boxer's Struggle', *An Phoblacht/Republican News*, Thursday 8 October 1987, p. 11.

15 *Struggle for Freedom*, unpublished script (FA: WCML).

16 Joe Reid, letter to the author, 12 October 1987.

17 Dan Baron Cohen, 'Participation and Resistance: Notes on the Tour of the North and South of Ireland of *Struggle for Freedom*', *Red Letters*, 22: March 1988, pp. 46–59, p. 56.

18 Derry Frontline: *Theatre of Self-Determination*, pp. 13–14.

19 Novelist, playwright and cultural theorist, Ngugi wa Thiong'o is currently Professor of Comparative Literature at New York University. In 1976 he became chair of the cultural committee that ran the Kamiirithu Community and Cultural Centre in rural east Kenya, and of its open air theatre. Denied permission for its performances by the then vice-president, Daniel Arap Moi, the theatre was burned to the ground by state sponsored vigilantes. Ngugi was jailed without trial, and went into exile in 1977. In his book *Decolonising the Mind*, Ngugi developed Franz Fanon's conception of liberation culture, arguing that the process of decolonization involved a 'decolonization of the

mind', an emptying of the 'European memory' through a willed reclamation by a people of 'the definition and production of their own culture'. Fanon and Ngugi's theorization of the relationship between language and power, and of the centrality of culture to liberation praxis was explored, as we have seen, in the literature and plays of the H-Blocks and the work of the People's Theatre and Belfast Community Theatre.

20 Derry Frontline, p. 16.

21 Programme notes for *Inside Out* (FA: WCML).

22 *Theatre of Self-Determination*, p. 9.

23 Ibid., p. 82.

24 Frontline: Culture and Education, 'Annual Report', 1990 (FA: WCML), p. 2.

25 *Time Will Tell*, in *Theatre of Self-Determination*, p. 92. All quotations in this section are from this text.

26 Undated review, *City Life*, 5–19 April 1989 (FA: WCML).

27 *Theatre of Self-Determination*, p. 10.

28 Valerie Morgan, *Peacemakers? Peacekeepers? Women in Northern Ireland, 1969–1995*, CAIN website, http://cain.ulst.ac.uk/issues/women/paper3.htm.

29 *Theatre of Self-Determination*, p. 10.

30 *20/20 Vision* leaflet (FA: WCML).

31 The massacre took place at the Sharpeville township, in the Transvaal, South Africa, on 21 March 1960, when police opened fire on a crowd protesting against pass laws.

32 Dan Baron Cohen, letter to Derry Frontline members, 10 October 1989 (FA: WCML).

33 Lionel Pilkington, 'From Resistance to Liberation with Derry Frontline: an interview with Dan Baron Cohen', *Drama Review*, 38: 4 (1994), pp. 17–47, p. 18.

34 *Threshold*, in *Theatre of Self-Determination*, p. 182. All quotations in this section are from this text.

35 Pilkington, 'From Resistance to Liberation', p. 41.

36 Padraig O'Malley, *Biting the Grave*, p. 109.

37 Pilkington, 'From Resistance to Liberation', pp. 24–5.

38 Ibid., p. 25.

39 *Theatre of Self-Determination*, p. 151.

40 All quotations in this section are from the company document, *Everything You Always wanted to Know About Derry Frontline (but were afraid to ask)*, 1992 (FA: WCML).

41 All quotations in this section are from the unpaginated pamphlet, *20/20 Dialogues* (FA: WCML).

42 For a consideration of the complexities and contradictions of cultural praxis within conflicts and neo colonial contexts, see, for example: Robert M'Shengu Kavanagh, *Theatre and the Cultural Struggle in South Africa* (London: Zed Books, 1985); Eugene Van Erven, *The Playful Revolution: Theatre and Liberation in Asia* (Bloomington: Indiana University Press, 1992); idem, 'Resistance Theatre in South Korea: Above and Underground', *The Drama Review*, 32: 3 (1988), 156–73; 'Spanish Political Theatre under Franco, Suarez and Gonzalez', *New Theatre Quarterly*, 4: 13 (1988), 32–52.

43 See the following essays by Dan Baron Cohen: 'Listening to the Silences: defining the language and the place of a new Ireland', in *Ireland in Proximity, history, gender, space*, edited by Brewster, Scott *et al.* (London: Routledge,

1999), pp. 173–88; 'Staging *Struggle for Freedom*', *Red Letters*, 21: December 1987, pp. 15–32; 'Participation and Resistance: Notes on the Tour of the North and South of Ireland of *Struggle for Freedom*', *Red Letters*, 22: March 1988, pp. 46–59. Another notable feature of these writings is Baron Cohen's construction of the war as a sectarian conflict, even though Frontline's work was validated by its appeal to an anti-imperialist politics.

44 Maloney, *A Secret History of the IRA*, pp. 180–5.
45 Maguire, *Making Theatre in Northern Ireland*, p. 21.
46 Pilkington, 'From Resistance to Liberation'.
47 A.Alexandra Jaffe, 'Involvement, detachment and representation' in C. Brettell (ed.) *When They Read What We Write: the politics of ethnography* (London: Bergin and Garvey, 1993), p. 62.

Notes to Derry Frontline – and the template for liberation

1 David Grant, *Playing the Wild Card*, p. 41. Maria Jones is a playwright, and was a co-founder of DubbelJoint Theatre.
2 Tom Magill, 'Between a Bible and a Flute band: Community Theatre in the Shankill and in Long Kesh', in *The State of Play: Irish Theatre in the Nineties*, ed. *Eberhard Bort* (Trier: WVT Wissenschaftlicher Verlag Trier, 1996), pp. 124–33, p. 127.
3 Grant, *Playing the Wild Card*, p. 41.
4 The fact that Ireland's indigenous amateur theatres were mainly centred in rural areas and dominated by priests only served to underpin this view.
5 Grant, *Playing the Wild Card*, pp. 41, 42.
6 Michael Hall (ed.), *Grassroots leadership (7): Recollections by Michael Hall* (Newtownabbey: Island Publications, 2006), op. cit.
7 All quotations from Hall in this section, unless indicated otherwise, are taken from: Michael Hall (ed.), *Grassroots Leadership*, pp. 1–24.
8 Ibid., p. 4.
9 All quotations in this section from the published play script: Michael Hall, *Expecting the Future: a community play focusing on the effects of violence* (Newtownabbey: Island Publications, 1993).
10 Ibid., pp. 3–4.
11 Jonathan Stevenson, *We Wrecked the Place – Contemplating an End to the Northern Irish Troubles* (New York: Simon and Schuster, 1996) p. 161.
12 A. Tyrie, S. Duddy, and M. Hall, *This Is It!* a community play (Newtownabbey: Island Publications, 2003), p. 3.
13 The 1974 Sunningdale Agreement set out proposals for power sharing within Northern Ireland, and for a north–south dimension to internal Irish relations. It was brought down through the Ulster Workers Council Strike, coordinated by Tyrie and the UDA leadership. Dissident Republicans call the Good Friday Agreement 'Sunningdale 2' to indicate a belief that Adams' leadership has secured nothing which had not been on offer twenty-five years earlier.
14 *This Is It!*, p. 3.
15 Ibid., p. 4.
16 Ibid., p. 2.
17 All quotations in this section from the play text of *This Is It!*
18 Howe, *Ireland and Empire*, p. 14.

19 Michael Hall in an email to the author, 1/8/2006. All quotations in this section are from that source.

20 Andy Tyrie, Sam Duddy, and Michael Hall, *This Is It!* (Newtownabbey: Island Publications, 2003), p. 5.

21 Ed Maloney, *A Secret History of the IRA*, p. 415.

22 Tom Magill, 'Between a Bible and a Flute Band', p. 124.

23 Ibid., p. 125.

24 Ibid., p. 126.

25 Ibid., p. 127.

26 Ibid., p. 127.

27 Ibid., p. 128.

28 Ibid., p. 127.

29 Tom Magill, email to author, 2 April 2008.

30 Tom Magill, 'Between a Bible and a Flute Band', p. 129.

31 Tom Magill in a letter to Jacky Hewitt, 13 October 1995.

32 John Coulter, 'Revolutionary Unionism', *Open Republic*, July/August/September 2005: http://www.openrepublic.org/open_republic/20050701_vol1_no1/articles/20050619_ru.htm, accessed 16 May 2007.

33 In a bizarre if alarming coda to the relation between theatre and Loyalism, on 24 November 2006, Michael Stone, one of Loyalism's most committed and infamous killers, attempted to assassinate the Sinn Féin leadership at Stormont. His lawyers argued in his defence that the attack was in fact a piece of Performance Art on the theme of contemporary terrorism.

Notes to The 'Long Peace'

1 Mulholland, *Northern Ireland*, p. 125.

2 A major site for dissident Republican analysis is *The Blanket*. The articles offer a trenchant and often witty commentary on Sinn Féin's leadership and current strategy. It can be accessed at http://www.phoblacht.net/lpltr.html.

3 Maloney, *A Secret History of the IRA*, p. 71.

4 Ibid., p. 127.

5 Stephen Hopkins, 'History with a Divided and Complicated Heart? The Uses of Political Memoir, Biography and Autobiography in Contemporary Northern Ireland'. http://cain.ulst.ac.uk/ethnopolitics/hopkins01.pdf, accessed 14 June 2007.

6 Brian Campbell, Laurence McKeown, and Felim O'Hagan, *Nor Meekly Serve My Time – the H-Block Struggle, 1976–1981* (Belfast: BTP Publications, 1994), p. xii.

7 Laurence McKeown, *Out of Time – Irish Republican Prisoners, Long Kesh 1972–2000* (Belfast: BTP Publications, 2001), p. xiii.

Notes to DubbelJoint at Amharclann na Carraige

1 From an interview with Pam Brighton given to the author, Belfast, 19 September 2006. All quotations from Brighton in this section are from this source unless otherwise indicated.

2 The commercial success of *Stones in His Pockets* led to a bitter court dispute between Brighton and Jones, with the former arguing that the original concept

and basic dramatic themes of the play had been hers, and that Jones had amplified these into a script during rehearsals in which Brighton had contributed significant dramatic material. Jones argued that the commercial productions were based on a fundamental reworking of the original text. The judge found for Jones in regard to this, but for Brighton on the issue of the original notes, which were implicitly copyrighted. A succinct legal analysis of the case can be found at http://www.harbottle.com/hnl/pages/article_view_hnl/689.php, Brighton and DubbelJoint versus Jones, accessed 23 September 2007. Brighton said that her motive for bringing the case was her anger that DubbelJoint's creative contribution to the play had never been acknowledged, or due royalties paid to the company. Jones did in fact pay over c. £30,000 in settlement of this aspect of the case.

3 Cited in profile of *DubbelJoint Theatre Company* on the Culture Northern Ireland website at http://www.CultureNorthernIreland.org, accessed 12 August 2007.

4 JustUs Theatre, *Strategic Development Plan*, 2000, p. 7.

5 On 6 March 1988 three unarmed Irish Republican Army (IRA) members were shot dead by undercover members of the Special Air Service (SAS) in Gibraltar. The episode sparked intense controversy and began a chain of events that led to a series of deaths in Northern Ireland on 16 March 1988 and 19 March 1988. The British government claimed that the SAS shot the IRA members because they thought a bomb was about to be detonated. Eye-witnesses claimed that those shot were given no warning. During the funerals of the IRA Volunteers, at Milltown Cemetery in Belfast, a Loyalist gunman, Michael Stone, launched a grenade and gun attack on mourners. Three people were killed and 50 injured. Stone was chased to a nearby motorway where he was attacked by a number of mourners. The police arrived in time to save his life.

6 Pam Brighton, Bridie McMahon and Brenda Murphy, interview with Liane Hanson, Weekend Edition Sunday, National Public Radio, WNYC, New York, 18 October 1998.

7 Ibid.

8 Tom Maguire, *Making Theatre in Northern Ireland*, p. 53.

9 Pam Brighton, 'Drama's Portrayal of Forgotten Injustices', *Irish News*, Thursday 14 August 1997, p. 8.

10 Tom Maguire, '*Binlids* at the boundaries of being: a West Belfast Community stages an authentic self', *KUNAPIPI*, http://www.uow.edu.au/arts/kunapipi/index.htm, accessed 4 July 2006.

11 Brighton, 'Drama's Portrayal of Forgotten Injustices', p. 8.

12 Mick Moroney, 'Just a Play', *Irish Times*, 29 July 1999, p. 12.

13 Imelda Foley, *The Girls in the Big Picture, Gender in contemporary Ulster theatre* (Belfast: Blackstaff Press, 2003). Pam Brighton had been an influential figure in Charabanc's early work, a contribution briefly covered in chapter 3 of Foley's book.

14 Amelia Gentleman, 'Dubbel Trouble', *The Guardian*, Thursday 5 August 1999, p. 14.

15 Ian Hill, 'The Arts Council are Wrong', *Fortnight*, September (1999), p. 21.

16 Malachi O'Doherty, 'This Isn't Art', *Fortnight*, September (1999), p. 22.

17 Padraig MacDabhaid, 'Arts Council Censorship', *An Phoblacht/Republican News*, Thursday 29 July 1999, p. 17.

18 HMG, House of Commons, Hansard Written Answers for 1 November 1999 (pt 11), p. 3.

19 Interview with Pam Brighton, September 19 2006.

20 Cited in *DubbelJoint Theatre Company*.

21 Joseph Sheehy, *Exile and the Kingdom*.

22 Cited in web based interview, Channel 4 Ideas Factory. http://www.channel4. com/4talent/ireland/, accessed 23 July 2006.

23 Ibid.

24 Gerassi, p. xx.

25 All quotations are taken from the version of Brian Campbell's *Des* printed in the DubbelJoint programme for the 2000 production.

26 Des Wilson in a letter to the author, 12 May 2001.

27 Anthony McIntyre, 'Brian Campbell, a Captivating Voice', *The Blanket*, http:// www.phoblacht.net/am2312058g.html, accessed 30 April 2006.

Notes to The plays of Laurence McKeown and Brian Campbell

1 Programme notes for DubbelJoint production of *Laughter of Our Children*.

2 David Beresford, *Ten Men Dead* (London: Harper Collins, 1987).

3 McKeown, *Out of Time*, p. 246.

4 Cited in DubbelJoint publicity release, May 2001.

5 Roy Garland, 'Challenging Roles We All Have to Play', *Irish News*, Monday 9 June 2003, p. 46.

6 Robert McMillen, 'People Will Leave this House Feeling Very Cold', *An Phoblacht/Republican News*, 31 May 2003, p. 18.

7 Press release for the 2003 production of *A Cold House*.

8 All quotations are taken from Brian Campbell and Laurence McKeown, *A Cold House*, unpublished version given to author by Laurence McKeown.

9 Garland, 'Challenging Roles', p. 46.

10 McMillen, 'People Will Leave this House', p. 18.

11 Cited in press release for the 2003 production.

12 Seth Liner, 'Political Drama Pulls No Punches', *Irish News*, Tuesday 17 June 2003, p. 13.

13 Gerry Kelly, 'Irish Slaves in America', http://www.scoilgaeilge.org/academics/ slaves.htm, accessed 11 October 2006.

14 Angelique Chrisafis, 'Racist war of the Loyalist Street Gangs', *Guardian Online*, Saturday 10 January, 2004. http://www.guardian.co.uk/race/ story/0,11374,1120113,00.html, accessed 13 October 2006.

15 Press release for the 2004 production of *Voyage of No Return*.

16 Quoted in programme notes for DubbelJoint production of *Voyage of No Return*.

17 Aisling McCrea, 'Play Goes Beyond Today's Headlines', *Irish Times*, 06/08/2004, online archive, http://www.ireland.com/cgi-bin/Voyage+of+no+return, accessed 24 November 2006.

18 Roisin de Rosa, 'Voyage Not to be Missed', *An Phoblacht/Republican News*, 5 August 2004, http://www.anphoblacht.com/news/detail/5943, accessed 25 November 2006.

19 Obituaries, Brian Campbell, *Times Online*, http://www.timesonline.co.uk/ article, accessed 27 March 2006.

20 From an interview with Pam Brighton given to the author, Belfast, 19 September

2006. All quotations from Brighton in this section are from this source unless otherwise indicated.

21 From an interview with Laurence McKeown given to the author, Belfast, 20 September 2006. All quotations from McKeown in this section are from this source unless otherwise indicated.

22 Programme for *The Official Version*.

23 All quotations in this section are from an unpublished copy of *The Official Version* given to the author by Laurence McKeown.

24 Bernadette Devlin McAliskey, *Damien Walsh Memorial Lecture*.

25 McKeown, Belfast, 20 September 2006.

26 'The Official Version', Reviews Section, *Irish Times Online*, http://www.ireland.com/cgi-bin/dialogserver, accessed 10 June 2006.

27 Ibid.

28 Bernadette Devlin McAliskey, *Damien Walsh Memorial Lecture*, http://www.victimsandsurvivorstrust.com, accessed 17 April 2006.

29 *The Official Version*, p. 72.

30 What is striking about this incident is that McKeown, who had only met me that day, was willing to bring me into the debate about his text. My experience in the community was always that if you were trusted then you were included. In any case McKeown would not have agreed to meet me without first checking that I was known and trusted. Joe Reid once said to me: 'You are watched over three times here my friend, first by us, then by the "Provies", and then by Her Majesty!' On another occasion he laughed as he told me, after the 1997 ceasefire, 'Of course they watched you! I'd go to the club, and your man's asking, "Is that wee bald lad one of yours, Joe?"'

31 DubbelJoint website, http://www.DubbelJoint.com/, accessed 3 March 2006.

32 In fact Sinn Féin did not choose the Culture portfolio following the May 2007 resurrection of the Northern Ireland Parliament. Instead it went to the DUP.

33 Dario Fo and France Rame's La Commune was founded in Milan in 1970 as a political and cultural collective positioned within Milan's working-class neighbourhoods. In 1986 Roland and Claire Muldoon, who had founded the socialist theatre company CAST in 1965, took over the Hackney Empire, an Edwardian theatre on Hackney High Street, which was at that time a bingo hall, and turned it into a vibrant centre for popular multicultural theatre, as well as a receiving house for productions by mainstream companies, such as the RSC.

Notes to The Politics of Process: insurgency, theatre and community

1 Badal Sircar, 'Letter from Calcutta', *Drama Review*, 25: 2 (1982), pp. 51–9, p. 51.

2 Pam Brighton, interview with author, Belfast 2006. All quotations from Brighton in this section are from this source unless otherwise indicated.

3 Jan Cohen-Cruz (ed.), *Radical Street Performance: an International Anthology* (London: Routledge, 1998), p. 243.

4 Sircar, 'Letter from Calcutta', p. 55.

5 Belfast Community Theatre, 1987.

6 Lionel Pilkington, 'From Resistance to Liberation with Derry Frontline: an interview with Dan Baron Cohen', *Drama Review*, 38: 4 (1994), 17–45 (p. 40).

7 Belfast Community Theatre, 1987.

8 Franz Fanon, *The Wretched of the Earth* (Harmondsworth: Penguin, 1990), p. 179.

9 Herbert Marcuse, *The Aesthetic Dimension* (London: Macmillan, 1979), p. 6.

10 Fanon, *The Wretched of the Earth*, p. 28.

11 The problem was not Baron Cohen's analyses of the role of cultural activism per se, derived from writers such as Freire and Ngugi, but his assumption that Ireland was a tabula rasa onto which such ideas needed to be inscribed. His dialogue with Eoghan MacCormaic, whom he visited in prison, was clearly important to both men.

12 Belfast Community Theatre, 1986.

13 Astrid Von Kotze, 'Workers' Theatre in South Africa', *New Left Review*, no. 163, May–June (1987), 83–92, p. 88.

14 The best account and analysis of the problems of sustaining cultural activism within neo-colonial and anti-imperial contexts remains Eugene Van Erven's *The Playful Revolution*.

15 Solomon Tsehaye and Jane Plastow, 'Making theatre for change: two plays of the Eritrean Liberation struggle', in Richard Boon, and Jane Plastow (eds), *Theatre Matters: Performance and Culture on the World Stage* (Cambridge: Cambridge University Press, 1998), pp. 36–54.

16 See Kennedy C. Chinyowa, 'More Than Mere Story-Telling: the pedagogical significance of African ritual Theatre', *Studies in Theatre and Performance*, 20: 2 (2000), 87–96, p. 89.

17 The parallels with the theatres of the South are not reflected in shared forms, exercises or methods. There is no consonance in performative contexts. There is no shared body of texts, techniques or methods. The values which link Pat McGlade of Belfast Community Theatre with Mi Hlatshwayo of the Dunlop Workers' Theatre are not *theatre values* but *political values*, derived from shared structures of experience: poverty, economic imperialism, state terror, unlawful imprisonment, torture, the suppression of minorities, racism, the abuse of judicial systems and human rights, etc. These values, which include a commitment to democracy, justice, human rights, freedom of speech, freedom from sexual and gender oppressions, and which are expressed through methods based upon inclusivity, dialogue, and the primacy of lived experience, defined the theatre processes. It is only with reference to these political values that we can understand the points of connection, and talk of a movement, a shared conception of political theatre.

18 Fanon, *The Wretched of the Earth*, p. 45.

19 John Willett, *The Theatre of Erwin Piscator: Half a Century of Politics in the Theatre* (London: Methuen, 1978), pp. 107–26.

20 Joe Reid, interview given to the author in Belfast, December 1998.

Select Bibliography

[1] **Primary Sources**

[a] Published Scripts
Derry Frontline, *Theatre of Self Determination, the plays of Derry Frontline Culture and Education, north of Ireland, 1988–1992*, ed. with an introduction by Dan Baron Cohen (Derry: Guildhall Press, 2001). Contains: *Inside Out*, 1988; *Time Will Tell*, 1989; *Threshhold*, 1992.
Hall, Michael, *Expecting the Future: A community play focusing on the effects of violence* (Newtownabbey: Island Publications, 1993).
Tyrie, A., Duddy S., and Hall, M., *This Is It!* (Newtownabbey: Island Publications, 2003).
Sheehy, Joseph (ed.), *The People's Theatre Vol. 1* (Belfast: Glandore Press, 1999).

[b] Unpublished Scripts
Where the text is held in a public archive I have indicated this with the abbreviations WCML (Working Class Movement Library, Salford) and LHB (Linenhall Library, Belfast). All other texts are held in the author's personal archive.
Belfast Community Theatre, adaptation of Samuel Beckett's *Eh, Joe* and *Not I*, 1986.
Belfast Community Theatre, 'Oxygen Plays' 1–3: *Willie Mandela, Thomas Jefferson, and George Jackson*, 1985.
Belfast Community Theatre, *On Education*, 1986.
Belfast Community Theatre, *Sign on the Dotted Line*, 1986.
Campbell, Brian, *Des*, 2000. (Printed in programme for production.) [LHB]
Campbell, Brian, *Voyage of No Return*, 2005.
Campbell, B. and McKeown, L., *The Laughter of our Children*, 2001.
Campbell, B. and McKeown, L., *A Cold House*, 2003. [LHB]
Ervine, Brian, *Somme Day Mourning*, 1995.
Frontline: culture and education, *Struggle for Freedom*, 1987. [WCML]
Klein, Michael, *In the Interest of Justice*, 1985.
Long Kesh POWs' Drama Group, *The Crime of Castlereagh*, 1996. [LHB]
McGlade, Jim, *Oh Gilbert*, 1984.
McGlade, Jim, *Belfast in Hell*, 1988.
MacCormaic, Eoghan, *Night at Clontarf*, 1985.
MacCormaic, Eoghan, *The Visit*, 1989.
McKeown, Laurence, *The Official Version*, 2006.

Murphy, B., Morrison, D., MacSiacais, J. and Poland, C., *Binlids*, 1997. [LHB]
Murphy, Brenda and Poland, Christine, *Forced Upon Us*, 1999.
Reid, Joe, *Ecce Homo*, 1989.
Wilson, Des, *You're Not Going to Like This! Part Two*, 1987. [LHB]
Wilson, Des, *Twenty Years: the best of the People's Theatre*, 1997.

[c] Archives
The following archives have provided invaluable sources for this study:
Manchester Frontline, Education and Culture company archive held at the Working
    Class Movement Library, Salford.
Northern Ireland Political Collection, Linenhall Library, Belfast.
Theatre and Performing Arts archive, Linenhall Library, Belfast. This is the most
    comprehensive and important set of holdings for research into the Troubles and
    its theatres.
Conflict Archive on the Internet (CAIN). By far the most important as well as the
    most comprehensive web resource for those seeking to study the Troubles.
Important newspaper archives include the online resources of the *An Phoblacht/
    Republican News*, *Irish Times*, *Irish News* and the *Belfast Telegraph*.
I have also drawn extensively on my personal collection of playscripts, letters and
    other ephemera.

[d] Cited Books by Principals
Campbell, B., McKeown, L., and O'Hagan, F., *Nor Meekly Serve My Time – the
    H-Block Struggle, 1976–1981* (Belfast: BTP Publications, 1994).
McKeown, Laurence, *Out of Time – Irish Republican Prisoners, Long Kesh
    1972–2000* (Belfast: BTP Publications, 2001).
Sands, Bobby, *Writings from Prison* (Dublin: Mercier Press, 1998).
Sheehy, Joseph, *Exile and the Kingdom, the authorized biography of Desmond
    Wilson, Ballymurphy Priest* (Belfast: Glandore Press, 1995).
Wilson, Fr Des, *An End to Silence* (Cork: Royal Carbery Books, 1985).
Wilson, Fr Des, *The Way I See It, an autobiography* (Belfast: Beyond the Pale, 2005).

[e] Cited Articles and Reflections by Principals
Baron Cohen, Dan, 'Listening to the Silences: defining the language and the place
    of a new Ireland', in *Ireland in Proximity, history, gender, space*, edited by
    Brewster, Scott and others (London: Routledge, 1999), pp. 173–88.
Baron Cohen, Dan, 'Staging *Struggle for Freedom*', *Red Letters*, 21: December
    1987, pp. 15–32.
Baron Cohen, Dan, 'Participation and Resistance: Notes on the Tour of the North
    and South of Ireland of *Struggle for Freedom*', *Red Letters*, 22: March 1988,
    pp. 46–59.
Brighton, P., McMahon, B., and Murphy, B., interview with Liane Hanson,
    Weekend Edition Sunday, National Public Radio, WNYC, New York, 18
    October 1998.
Brighton Pam, 'Drama's Portrayal of Forgotten Injustices', *Irish News*, Thursday 14
    August 1997, p. 8.
Campbell, Brian, 'Power and Confidence in Outstanding Drama', *An Phoblacht/
    Republican News*, 19 September 1996, p. 10.
Campbell, Brian, 'Editorial', *An Glór Gafa/ The Captive Voice*, Vol. 1, No. 1
    (1989).

Devenny, P., Fox, P., Higgins, E., Jamison, S., Kelly, D., Mac Giolla Ghunna, M., Og Meehan, M., Quinn, F., Morris, M., McCann, J., 'Personal Thoughts', *Crime of Castlereagh*, Féile an Phobail programme, September 1996, unpaginated.

Kelly, Dan, 'Diary of a Drama Project', *An Glór Gafa/ The Captive Voice*, Vol. 8, No. 1 (1996), pp. 11–18.

MacCormaic, Eoghan, 'Revolutionary People's Theatre', in *Iris Bheag* (Dublin: Sinn Féin Education Department), December, 1988, pp. 31–4.

MacGiolla, Gunna Micheal, 'Cultural Struggle and a Drama Project', in *Journal of Prisoners on Prisons*, Vol. 7, No. 1 (1996), pp. 71–4.

MacGiolla, Gunna Micheal, 'The Politics of Cultural Struggle', *An Glor Gafa*, Winter (1996), pp. 10–11.

McKeown, Laurence, 'Writing our own History', paper given at *Prison Writings: Probing the Boundaries* conference held in Vienna, September 2002. Source held at http://www.inter-disciplinary.net/Mckeown%20paper.pdf.

Magill, Tom, 'Between a Bible and a Flute band: Community Theatre in the Shankill and in Long Kesh', in *The State of Play: Irish Theatre in the Nineties*, ed. By Eberhard Bort (Trier: WVT Wissenschaftlicher Verlag Trier, 1996), pp. 124–33.

Magill, Tom, 'Theatre as Democracy: Boal in Belfast', *Fortnight*, November (1988), pp. 21–2.

O'Dowd, Paddy, 'Festival Drama in the Blocks', *An Glór Gafa/ The Captive Voice*, Vol. 8, No. 1 (1996), pp. 18–19. Also printed in *Journal of Prisoners on Prisons*, Vol. 7, No. 1 (1996), pp. 74–9.

[f] Cited Pamphlets, Programmes and Documents written/edited by Principals

Both during the war and in the post-conflict period, Springhill Community House produced a remarkable range of pamphlets covering social and political issues and cultural production. Some were later published by small local publishers. Another prodigious achievement has been the series of Island Pamphlets, edited by Michael Hall. Launched by the Farset Think Tank in 1993, the series were conceived, says their publicity, as a means to 'open up debate on historical, cultural, socio-economic, political and other matters pertinent to Northern Irish society'. Numbering some one hundred titles to date, Hall's project has been a critical contribution to the post-war dialogue between the communities. Information can be accessed at http://cain.ulst.ac.uk/islandpub-lications/index.html. In addition there are the theatre programmes, some of which are substantial acts of documentation, produced by Féile an Phobail and DubbelJoint, in which principal actors, political and theatrical, have set down their reflections. Some programmes, for example the DubbelJoint production of *Des*, contain a full script. Documents taken from the Derry Frontline archive include annual reports, letters and other ephemera, and these are referenced in the main text. The Republican Movement also produced a vast number of internal documents, as well as publications such as *An Glor Gafa*.

This study has drawn on the following published works from these sources:

An Glór Gafa/The Captive Voice, written and illustrated by Irish Republican prisoners of war (Dublin and Belfast: Republican Publications, 1989–99).

Hall, Michael (ed.), *The Cruthin Controversy: A response to academic misrepresentation* (Newtownabbey: Island Publications, 1993).

——, *Ulster's Shared Heritage: Exploring the cultural inheritance of the Ulster people* (Newtownabbey: Island Publications, 1993).

——, *Beyond King Billy? East Belfast Protestants explore cultural and identity-related issues* (Newtownabbey: Island Publications, 1999).

——, *Grassroots leadership (2): Recollections by Fr Des Wilson and Tommy Gorman* (Newtownabbey: Island Publications, 2005).

——, *Grassroots leadership (7): Recollections by Michael Hall* (Newtownabbey: Island Publications, 2006).

Republican Prisoners, *Scairt Amach* (Long Kesh Prison: 1989).

Wilson, Fr Des, *A Diary of Thirty Days, Ballymurphy July–December 1972*, edited by Joseph Sheehy (Springhill Community House: Local Heritage Series).

——, *A Political Catechism* (Belfast: Cuig Chead Publications, 1990).

Wilson Fr D., and Sheehy, J., *The People's Theology at Whiterock College* (Springhill Community House: Local Heritage Series).

[2] Selected Secondary Sources

Adams, Gerry, *Before the Dawn: an autobiography* (New York: William Morrow and Company, 1996).

——, *The Politics of Irish Freedom* (Co. Kerry: Brandon Books, 1986).

Balfour, Michael, and Somers, John, eds, *Drama as Social Intervention* (Ontario: Captus Press, 2006).

Bannerji, Himani, *The Writing on the Wall: Essays on Culture and Politics* (Toronto: TSAR, 1993).

Barucha Rustom, *Theatre and the World: Performance and the Politics of Culture* (London: Routledge, 1993).

——, *Rehearsals of Revolution: the Political Theatre of Bengal* (Hawaii: University of Hawaii Press, 1983).

Baulhan, Hussein Abdilahi, *Franz Fanon and the Psychology of Oppression* (New York: Plenum Press, 1985).

Bew, Paul and Gillespie, Gordon, eds, *Northern Ireland, a chronology of the Troubles, 1968–1993* (Dublin: Gill and Macmillan, 1993).

Bond, Steven and others, *Learning From Each Other*, a report on the visit of Sheffield Adult Education Delegation to Belfast, October 1986.

Boon, Richard and Plastow, Jane, eds, *Theatre Matters: Performance and Culture on the World Stage* (Cambridge: Cambridge University Press, 1998).

Biggs, Jill and others, *Nothing But the Same Old Story: the Roots of Anti Irish Racism* (London: Information on Ireland, 1985).

Boal, Augusto, *Theatre of the Oppressed*, trans. by Maria Leal McBride, first published as *Teatro de Oprimido*, 1974 (London: Pluto, 1979).

Boal, Augusto, *Games for Actors and Non Actors*, trans. by Adrian Jackson (London: Routledge, 1992).

Boff, Clodovis, 'The Nature of Basic Christian Communities', *Conciliana Magazine*, no. 144 (1981), pp. 53–64.

Boon, Richard and Plastow, Jane, eds, *Theatre Matters: Performance and Culture on the World Stage* (Cambridge: Cambridge University Press, 1998).

Brecht, Bertolt, *Brecht on Theatre: the development of an aesthetic*, ed. and trans. by John Willett (London: Methuen, 1978).

Bulhan, Hussein Abdilahi, *Frantz Fanon and the Psychology of Oppression* (New York: Plenum Press, 1985).

Chinyowa, Kennedy C., 'More Than Mere Story-Telling: the pedagogical significance of African ritual Theatre', *Studies in Theatre and Performance*, 20: 2 (2000), 87–96.

Cohen-Cruz, Jan (ed.), *Radical Street Performance: an International Anthology* (London: Routledge, 1998).

Curtis, Liz, *Ireland – the Propaganda War* (London: Pluto, 1984).

Curtis, Liz, *Nothing But the Same Old Story* (London: Russell Press 1985).

Daly, Edward, *Mister, Are You A Priest?* (Dublin: Four Courts Press, 2000).

De Baroid, Ciaran, *Ballymurphy and the Irish War* (London: Pluto Press, 2000).

Dutt, Uptal, *Towards a Revolutionary Theatre* (Calcutta: Sarkar, 1982).

Eagleton, Terry, *Ideology* (London: Verso, 1991).

Fanon, Franz, *The Wretched of the Earth* (Harmondsworth: Penguin, 1990).

Farrell, Michael, *Northern Ireland: the Orange State* (London: Pluto, 1980).

Fitzgerald, Mary (ed.), *The Selected Plays of Lady Gregory* (Washington D.C: Catholic University of America Press, 1983).

Ford Smith, Honor, 'From Sistren – Jamaican Women's Theatre', in *Twentieth Century Theatre: a sourcebook*, ed. by Richard Drain (London: Routledge, 1995), pp. 331–4.

Foley, Imelda, *The Girls in the Big Picture, Gender in contemporary Ulster theatre* (Belfast: Blackstaff Press, 2003).

Foster, R.F., *Modern Ireland, 1600–1972* (London: Penguin, 1989).

Freire, Paulo, *Pedagogy of the Oppressed*, trans. by Myra Bergman Ramos (Harmondsworth: Penguin, 1972).

——, *Cultural Action for Freedom*, trans. by Myra Bergman Ramos (Harmondsworth: Penguin, 1972).

——, *Pedagogy of the Heart*, trans. by Donaldo Macedo and Alexandre Oliveira (New York: Continuum, 1998).

Funnemark, Bjorn and Borg, Arne, *Irish Terrorism or British Colonialism? The Violation of Human Rights in Northern Ireland* (Norwegian Helsinki Committee, 1990).

'Fury at Parole Drama', Editorial, *Newsletter*, Monday 16 September 1996, p. 1.

Garland, Roy, 'Challenging Roles We All Have to Play', *Irish News*, Monday 9 June 2003.

Gentleman, Amelia, 'Dubbel Trouble', *The Guardian*, Thursday 5 August 1999, p. 14.

Gramsci, Antonio, *Selections from the Cultural Writings*, ed. by David Forgacs and Geoffrey Nowell-Smith, trans. by William Boelhower (London: Lawrence and Wishart, 1985).

Grant, David, *Playing the Wild Card, a survey of community drama and smaller scale theatres from a community relations perspective* (Belfast: Community Relations Council, 1993).

Harrington, John P. and Mitchell, Elizabeth J., editors, *Politics and Performance in Contemporary Northern Ireland* (Amherst USA: University of Massachusetts Press, 1999).

Harrington, John P. (ed.), *Modern Irish Drama* (New York and London: WW Norton, 1991).

Hill, Ian, 'The Arts Council are Wrong', *Fortnight*, September (1999).

Hopkins Stephen, *History with a Divided and Complicated Heart? The Uses of Political Memoir, Biography and Autobiography in Contemporary Northern Ireland*. http://cain.ulst.ac.uk/ethnopolitics/hopkins01.pdf. Accessed 14/06/2007.

Howe, Stephen, *Ireland and Empire, colonial legacies in Irish history and culture*

(Oxford: OUP, 2000).

Jennings, Alan (ed.), *Justice Under Fire – the Abuse of Civil Liberties in Northern Ireland* (Pluto: London, 1988).

Jordanova, Ludmilla, *History in Practice* (London: Arnold, 2000).

Kavanagh, Robert Mshengu, *Making People's Theatre* (Johannesburg: Witwatersrand University Press, 1997).

Kee, Robert, *The Green Flag, a history of Irish Nationalism* (London: Penguin 2000).

Kelley, Kevin, *The Longest War – Northern Ireland and the IRA* (London: Zed Books, 1982).

Klein, Michael, 'Life and Theatre in Northern Ireland, an interview with Martin Lynch', *Red Letters: a Journal of Culture and Politics*, vol. 16, Spring–Summer (1984), pp. 26–31.

Kiberd, Declan, *Inventing Ireland, the literature of the modern nation* (London: Vintage, 1996).

Lawyers Alliance for Justice and others, *Transcript of Evidence About the RUC*, presented at a hearing in Belfast, 26 February 1999.

McCann, Eamonn, *War and an Irish Town* (London: Pluto Press, 1975).

MacDabhaid, Padraig, 'Arts Council Censorship', *An Phoblacht/Republican News*, Thursday 29 July 1999.

McKittrick, David and others, *Lost Lives: the stories of the men, women and children who died as a result of the Troubles* (Edinburgh: Mainstream Pub., 1999).

McMillen, Robert, 'People Will Leave this House Feeling Very Cold', *An Phoblacht/Republican News*, 31 May 2003, p. 18.

McPhilemy, Sean, *The Committee: Political Assassination in Northern Ireland* (Colorado: Roberts Rinehart, 1998).

Marcuse, Herbert, *The Aesthetic Dimension* (London: Macmillan, 1979).

Maguire, Tom, *Making Theatre in Northern Ireland: Through and Beyond the Troubles* (Exeter: UEP, 2006).

——, '*Binlids* at the Boundaries of Being: a West Belfast Community stages an authentic self', *KUNAPIPI* Journal of Postcolonial Writing 22 (2), pp. 106–17.

Mallie, Eamonn and McKittrick, David, *The Fight for Peace – the secret story behind the Irish Peace Process* (London: Heinemann, 1996).

Maloney, Ed, *A Secret History of the IRA* (London: Penguin, 2003).

Martin, Randy, *Performance as Political Act* (New York: Bergin and Garvey, 1990).

Miller, David, *Don't Mention the War, Northern Ireland, propaganda and the media* (London: Pluto Press, 1994).

Millet, Kate, *The Politics of Cruelty: an Essay on the Literature of Political Imprisonment* (London: Viking, 1994).

Mulholland, Marc, *Northern Ireland – a very short introduction* (Oxford: OUP, 2002).

Murray, Fr Raymond, *State Violence – Northern Ireland, 1969–1997* (Dublin: Mercier Press, 1998), p. 34.

O'Callaghan, Sean, *The Informer* (London: Corgi, 1998).

O'Connor, Maureen, 'In the Frontline', *The Guardian*, Tuesday 30 June 1987, p. 11.

O'Doherty, Malachi, 'This Isn't Art', *Fortnight*, September (1999), p. 22.

O'Malley, Padraig, *Biting at the Grave, the Irish Hunger Strikes and the Politics of Despair* (Belfast: Blackstaff Press, 1990).

Pilkington, Lionel, *Theatre and the State in Twentieth-Century Ireland* (London:

Routledge, 2001).

——, 'From Resistance to Liberation with Derry Frontline: an interview with Dan Baron-Cohen', *Drama Review*, 38: 4 (1994), pp. 17–47.

——, 'Theatre and Cultural Politics in Northern Ireland: the Over the Bridge Controversy', *Journal of Irish Studies*, 30: 4 (1996), pp. 76–93.

——, 'Theatre and Insurgency in Ireland', *Essays in Theatre/Etudes Theatrales*, Vol. 12, No. 2 (May 1994), pp. 128–40.

Plunkett, Jane, 'A Boxer's Struggle', *An Phoblacht/Republican News*, Thursday 7 October 1987.

Prince, Simon, *Northern Ireland's '68: civil rights, global revolt and the origins of the Troubles* (Dublin: Irish Academic Press, 2007).

Samuel, Raphael, *Theatre of Memory, Vol. 1, past and present in contemporary culture* (London: Verso, 1994).

Schaeffer, Karine, 'The Spectator as Witness? *Binlids* as case study', *Studies in Theatre Production*, Vol. 23, No. 1 (2003), pp. 5–20.

Seymour, Anna, 'Welcoming in the New Millennium: The Possibilities of Brecht's Days of the Commune for Northern Ireland', *Modern Drama*, 42: 2 (2001), 176–84.

Sharrock, David and Davenport, Mark, *Man of War, Man of Peace, the unauthorized biography of Gerry Adams* (London: Pan Books, 1997).

'Short Strand Visit added to Frontline Itinerary', *Andersontown News*, Saturday 3 October 1987, p. 8.

Sinn Féin, Official Website, www.sinnfein.

Sircar, Badal, 'Letter from Calcutta', *Drama Review*, 25: 2 (1982), pp. 51–9.

Soyinka, Wole, *Art, Dialogue and Outrage: essays on literature and culture* (London, Methuen 1993).

——, 'A letter from Kingston', in R. Boon & J. Plastow, eds, *Theatre matters: performance and culture on the world stage* (Cambridge: Cambridge University Press, 1998).

Stevenson, Jonathan, *We Wrecked the Place – Contemplating an End to the Northern Irish Troubles* (New York: Simon and Schuster, 1996).

Toolis, Kevin, *Rebel Hearts* (London: Picador, 1995).

Tombs, David, *Latin American Liberation Theology* (Boston: Brill Academic Publishers inc., Leiden) 2002.

Torres, Camilo, *Revolutionary Priest, the complete writings and messages of Camilo Torres*, edited by John Gerassi (London: Jonathan Cape, 1971).

Van Erven, Eugene, *Radical People's Theatre* (Bloomington: Indiana University Press, 1989).

——, *The Playful Revolution: Theatre and Liberation in Asia* (Indiana: Indiana University Press, 1992).

Von Kotze, Astrid, 'Worker's Theatre in South Africa', *New Left Review*, no. 163, May–June (1987), pp. 83–92.

wa Thiong'o, Ngugi, 'The Language of African Theatre', in *Radical Street Performance*, ed. by Jan Cohen-Cruz (London: Routledge, 1998), pp. 238–44.

——, *Moving the Centre, the struggle for cultural freedom* (Oxford: James Curry, 1993).

——, *Writers in Politics* (London: Heinemann, 1981).

——, *Decolonising the Mind: the politics of language in African Literature* (London: Heinemann, 1986).

Williams, Raymond, *Modern Tragedy* (London: Verso, 1979).

Index